Competitiveness
and American Society

Research in Technology Studies

Competitiveness
and American Society

Research in Technology Studies
Volume 7

EDITED BY
Steven L. Goldman

Bethlehem: Lehigh University Press
London and Toronto: Associated University Presses

Associated University Presses
440 Forsgate Drive
Cranbury, NJ 08512

Associated University Presses
25 Sicilian Avenue
London WC1A 2QH, England

Associated University Presses
P.O. Box 338, Port Credit
Mississauga, Ontario,
Canada L5G 4L8

The paper used in this publication meets the requirements
of the American National Standard for Permanence of Paper
for Printed Library Materials Z39.48-1984.

Library of Congress Cataloging-in-Publication Data

Competitiveness and American society / edited by Steven L. Goldman.
    p.   cm.   (Competitiveness and American society ; v. 7)
    ISBN 0-934223-28-9
    1. United States—Foreign economic relations.   2. Competition—
United States.   3. Competition, International.   4. International
economic relations.   I. Goldman, Steven L., 1941–   . II. Series.
HF1455.C724   1993
336.6'048—dc20   92–54262
                                                                      CIP

Contents

6 *Contents*

Foreword

LAURENCE W. HECHT

Is economic competition today a greater threat to the American way of life than military confrontation? Is the United States losing its economic war with foreign rivals while U.S. armed forces triumph in conflicts such as the recent war with Iraq? Is U.S. manufacturing improving its competitive position in domestic as well as in global markets, or is it becoming a hollowed-out distribution channel for foreign manufacturers?

The Iacocca Institute at Lehigh University is dedicated to improving the competitiveness of American industry, yet we have no definitive answers to these questions—nor does anyone else at this time. America has many resources that it can bring to bear on improving its manufacturing competitiveness, but an honest, open debate is needed to clarify policy alternatives, engage public opinion, and catalyze political action.

If no consensus exists among the American people with respect to the competitive strength or weakness of our manufacturing base, or on what should be done to improve its competitiveness if it is weak, then it is unrealistic to expect decisive national political action. The U.S. Congress today, reflecting the absence of such a public consensus, seems confused about the state of our manufacturing industries. Is there a national competitiveness problem or is it only individual companies that have lost their competitive edge? If the problem is national, do we solve it through education? By implementing a national industrial policy? By enacting specific legislation in support of particular industries? By reforming macroeconomic policies? By reforming the entitlement system within the federal budget? By igniting a thousand points of light?

The Iacocca Institute believes that a national debate on the competitiveness of U.S. industry is important and that it must be as informed a public debate as it can be made to be. To that end, we invited a group of Lehigh University faculty from a variety of disciplines to examine the concept of industrial competitiveness in the American social context. We are proud of the result and hope that through this contribution to the competitiveness debate we are also contributing to focusing our efforts as a nation on the critically important issues that are its subject matter.

Introduction

STEVEN L. GOLDMAN

The debate over the competitiveness of American industry is, above all else, a social phenomenon opening a window onto American society. The participants, the positions taken (and the positions avoided), the assignment of blame for causing the problem and of responsibility for leadership in solving it, all reveal a great deal about the distribution of power among American social institutions. At the same time, the disparate conceptions of what the competitiveness problem is, or even whether there is such a problem, of whose problem it is and how it should be solved, reveal a great deal about American social values.

The claim that U.S. industry is in crisis, that it stands at a turning point in its competitiveness with foreign rivals, seems on the face of it an objective description of the prevailing state of affairs. The gap between imports and exports of manufactured goods is large and persistent. The loss of market share, indeed of whole markets, especially in highly visible consumer products as well as in such ordinarily invisible products as machine tools, seems irreversible. The decline in manufacturing employment, the rise in corporate bankruptcies and losses of profitability, and the explosive growth of foreign, particularly Japanese, ownership or control of American industrial assets, seem factual evidence enough that we confront a true crisis. Either American industry responds aggressively to foreign manufacturers and regains lost market shares at home and abroad, or it faces a decisive contraction.

But what does "competitiveness" mean when predicated of an entire industry, an economy, a nation? What is the relationship between industrial competitiveness and the personal and social value placed on competition? What are the social roots of competition that have made it an enduring American value? How does the competitiveness debate serve special interests seeking to preserve or extend their social power, and in what ways? Is there a "correct," a "natural," status for the American economy vis-a-vis other national economies and, if so, is it dominance? How did America achieve the industrial dominance it enjoyed until recently, and how was that dominance lost?

On the view that America's industrial competitiveness is declining, what is the relationship between this decline and the pursuit of American political and military objectives? Between this decline and declines in other measures of American social well-being: the state of the natural environment, the quality of urban life, drug and alcohol abuse, public education, health care, the distribution of income, urban crime, the standard of living? How does competitiveness relate to the globalization of industrial activity, with its attendant blurring of the national identity of corporations?

If American firms achieve growth and profitability by manufacturing abroad, then importing many of those goods back into the United States, will improving their competitiveness generate prosperity for American society? If foreign-owned firms open U.S.-based facilities that employ Americans and export some of their production, are they harming American prosperity? To what extent is the current state of U.S. industrial competitiveness the product of deliberate managerial choices, including subordinating design and manufacturing decisions to maintaining control of the work force, to short-term maximization of stock price or earnings, or to competing on the basis of cost rather than of quality?

To the extent that these questions have been addressed at all, and all are addressed by the essays in this volume, the answers quickly reveal the political character of the competitiveness debate. They reveal as well the complexity and the ambiguity of the value judgments with which competitiveness issues are entangled. To highlight the central role played by value judgments in shaping our understanding of these issues, the essays are grouped into three broad categories, distinguished by the value commitments that the authors bring to their conceptualization of competitiveness: Competitiveness and Economic Values; Competitiveness and Insititutional Values; Competitiveness and Social Values. The objective in offering these essays is not to resolve the competitiveness "crisis", but to broaden, and to deepen, the terms of the debate.

In the opening essay, Anthony O'Brien and Robert Thornton argue that the competitiveness debate suffers from major misconceptions of underlying economic issues, exacerbated by highly selective media attention. Because of the influence of such factors as massive federal budget deficits, changes in the value of the dollar against foreign currencies, and the decline of the U.S. savings rate, the trade deficit is not by itself a good indicator of the non-competitiveness of American manufacturing. Even falling market share and low rates of growth in industrial productivity, they claim, do not imply non-competitiveness. Examined dispassionately, individual U.S. companies are having trouble competing with individual foreign companies. This can have significant implications for communities and even for society, but it does not imply a general loss of competitiveness.

The growth of the U.S. economy was the same from 1965–1989 as it was from 1950–1964. U.S. employment growth during the "competitiveness crisis" of the 1980s was "well above that in any other major country," except Canada. Furthermore, contrary to public perceptions, almost half of these jobs (46.1%) were high wage jobs, not the stereotypical fast food restaurant service jobs: 94% were above minimum wage. The average annual growth rate of the real GNP per employee did drop sharply, from 2.2% in 1950–1964 to 0.7% from 1965–1989, but O'Brien and Thornton attribute this decline to two factors quite independent of industrial competitiveness. First, female participation in the work force doubled between 1950 and 1985. Most of this increase has come since 1965, and O'Brien and Thornton attribute part of the decline in the GNP growth rate to the fact that women are paid less than men for the same jobs—until recently much less. Second, the decline in the GNP per employee has been "largely confined" to the service sector. Manufacturing output per (manufacturing) employee was down only slightly between 1965 and 1985 compared with the earlier period, and recent U.S. Department of Commerce statistics suggest that it may have risen sharply in the past five years. But assigning the decline to the service sector is misleading. The quality of services provided today is much higher than it was forty years ago and this component has not been factored into the GNP per employee figure.

The competitiveness debate, then, is misguided. If it were informed by a correct understanding of relative competitive advantage, the debate would take on an altogether different tone. O'Brien and Thornton do not mean to imply that American industry suffers from no competitiveness problem at all. It is "worrisome" to them that foreign companies "have been able to establish production facilities in the United States that turn out products that American consumers prefer to those turned out by U.S. companies." But the causes of this problem cannot be any of those that dominate the competitiveness debate, while the solutions proposed "are much more likely to reduce the American standard of living than to raise it."

In Europe, at least, the subject of industrial competitiveness has gone far beyond the confines of debate. It has precipitated a multinational industrial policy in pursuit of competitive equality with Japan and the United States: the European Community unification initiative scheduled for consummation in 1992. Michael Hodges outlines in his essay the recent history of the European integration movement and the role played in the integration movement by the post-war quest for industrial competitiveness.

By 1958 the six member states of the European Economic Community agreed that post-war economic recovery had been accomplished and the stability of democratic government in western Europe assured. Their economic agenda for the future then included "emulation of the continental market of the United States." The cultural and political barriers to creating such a market, however, were formidable. The "American Challenge," as Jean-Jacques Servan Schreiber styled it in a best-selling book of the mid-1960s, and the perception that the United States–USSR space and arms "races" were creating a technology gap between the United States and western Europe, lent a sense of urgency to the formulation of a joint industrial policy.

Initially it was thought sufficient to harmonize commercial company law among member states to facilitate transnational mergers and joint ventures. This approach had the advantage of avoiding the political and cultural issues implied by true economic integration. With the expansion to nine nations and the admission of an integration-shy Britain (in 1973), major joint policies were almost invariably frustrated by the requirement of a unanimous vote for decisions to be binding. In addition, the assumption that "reducing internal trade barriers would by itself lead to the restructuring of European industry" proved incorrect. A series of efforts in the 1970s to press more active industrial policies, in effect "picking winners," achieved little. Britain, France, and West Germany had exclusive economic agendas, perhaps because the last two, at least, still hoped to achieve competitive parity with the United States on their own.

The threat of American economic dominance did not inspire union in the face of a common "enemy." The decline of American economic and political power, however, concurrent with the startling rise of Japan and the dissolution of the Russian threat to western Europe, did. The major European industrialists recognized that a single domestic market permitted vital economies of scale and scope. It was necessary to form such a market to keep Japan at bay. Once formed, however, this market could also serve as a springboard for global competitiveness. At the same time, major European political figures saw in the mutual decline of the United States and the USSR an opportunity for an integrated western Europe to rise to political parity with the "superpowers."

A 1985 "white paper" for the Commission of the European Community, then with eleven member nations, outlined "some 300 measures" that needed to be taken if the nations of the EC were to achieve economic integration. In 1987 the Single Europe Accord was ratified and a crucial procedural change was adopted. After 1987, except for fiscal and social matters, EC rulings only required a majority vote to be binding. By December 1990, 281 of the 300 "white paper" measures had been drafted, were submitted to the Council of the EC—which had not met to discuss industrial policy once during the preceding seventeen years—and two-thirds were approved (though implementation lies ahead). "It is business," Hodges writes, "not member governments, that is making a reality of the single market in Europe." And business in this context includes American multi-national corporations such as GM, Ford, and IBM, companies that pioneered pan-European corporate strategies in the 1960s. The unification program has been driven by "market-led dynamics of the globalization of competition and the escalating cost of technological innovation," together with "policy-led factors that have a micro-economic impact at the level of the individual firm."

Geraldo Vasconcellos and Richard Kish argue in their essay that the "motivations involved in the complex web of international capital flows represent an important dimension of competitiveness." Foreign direct investment in the U.S. economy has become an increasingly significant factor in U.S. industrial competitiveness and a strident theme in the competitiveness debate. "Accordingly, the study of [cross-border mergers and acquisitions] . . . complements and illustrates the several angles from which the competitiveness question is examined in this volume." In particular, Vasconcellos and Kish address the motivations underlying acquisitions involving U.S. and Japanese companies from 1982–1989. Applying a statistical model they have developed for assessing corporate merger-acquisition decisions, they conclude that the anti-Japanese rhetoric provoked by recent acquisitions is unjustified.

Which variables explain why Japanese companies, in the second half of the 1980s, increased the rate at which they acquired U.S. companies, while U.S. companies decreased the rate at which they acquired Japanese companies? Until the recession of 1981–82, for example, U.S. companies were the acquiring companies in 56% of United States–Japan cross-border mergers and acquisitions. By 1989 this figure had declined to 26%. Broadly speaking, the attractiveness of the U.S. market to foreign investors is a function of its size, its openness—"the generally benign set of rules and regulations concerning foreign businesses"—and the political stability of U.S. society. In addition, access to technology is an important factor "in industries where frontier technologies are crucial to competitive advantage."

Because of corporate cultural factors, Japanese companies believe that they have a special opportunity to succeed in the U.S. market. Japanese corporate management practices since World War II have been a blend of assimilated U.S. managerial expertise and Japanese communitarian values. Together with the much longer investment horizons of Japanese, as opposed to U.S. management, the "foreignness" of acquiring U.S. companies was substantially diminished. In addition, the frenzy of U.S. corporate restructuring in the period, coming at a time of successive record high profits for Fortune 500 companies and swelling cash balances in Japanese companies, provided a compelling opening for Japanese investment.

To these factors must be added the fluctuating dollar-yen exchange rate and the opportunity to balance vulnerability in the home market by cross-economy diversification, as well as such negative factors as a possible lack of relevant information about a foreign company and the cost of replacing its inefficient, or now redundant, management. In the end, for Vasconcellos and Kish, mergers and acquisition decisions are to be "evaluated like any other project" and, in particular, in relation to the framework of capital budgeting decisions made by a firm. They present a statistical model for assessing such decisions and its application to U.S.–Japan acquisition data for the period 1982–1989. They conclude that there is no need to resort to ideological, political, or conspiratorial explanations. The "combined impact of the exchange rate, cost of debt (that is, bond yields), and equity prices explains quite well the trends of cross-border acquisitions in the U.S.-Japan case."

More generally, when combined with their application of this model to direct investment by U.S. and British companies in one another's economies, it emerges that currency exchange rates are accurate predictors of trends, while cost of debt and equity prices are decisive when individual decisions need to be made. To the extent that exchange rates and corporate bond and equity prices are symptomatic of competitiveness, given the complex of relevant factors Vasconcellos and Kish identify, the rate of cross-border mergers and acquisitions is an index of competitiveness.

John Gatewood's essay reveals that marine fisheries management policies hold profound lessons for students of industrial policy. Competing for fish in an open access marine fishery and competing for customers in an international free trade environment have strong similarities. Fisheries and consumer markets are both necessarily limited in size and restore themselves at rates unconnected with the rate at which they can be exploited using modern technology. Open access to both promotes the "natural" response of developing increasingly powerful exploitative technologies to harvest the maximum yield before competitors move in. This tactic, however, threatens to "overfish" markets no less than fisheries. It also drives up the investment needed to compete. The end result is an instance of the "tragedy of the commons": everyone's economic harvest suffers in the wake of over-exploitation and over-capitalization.

Gatewood begins his essay by discussing several different models that aim at explaining why fisheries inevitably are over-exploited and the fishing industry over-capitalized. Value-free models based on the dynamics of biological populations contrast with models incorporating competing values of economic yield, resource sustainability, and "socially optimal" yield. As amorphous as social optimality may seem, the 1977 Magnuson Fisheries Conservation and Management Act requires that U.S. fisheries management policies take into account social and ecological, as well as economic, factors.

Any attempt to manage access to what is perceived to be an open resource runs counter to traditional American values such as equal opportunity. Doing nothing, however, guarantees short-term profitability at best, exhaustion of the resource base, and the need to move to another fishery, for as long as other unexploited fisheries are available to move onto! Scientific management policies quickly bump up against the conflicting demands of efficient use of the resource, of labor, and of capital and equipment. How can capital investment in technology, access to an open resource, pursuit of maximum profit, and prevailing social values concerning the distribution of resources all be balanced in an intensely competitive environment so as to provide sustained prosperity?

Gatewood explores that question by way of six regulatory tactics that U.S. fisheries managers have in their management "toolkits." Each of these tactics balances, in a different way, resource conservation values, economic efficiency values, and social justice or

equity values. Fleet size quotas are capable of conserving the resource, but only at the expense of optimal economic efficiency and
social equity. Sole ownership of fishing rights can be economically
efficient, but social equity values must be ignored and resource
conservation is by no means guaranteed.

International price competition adds another level of complexity.
American consumers have been buying fish from foreign vendors
at a rate that in 1989 generated a $5 billion trade deficit in fresh and
processed fish alone. U.S. fisheries cannot, therefore, be managed
without taking into account the impact of management policies on
the cost of American fish relative to the prices at which foreign
competitors offer fish in U.S. as well as in global markets.

Domestic U.S. and global markets for industrial and consumer
goods and services display the same kinds of features that fisheries
do. Management policies for industrial markets give rise to the
same sorts of issues, the same need for compromises between conflicting and competing values, the same penalties for inaction or
narrowly conceived regulatory action, that fisheries management
gives rise to. In the nineteenth century, for example, industry
shifted from a historically labor intensive, wealth distributing activity to a capital intensive, wealth consolidating activity. In the first
half of the twentieth century, commercial fishing went through precisely the same transition. For both, issues of domestic equity seem
to conflict with the ability to "compete in a free trade global market." For both, the price exacted by policy inaction—over-capitalization, natural resource/market depletion, loss of profitability—is
the same and unacceptably high. Management policies, however,
require deliberate, overt, value judgments that exact a political
price of their own. Because fisheries management issues implicate
a narrower range of vested interests than industrial policy issues
do, they have developed further and without provoking broad public debate. As a result, they offer an interesting miniature for industrial policymakers to consider.

Carole Gorney's essay assesses the impact of federal regulation
on U.S. industrial competitiveness and addresses the issue of a role
for the public in shaping regulatory initiatives. On the one hand,
Congress expresses concern about the competitiveness of U.S. industry and takes concrete action to support it. Congress has selectively relaxed anti-trust laws, liberalized patent assignment
agreements for federally funded research, created programs for
transferring technology from federal laboratories to the private
sector, and funded the development of important new technologies.
On the other hand, Congress enacts regulatory legislation that Gor-

ney claims has increased the competitiveness burden on U.S. industry.

Congress has also pursued a distinctive approach to regulation, responsive to the tug-of-war among competing special interests that is a feature of American-style, single-issue politics. Congress maintains centralized control of the regulatory process, specifies pollution control processes to be employed, and lays down detailed rules and regulations for complying with its mandated standards. Japanese and western European governments, by contrast, set limits and allow affected companies to decide on the means they will use to comply with them. Their regulatory legislation is largely procedural and is formulated cooperatively rather than adversarially, with few "legally enforceable codes." The result is that the American response to environmental, health, and safety regulation "has proven itself to be costly and ineffective, placing American business and industry at a comparative competitive disadvantage with the rest of the world." Worse, Congress is not adequately representing the right of the public, in a democracy, to influence decisions that profoundly affect their lives. Congress' approach to regulatory public policy is simply too vulnerable to special interests, too adapted to political compromise, for the public to feel that they have participated "meaningfully" in industrial managerial decision-making processes.

Gorney defines "public," in this context, as a "loosely structured" set whose members "detect the same [industrial activity-related] problem or issue" and "behave as though they were one body." She identifies "meaningful" participation as entailing "two-way symmetric communication in which concerned parties . . . mutually pursue solutions [to common problems] that take all relevant factors into consideration." This does not imply that industrial decision makers will always adopt the positions argued by public activists. It does imply that public opinion will be factored into proprietary decision-making processes before, rather than after, decisions are made.

Gorney cites the Public Advisory Committees of Pennsylvania Power and Light and South Carolina Bell as positive instances of corporate efforts to identify public interests and concerns, and to respond to them proactively. Both utilities discovered that time and money could be saved by working with the public in advance of costly planning, or of actual facilities investments that could provoke controversy. Gorney reviews five citizen-participation mechanisms that emerged out of a 1970s study at the University of Michigan, but she concludes that all of the mechanisms reviewed "are flawed in terms of the two-way symmetric model" that she has identified as the ideal.

Two programs exemplify the best current provision of a meaningful public role in setting industrial managerial agendas: the Office of Public Participation within the Department of Environmental Protection of the State of New Jersey and the "Responsible Care" program of the Chemical Manufacturers Association. Both programs require the systematic engagement of widening circles of affected citizens before institutional policies can be finalized. In the case of the State of New Jersey, the process is restricted, so far at least, to setting groundwater quality regulations. The Chemical Manufacturers Association, however, includes over 90% of the "basic" chemical industry capacity in the United States. Its members are now "obligated to participate" in a network of Community Advisory Panels linked to a national-level Public Advisory Panel designed to give citizens a voice in chemical manufacturing agendas. These programs must be taken up as models, Gorney argues, if community involvement in corporate decision making is to become efficacious, and offer an alternative to federal regulation of industrial activity, with positive consequences for U.S. competitiveness.

Steven Goldman and Roger Nagel argue in their essay that the form and the content of technological innovation is driven by the selective utilization of technical knowledge within individual firms. If innovation is a factor in a firm's competitiveness, then it becomes important to identify the subjective value judgments embedded in the selection criteria employed by management in assigning to technical knowledge the role it is to play in corporate planning and in deciding which knowledge to utilize, in what forms, and on what scale. Furthermore, a complex interdependence exists among the organizational structure of an industrial corporation, the enterprise-specific "logic" of its managerial decision-making processes, and the utilization of technologies and technical knowledge. Ultimately, the impact of innovations on the competitiveness of firms, industries, and societies depends on the deliberate mutual adaptation of management values and technical resources.

Goldman and Nagel focus on manufacturing enterprises because of the centrality of technology to their competitiveness. They refer to the historical development of a broad range of technologies, and to philosophical and sociological studies, that support their characterization of innovation as a social process driven by the self-serving agendas of public, no less than of private, institutions. That is, each of these institutions reflects in its changing agenda its management's judgment, at that time, of which objectives are in the best interests of that institution, given its distinctive relationship to society, and of how those objectives ought to be pursued by that institution. The decisions management makes concerning the utilization of technical knowledge cannot be derived formulaically, however. Goldman and Nagel refer to a Technological Innovation Function that management must solve in making those decisions. Unfortunately, no algorithm can be given for the solution of this function, nor does it possess a unique solution.

Managerial decision making is, in this respect at least, very much like engineering design. Both require assigning weights in accordance with subjective value judgments to solution parameters whose identification as necessary and sufficient to the solution of a given problem is itself to a significant degree subjective. The problems addressed by industrially employed engineers are defined by the particular interests of their employers and those same interests determine what will constitute acceptable solutions to those problems. The very same is true of managerial decision making vis-a-vis technological innovation: how shall it enter into the management "design" problem of operating the corporation (or governmental agency) "successfully?"

Goldman and Nagel emphasize the importance of the mutual adaptation of management organization and technical knowledge to the competitive power of an enterprise. The decisive competitive power of early industrial corporations, for example, derived from the synthesis of a set of existing production, communication, and transportation technologies, and a new commercial managerial structure: the centrally administered, hierarchically organized, vertically integrated corporation. Without the telegraph and telephone, steamships and railroads, steam and electric power, these industrial corporations would not have come into being. But all of these separate technologies, although they existed, had the transformative impact they have had on commerce, politics, and the forms of modern social life only through their integration into an adapted organization, namely, the mass-production manufacturing enterprise. Current anti-trust legislation is a testimony to the competitive power that integration achieved.

After 100 years of commercial dominance, mass-production enterprises are today being challenged by a new form of manufacturing called "agile" manufacturing. In place of achieving low cost through the mass production of uniform products, agile manufacturing produces high quality, highly customized products at low cost, and brings new or improved products to market quickly. Mass-production manufacturing required long production runs in order to amortize the high cost of dedicated production facilities. It thrived on short-lived, discontinuous, product generations: new models of the same product were meant to replace earlier models as part of the rationale for their production. Agile manufacturing thrives on short production runs and extended product longevity through products that can be upgraded and reconfigured as user requirements change. Goldman and Nagel offer a "vision" of what the emerging reality of agile manufacturing will look like when it matures. They argue that, essential as new production and information processing technologies are to accomplishing the goals of agile manufacturing, its latent competitive power will only be realized if these technologies are integrated into an organizational structure whose managerial values are matched to the distinctive requirements of the technologies being utilized.

Gail Cooper offers a complementary perspective to that of Goldman and Nagel on the influence of managerial values on competitiveness. She describes value judgments that have shaped U.S. and Japanese management practices in contrasting ways. American leadership, nationally as well as at the level of the individual firm, places a premium on invention, on achieving competitive advantage by breakthrough research and innovations. Japanese leadership, especially at the level of the firm, places a premium on manufacturing and production values that yield competitive advantage through constantly improved applications of science and technology. In the United States, science and technology serve international political goals in the "hope that domestic economic prosperity and civilian technological leadership" will be by-products. The American obsession with Nobel Prize awards as a validation of "the American way," the dominance of defense-based R&D, the focus on Big Science, and with projects that are the first, the biggest, the best achievements in their field, are all symptomatic of this policy. Since World War II, Japanese leaders have consistently "pursued economic goals in the belief that they will be a means of implementing international political ends." Japanese leaders have made technology-based domestic economic growth and aggressive exporting the bases of Japan's international influence.

Political rhetoric to the contrary notwithstanding, the United States does have an industrial policy. This policy has for forty years been dominated by "strategic concerns and the drive to contain communism," by defense spending, by patent policies, tax laws, export restrictions, and environmental, health, and safety legislation. In Japan, government and industry found mutual reinforcement for cooperating to achieve commercial success by using new technologies to gain footholds in international markets. The development of Japanese industry was, for example, powerfully reinforced by their systematic enhancement of mass-production manufacturing, eventuating in a "new system of production, one that differs significantly from Henry Ford's . . . system."

The Ford-based moving assembly line "pushed" materials through the production process to stockpile and sell. The rate of production determined the speed with which workers had to complete their tasks as well as the rate of consumption of the materials used. Together with such factors as delivery schedules, availability, and seasonal price variations, the rate of production also dictated inventory requirements to sustain that rate. During World War II, the U.S. War Production Board had experimented with a "pull" system of production for manufacturing aircraft, in which workers pulled materials out of inventory as they needed them. This system dramatically reduced inventory requirements while focusing attention on the quality of materials supplied and on the production process itself. After the war, U.S. manufacturers returned to the traditional "push" system, but in the late 1950s, engineer Ono Taiichi introduced a "pull" system of production, identified today with Just-in-Time (jit) inventory management, at Toyota. Ono devoted himself to perfecting the system and enhancing it. He also developed non-scale based economies of production such as faster die changes, and he explored the impact of providing workers with more, and more varied, machine tools, moving toward the objective of a more flexible production system.

Concurrently, Japanese manufacturers introduced statistical quality control (sqc) on a comprehensive basis. In addition, Japanese management drew from the concurrent implementation of jit and sqc the lesson that quality could be uncoupled from cost of production. High quality products could be manufactured on a mass-production basis at low cost. It took a long time before American management was receptive to this, by then all too obvious, new truth. And furthermore, while the "general direction of American industrial management, such as Taylorism, has contributed to the deskilling of factory workers, sqc as it is practiced in Japanese quality control circles enriches the skills of workers."

Cooper contrasts the differential impact on competitiveness of U.S. and Japanese managerial values relating to production. In his essay, John Smith contrasts U.S. and Japanese social values with respect to competition and relates the different managerial attitudes toward production that Cooper noted to the institutionalization of these values in Japanese and American versions of the modern industrial corporation. Smith argues that the American public is "obsessed" with Japanese success, and the cost to America with which that success has been won, because Japanese society is a "distant mirror" of our own. We can easily recognize features of U.S. society in Japanese society, but there are curious "inversions," as in all mirror images, that render the familiar puzzlingly alien. Smith reflects on the Japanese passion for baseball as an illustration of this familiarity-cum-alienness. Baseball, like manufacturing, has a sequential form of action that focuses at any moment on an individual player's skillfulness. Success, however, comes only from the complementary cooperative behavior of the other players on the team. In the U.S., reward of individual excellence, in fact, dominates despite the rhetoric that lauds team play. In Japan, team play dominates in ways that invariably startle and disorient American stars who play for Japanese teams.

Smith relates this contrast to the choices offered by Jefferson and Hamilton, respectively, for the founding principle of American society. Jefferson championed individual initiative, Hamilton cooperative endeavor, as the key to a healthy and productive society. Every society requires some combination of both principles to function well, but inevitably one or the other dominates. In the United States, people admire consistent high individual achievement, but commonly resent consistent team success. Babe Ruth was a culture hero of almost mythic proportions despite his well-known vices, but the Yankees as a corporate entity were widely disliked. John D. Rockefeller was a popular hero, but not Standard Oil. In Japan, however, people admire the power and success that institutions achieve and honor individuals for contributing to that success.

The Sherman Anti-Trust Act, reflecting prevailing American social values, "codified cultural beliefs about the inherent goodness of competition." Competition became an end in itself, a Darwinian regulator of industry as it was of nature, uncoupled from the social impact of the object of the competition. At the same time that competition was being enshrined by Congress and the Supreme Court as a sacred American value, it became obvious that unbridled competition was, in a number of areas at least, insupportable. The creation of regulated public utilities for the provision of telephone service, electricity, water, gas, and mass transportation reflected this realization. So did the requirement of professional licensing, of governmental accreditation for educational institutions, and the "benign neglect" of obvious non-competitive production and pricing practices in many industries.

With the onset of the Cold War, and later the space and arms races, the U.S. government initiated massive government intervention in social affairs even as it continued to proclaim the sanctity of individualism and competition. It is no wonder, then, given this profound ambivalence toward competition in American social history, that the Japanese fascinate us as competitors with the United States. Although they play the same industrial "game" we play, the weights they assign to the elements of the game are practically the inverse of the weights we assign. This becomes quite clear in a comparison of U.S. and Japanese corporate structures.

Smith argues that the industrial competitiveness issue is "probably best addressed at the level of the corporation, the actual producer of wealth in America and Japan." As cultural institutions, corporations must balance individual initiative and cooperative endeavor, and the balance they strike is embodied in their structures. Smith builds on Alfred Chandler's approach to the study of the competitive success of the modern corporation. Chandler focused not on economic or market parameters, but on organizational structures as vehicles for realizing managerial objectives. Smith applies Chandler's "analytical framework" to British industry in the late nineteenth century, and to U.S. and Japanese industry in the late twentieth century. Smith calls special attention to the power of vertical integration, which Japanese keiretsu have carried to new levels, and to product diversification. Using the machine building and chemical manufacturing industries as examples, he argues that this combination is manifestly very hard to beat. The result of Smith's analysis, then, is that the success of individual Japanese firms cannot be understood apart from understanding how individualism and cooperation are balanced within a firm and how that firm itself functions cooperatively within a complex of other firms in a coherent larger whole validated by prevailing Japanese social values.

Edward Morgan and Robert Rosenwein offer a taxonomy of the rhetoric of the competitiveness debate. Their objective is to expose the ideological underpinnings of the most prominent positions taken, whether by defenders of management or defenders of labor. The rhetoric from the supporters of each position displays characteristic features of propaganda. Propagandists seek to hide aspects of their intent in order to avoid alienating certain potential supporters, and they attempt to suppress the "critical capacity" of audiences by selective misrepresentation. Because propagandists seek to "marginalize any counter-constituency of the[ir] recommended policies," Morgan and Rosenwein are concerned about the implications of the competitiveness debate for the practice of democracy in America.

A distinction needs to be made between "direct" propaganda and "sociological" propaganda. Although both play a role in the competitiveness debate, they play different roles and the relationship between them must be appreciated. Direct propaganda attempts to mobilize a public response to a crisis, in the process subordinating private gain to the public good. Sociological propaganda "refers to those assumptions, principles and 'tacit understandings' that provide a set of culural resources on which elites can draw in using direct propaganda." The value attributed to a free market in a capitalist society, for example, is supported by four convergent elements: atomistic individualism, an ostensibly classless society, a distinction of economic rights from economic opportunities, and the legitimization of resource control in a context of selectively managed competition and cooperation. Public internalization of the free market as a good pulls these elements in its train, so that all are available without having to be justified in defending the establishment position against challenges to the free market.

Morgan and Rosenwein do not claim that the participants in the competitiveness debate consciously intend to propagandize. They argue, rather, that the crisis tone of the debate implicitly aims to maintain the structure and the operation of American capitalism "by mobilizing support and repressing, derogating, or marginalizing dissent." The force of sociological propaganda is such that few of the participants in the debate are prepared to challenge the root assumptions of the problem debated. If U.S. industry is suffering from a decline in competitiveness, that is because the fundamental supports of the post-WW II U.S. economy steadily eroded in the course of the 1960s and 1970s, quite independent of industrial competition from abroad. These supports were "a tripartite . . . system consisting of global military interventionism . . . , the resolution of severe capital-labor strife through consumption-stimulating higher wages (in exchange for managerial control of the workplace), and a governing ideology that often rendered invisible the social costs of business' quest for profits."

As the war against Iraq demonstrated, the context of U.S. global military intervention has changed dramatically with the collapse of the Soviet Union as a military threat to the West. Public support for U.S. military intervention abroad waned considerably after Vietnam. U.S. wages in constant dollars have been in decline since the late 1960s, and consumption for the sake of consumption continues to lose public support. As a result, the social costs of the quest for profits are far more visible and more openly contested today than in the early 1960s. The same is true for managerial control of the workplace. The success of the Japanese in American markets was thus symptomatic of an erosion that had already taken place, it was not the cause of that erosion. Nevertheless, the competitiveness debate proceeds as if the symptom were the cause and as if alleviation of the symptom would dissolve the cause. This distortion reduces the debate to a contest between special interests wherein the public's interest is explicitly not the central concern. If the public acquiesces in the conduct of the debate in these terms, then there is no forum for determining what the public interest is in industrial competitiveness issues or of how that interest should be protected.

In her essay, Laura Olson argues that the "concepts of, and goals for, competition" in U.S. society "are seriously at odds with the values, objectives, and strategies of other industrialized nations in the 1990s, disadvantaging the U.S. in the global market economy." Olson points to the counter-competitive consequences of the primacy placed on individualism in U.S. culture and on a constellation of collateral values linked to American capitalism. John Smith described how the Sherman Anti-Trust Act enshrined competition as an end in the American pantheon of values. Olson warns that U.S. industry will not recover competitiveness in the global marketplace unless it transforms competition into a means to "larger ends" rather than merely success at competing. Some of these larger ends are: rising living standards, a more equitable distribution of wealth and income, improved employment opportunities (especially for working class Americans), and enhanced working and living environments.

For Olson, "U.S. institutional arrangements, under capitalism, are simply ill-suited to the needs of modern industrial society." Privileging individualism and the proprietary rights of individual firms makes it impossible to set national economic goals that individual firms can cooperate in meeting. Instead of working toward communal goals, firms pursue their own self-interest and, in the name of a competitiveness crisis threatening all of society, demand communal help in pursuing their self-interest! These same American firms will, however, have to compete, even in the domestic marketplace, with foreign firms whose managerial decision-making reflects communitarian values and commitments that confer competitive advantages. The Japanese view of the industrial corporation is that of a complex partnership among management, labor, and financial backers at one level, and at another level among the firm, the family of firms with which it interacts, and various Japanese social institutions. This situation is not an intellectual or social abstraction. It becomes concrete in the firm's ability to pursue long-term growth and market share in the face of persistent low corporate earnings, in its readiness to invest heavily in both work-force training and new technologies of production, and in support for improvements of the production process.

Similarly, European industrial corporations have explicit obligations to the communities in which they operate, as well as to customers, workers, and supplier networks. These are reciprocal commitments that provide management with resources they can translate into competitive advantages. American corporate management, by contrast, spent much of the 1980s achieving new capacity and growth through mergers and acquisitions, improved profitability through lowering labor costs by moving facilities abroad, and improved competitiveness through buying, or buying into, foreign firms. The current internationalization of economic activity, and of manufacturing in particular, implies that the United States needs to adapt its cultural and economic values to "the prevailing cultural and corporate values, and the economic, social, and political structures" supporting them. Exporting our manufacturing sector by manufacturing abroad, while keeping research, development, design, and related service jobs in the United States is not an option. The service sector is not a substitute for a profitable, and hence a competitive, manufacturing sector because the two are significantly interdependent. Olson concludes, all of her criticisms of its industrial capitalist institutionalization notwithstanding, that competition can be a means to socially ameliorative ends and still be profitable for corporations. But it seems to her "problematic as to whether the United States is capable of confronting [the] formidable challenges" posed by the transformation of current practices required to accomplish this goal.

Today individual American firms find themselves competing not so much against individual foreign firms as against whole nations to which individual firms stand as the tip of an iceberg stands to its body. The blow that an iceberg can deliver in a collision is a function of the mass of the whole iceberg, not just the mass of the tip. Similarly, the ability of firms to compete against rivals is a function of the total "mass" of social resources—industrial policy commitments in the broadest sense—upon which companies are able to draw. When the rivals are foreign firms, constrained by a significantly different set of social resources, the competitiveness equation changes dramatically from the case of domestic competition.

The essays in this volume address the complex social rootedness of industrial competitiveness, a rootedness made still more complex by the intensifying globalization of industry that obscures the national identities and the social ties of corporations. The perspectives of the authors of these essays range from the austerely economic through the political and managerial to the richly sociological. Their common denominator is an engagement with the role that social value judgments play in determining the competitiveness of individual firms. For some of the authors this role is broad and definitive; for others it is narrowly circumscribed. Taken together, the essays establish the need for wider participation in a more wide-ranging competitiveness debate than has been held so far. What is needed is a debate in which the competitive strengths and weaknesses of American industry are identified—a debate that addresses the interdependence of the quality of American life and the health of the industrial sector of the U.S. economy, that opens for public deliberation the changes in values and institutions that need to be made. The extraordinary support of the Iacocca Institute, and especially of its Executive Director Larry Hecht, made this project possible, and contributed significantly to creating the collegial atmosphere in which it was executed.

Contributors

GAIL COOPER is Assistant Professor in the Department of History at Lehigh University. Her research is in the transfer of technology between the U.S. and Japan, with a special focus on statistical quality control techniques.

JOHN B. GATEWOOD is Professor and Chair of the Department of Sociology and Anthropology at Lehigh University, where he is affiliated with the Cognitive Science Program, the Environmental Studies Center, and the Center for Social Research. His principal research areas are decision-making, language, thought and culture, and commercial fisheries. (He worked as a commercial fisherman in Alaska for three seasons to acquire his research data firsthand.)

STEVEN L. GOLDMAN is Andrew W. Mellon Distinguished Professor in the Humanities at Lehigh University and a member of the Departments of Philosophy and of History. His research interests are the social relations of modern science and technology, and the relationship of technical knowledge to technological innovation.

CAROLE GORNEY is Associate Professor and Director of the Public Relations Program in the Department of Journalism at Lehigh University. She is a consultant in media relations and crisis planning and management and has published numerous articles in the *Journal of Communication, Public Relations Quarterly,* and *Public Relations Journal.*

LAURENCE W. HECHT is Executive Director of the Iacocca Institute at Lehigh University. Prior to joining the Iacocca Institute, he was Senior Vice President for Owens-Illinois Inc., with responsibility for manufacturing plants in the U.S., Europe, and the Far East. He serves on the Council on Competitiveness, a National Research Council committee, and a committee of the National Planning Association.

MICHAEL HODGES is Senior Lecturer in International Relations at the London School of Economics. He was for twelve years a member of the Department of International Relations at Lehigh University. His research area is international political economy, especially relations among Japan, the U.S., and the European Community. He is the author of *Multi-National Corporations and National Government* and of *The Development of the International Oil Industry,* as well as numerous papers and edited collections.

RICHARD J. KISH is Assistant Professor of Economics at Lehigh University. His primary research interest is debt securities and he has co-authored with his collaborator in this volume, Geraldo M. Vasconcellos, a related article on U.S.-U.K. cross-border acquisitions.

EDWARD P. MORGAN is Professor of Government at Lehigh University. His research area is urban politics and public policy with a special focus on the politics of the 1960s. His most recent publication is *The Sixties Experience: Hard Lessons About Modern America.*

ROGER N. NAGEL is the Harvey E. Wagner Professor of Manufacturing Systems Engineering at Lehigh University. His research is in industrial robotics, intelligent control systems, and the integration of manufacturing enterprises. He is a member of the (U.S.) National Research Council Manufacturing Studies Board and the author or co-author of numerous books and papers in his fields of interest.

ANTHONY PATRICK O'BRIEN is Associate Professor of Economics at Lehigh University. He has published widely in leading economics journals on a variety of subjects.

LAURA KATZ OLSON is Professor of Government at Lehigh University. Her research interests are in political economy and gerontology, especially private and public policies affecting the elderly, with a focus on long-term care issues. Her books include *The Political Economy of Aging: The State, Private Power, and Social Welfare; Aging and Public Policy; The Graying of the World* (forthcoming). She has been a Gerontological Fellow, a NASPAA Fellow, and a Fulbright Scholar.

ROBERT E. ROSENWEIN is Professor of Social Psychology in the Department of Sociology and Anthropology at Lehigh University.

His research is in human communication, the exercise of social influence in groups, the social psychology of politics, and the sociology of science. He is co-author, with Carol Barner-Barry, of *Psychological Perspectives on Politics.*

JOHN KENLY SMITH, JR. is Associate Professor of History at Lehigh University. His research area is the history of technology in America, with a special focus on the chemicals industry. He is the co-author of *Science and Corporate Strategy: DuPont R&D, 1902–1980.*

ROBERT J. THORNTON is Professor and Chair of the Department of Economics at Lehigh University. He is the author or editor of eight books, and has written more than fifty articles dealing with such diverse topics as unionism, collective bargaining, the economics of the public sector, and litigation economics. He has served as President of the National Association of Forensic Economists and currently serves on the editorial boards of the *Journal of Collective Negotiations,* the *Eastern Economic Journal,* and the *Journal of Forensic Economics.*

GERALDO M. VASCONCELLOS is Assistant Professor of Finance at Lehigh University. His primary research interests are multinational business finance, international financial markets, and Latin American economic and financial issues. He has co-authored with his collaborator in this volume, Richard J. Kish, a related article on U.S.-U.K. cross-border acquisitions.

Competitiveness
and American Society

Part I
Competitiveness and
Economic Values

How Serious Is the U.S. Competitiveness Problem? An Economic Perspective

ANTHONY PATRICK O'BRIEN AND
ROBERT J. THORNTON

Until about 1980 most Americans, economists included, tended to pay little attention to the position and role of the United States in the international economy. Indeed, there seemed to be little point to doing otherwise. Imports and exports together amounted to a relatively small percentage of U.S. GNP, and our normal trade account was either in balance or marked by a deficit too small to be of concern.[1] U.S. manufacturers in general had few worries about their ability to sell their products to the rest of the world.

How quickly things have changed. Few economic topics have been more widely discussed during the last decade than America's "competitiveness." Against a backdrop of a growing U.S. trade sector and the emergence of chronic and sizeable trade deficits, the fear has emerged that the United States possesses an economy in a state of competitive decline, with many of its products—automobiles, steel, textile, apparel, footwear—unable to "hold their own" in the international marketplace. And there is no shortage of explanations for the decline. The list includes (to name just a few):

- a decline in R&D spending in the United States;
- inadequate investment in new factories, machinery, and equipment due to federal budget deficits and the high cost of capital;
- the neglect of human resources and an educational system which is failing in its mission to educate and train future workers;
- the overhead burdens of excessive legal, health care, and regulatory costs;

- poor labor-management relations;
- a slow diffusion of new manufacturing technologies;
- unfair foreign trade practices;
- the short-sightedness of American management.

In fact, the list of ailments seems endless.[2] To use a somewhat gruesome analogy, a hospitalized patient as sick as the American economy is alleged to be would long ago have "had the plug pulled."

But are things really as bad with the American economy as popular opinion and conventional wisdom seem to indicate? In this essay we analyze the issue of American competitiveness from the economist's perspective. We address the question of the various meanings as well as the misconceptions of the term "competitiveness." We find not only that the concept is a surprisingly elusive one, but that many of the concerns about the alleged decline of the U.S. economy are not supported by the evidence.

DEFINING COMPETITIVENESS

Can a Nation Be Noncompetitive?

There is an amazing amount of ignorance and confusion over just what the term "competitiveness" (or its converse) means when applied to an entire economy. Notice that there is no such problem of meaning at the microeconomic level. A firm is said to be noncompetitive if it is unable to market its products as successfully as its rivals because of problems of price, quality, delivery, or whatever. The same is true of an industry. But it is another matter entirely to question the competitiveness of an entire economy, as has been the custom of many journalists and other observers. No nation can be noncompetitive—or competitive, for that matter—in *every* category of goods and services it produces. Even Japan, the country to which the United States is most often unfavorably compared in the competitiveness debate, has many industries that can't compete. The reason lies in one of the oldest principles in economics: comparative advantage.

According to comparative advantage, nations are better off specializing in the production of those goods and services in which they are relatively more efficient, and trading for those goods and services in which they are relatively less efficient. Quite simply, it is logically impossible for a nation to be *relatively* inefficient in the production of *all* goods and services. To use a simple analogy, an attorney might be a better typist than his secretary, but he would not find it in his best interest to do all the legal work *and* all the typing. Rather, he would be better off to specialize in the area in which he possesses the comparative advantage (presumably the practice of law) and to allow the secretary—though perhaps a slower typist—to toil away at the word processor.

All too often, though, critics of the U.S. economy have ignored the principle of comparative advantage in their analyses of the competitiveness issue. Others have acknowledged the principle, but nevertheless continue to express grave concern at how U.S. dominance in certain industries (for example, steel) or in certain products (motorcycles) is deteriorating or has been lost. In fact, too much of the case in support of the declining U.S. competitiveness thesis is based on anecdotal evidence. Although such evidence has some value, it is difficult to accept it as proof of a general decline in competitiveness. The major difficulty with anecdotal evidence is that in the absence of a clear-cut definition of competitiveness, it is not at all clear what such evidence is telling us, much less what solutions are appropriate.

What About the Trade Deficit?

Probably no other evidence has been more often cited as proof of the deterioration of U.S. competitiveness than has the sizeable U.S. trade deficit. Since the early 1980s the merchandise trade deficit has risen sharply, peaking at $152 billion in 1986 and 1987. By way of contrast, the average annual merchandise trade deficit in the 1970s was only $9.6 billion, while during the 1960s the U.S. trade position was typically one of surplus.[3]

Contrary to the popular impression, however, the massive trade deficits of the U.S. are *not* primarily a consequence of any "competitiveness" problem that the United States might have. This is a point all too often ignored or misunderstood. Rather, these trade deficits are mainly due to a low level of domestic savings combined with a sizeable federal government deficit. These circumstances have brought about higher interest rates, which in turn have attracted a sizeable inflow of capital from abroad. This inflow of capital has substantially increased the price of the U.S. dollar. Higher priced dollars, of course, make American goods more expensive in world markets and foreign goods cheaper to American consumers—hence the trade deficit.

What evidence is there that the low U.S. savings rate, the high federal government deficit, and the consequently strong dollar are at the root of the U.S. trade deficit?

1. Between 1979 and 1985 (the period during which the U.S. trade deficit began to mushroom) the dollar rose about 50% against foreign currencies. As a consequence, the price of a typical American export good rose more than 25%.[4] Consequently, the rise of the dollar affected the competitiveness of American goods in world markets in the most basic possible way, by raising the prices of American goods relative to the prices of the goods of other countries.
2. The trade deficit itself emerged on the scene far too suddenly for a decline in competitiveness (supposedly caused by the various factors already alluded to) to have played much of a role. The early 1980s saw no marked changes in any of the relevant factors (government regulation, education, labor quality, and so forth) alleged to be at the root of the competitiveness problem. Hence, these factors are simply incapable of explaining either the magnitude or the sudden emergence of the trade deficit.
3. The level of saving in the United States fell sharply during the 1980s to about 3 to 4% of disposable personal income, down from levels that were double that just a decade earlier. U.S. savings levels now compare unfavorably with those of most other developed economies: Japan, 15%; France, 12%; West Germany, 13%.[5] At the same time, the federal government deficit has risen sharply (from $40 billion in fiscal 1979 up to $221.2 billion in fiscal 1986, down to $152.0 billion in fiscal 1989, and then back to $220.0 billion in fiscal 1990). Again, what all this means is that the United States—its people and its government—is spending beyond its means and is borrowing heavily from abroad to do so. The consequent high interest rates have kept the value of the dollar and the prices of U.S. goods on world markets high. The simple fact is that no matter how competitive a nation is, it will run a trade deficit if the nation's consumption is greater than its production.[6]

If Not the Trade Deficit, Then What?

We have been arguing two points so far: that comparative advantage renders meaningless the notion of competitiveness at the macroeconomic level, at least in the sense that not all of a nation's firms can be noncompetitive; and that however one tries to define competitiveness, the U.S. trade deficit is not a good indicator. What other definitions have been offered for competitiveness (or its converse)? Rachel McCulloch notes at least three additional meanings—or, better, indicators—of competitiveness:[7]

1. sectoral trade imbalances in certain industries (for example, autos) with certain trading partners (Japan);
2. falling market share (in total or by sectors);
3. low rates of productivity growth.

Closer analysis of "sectoral trade imbalances in certain industries with certain trading partners" reveals a logical difficulty. There is no reason to suppose that a country's economic fortunes require that a certain "balance" exist with specific trading partners. For example, because Japan is a resource-poor country, she will always have a sectoral trade imbalance with certain other countries, particularly oil exporting countries. Trade imbalances (deficits) with some trading partners will be offset by trade imbalances (surpluses) with others. This is as true for the United States as it is for any other country. Some may, of course, argue that it is *politically* undesirable to be at the mercy of foreign suppliers of key products. This is a point to which we will return. In fact, however, such imbalances are an unavoidable consequence of the trading process.

Another definition of competitiveness that has been put forth is that of a falling market share, either for total trade or for specific sectors. This, too, is a rather troublesome definition. As McCulloch states, "Many concerns about competitiveness are actually concerns about changes in the composition of output relative to some unspecified ideal."[8] Not only is the ideal, as McCulloch notes, usually unspecified, but also in a growing world market it is possible to have a decline in relative "share-competitiveness" at the same time that the absolute sectoral trade level is rising, which occurs if a country fails to capture a proportional increase in the growth of world demand for a particular category of products. This has been the case for the United States in several product categories over the 1980s. The total volume of U.S. exports in the machinery product category, for instance, rose from $57.1 billion in 1980 to $94.6 billion in 1988, an increase of 66%. Yet the U.S. share of world exports in this category fell from 21.4% to 18.9% over this same period. A similar phenomenon took place for transportation equipment (a 65% rise in U.S. exports, yet a decline in world share from 18.3% to 16.6%) and for chemicals (a 57% rise in exports, but a decline in world share from 17.9% to 16.0%).[9]

One last commonly offered definition of competitiveness—again, "indicator" probably is a better term here—concerns productivity growth. It is a matter of widespread concern that the rate of productivity growth in the United States appears to have slowed in the last several decades. In fact, since 1950 the U.S. has lagged behind other industrial countries in one measure of productivity growth: increases in gross domestic product (GDP) per worker.[10] However, several qualifications are in order:

1. Although increases in productivity appear to have lagged in the United States, the *level* of productivity remains well above the levels of its major trading partners. In 1987 the average American worker produced 18.9% more than the average German worker and 29.3% more than the average Japanese worker.[11]

2. Much, though not all, of the difference in growth rates in GDP per worker between the United States and other industrial countries reflects, until recently, "catch-up" from the very low starting points of the other countries. As Bosworth and Lawrence note, "It is far easier to copy than to innovate. In the past foreigners were able to increase productivity by adopting U.S. technologies, while productivity gains in the United States came from pushing out the frontiers of knowledge."[12]

3. As the levels of GDP in other countries have risen, the gap between productivity growth in these countries and productivity growth in the United States has narrowed. John Kendrick, one of the foremost researchers of U.S. productivity trends, has compared U.S. productivity growth trends with those of eleven other countries.[13] He has found that the growth rate of GDP per worker for the average of the other eleven countries was two percentage points higher than for the United States for the whole of the period 1950–1986, but only about 0.8 percentage points higher for the years 1979–1986. The gap in growth rates in manufacturing output per worker fell from 2.2 percentage points to zero. That is, during the most recent period for which data were available, manufacturing productivity in the United States grew at a rate equal to that of the average of the other eleven countries.[14]

We must be careful, though, to note the somewhat tenuous link between productivity growth and competitiveness on the macro-economic scale. Productivity is only one element in price level determination, and the favorable effects of productivity growth on competitiveness can easily be neutralized by adverse changes in exchange rates or wage increases. Moreover, it is not always the case that productivity growth and competitiveness are mutually compatible goals. Some macroeconomic policies that have been advanced for the purpose of increasing competitiveness would do so at the expense of future gains in productivity, restrictive trade policies being the obvious example here.

We have noted, then, the slipperiness of competitiveness as a macroeconomic concept. At this point some might think it para-doxical that a concept considered to be so "obviously" important can also be so difficult to define. To this the answer is quite simple: competitiveness is *not* a goal that is important *per se*. Rather, com-petitiveness is merely a secondary goal, a means to other ends, rather than an end in itself. And one end—some would argue the major end—to which competitiveness must take a back seat is the goal of higher living standards.[15]

THEN WHY THE CONCERN?

As we have seen, "competitiveness" is a rather elusive concept, one that lacks a precise meaning at the macroeconomic level. How-ever, this fact has not deterred journalists and many other observ-ers from asserting that America has a serious competitiveness problem. When journalists write about America having a competi-tiveness problem, though, they usually appear to be referring to the belief that there are certain American companies, for example, steel producers and automobile manufacturers, whose sales ought to be higher than they are relative to foreign companies selling similar products. Although this point is not always explicitly stated, the poor relative performance of these companies is held to be "bad" for the American economy. That is to say, it is presumed that the standard of living of the average American would be higher if these companies improved their sales relative to their foreign competitors. Such a presumption is not necessarily true, though, as some elementary economic analysis will reveal.

The general presumption among economists is that companies that possess the necessary technology, management skills, market-ing skills, and so forth to enable them to earn at least a normal rate of return on their invested capital will thrive and prosper, while those that cannot earn a normal rate of return will go out of business. The failure of companies that are unable to sell their products for a normal profit has always been considered a good thing. The resources (workers, machinery, and so forth) that such companies were employing become available to other companies more capable of selling their products at a profit. This is not to say that bankruptcies are an unalloyed blessing. Those persons formerly employed at a bankrupt firm must find jobs elsewhere; investors in the company have lost some part of their wealth; firms that had been supplying products to the bankrupt company see their sales decline. From the point of view of the economy as a whole, however, bankruptcies are the market's way of ensuring that scarce resources are employed in the best way. Donald Dull cannot make a profit running a diner at 4th and Main, but Sally Sharp realizes that the business that corner really needs is a pharmacy. She buys Dull's building at a foreclosure sale, and her venture becomes successful. Economicst believe that the most important factor in explaining the economic prosperity of the United States is the willingness of the American government to refrain from impeding the free flow of resources to their most productive uses. By and large the American government has been willing to step aside and allow those incapable of earning a normal profit to go into bankruptcy.[16] The economy is better off for these inefficient firms having disappeared.

But what if an American firm goes bankrupt because it is losing sales to competitors outside of the United States? The popular belief is that such bankruptcies hurt the American economy. Again, most economists disagree. If an American firm is incapable of producing television sets as efficiently as a Korean firm, the level of income in the United States will be higher if the American consumer is allowed to buy the Korean television set and the resources previously used by the American firm are made available for use by some other firm. Contrary to popular belief, the level of income in the United States will be *lower,* not higher, if the American government interferes with the freedom of American consumers to buy television sets from the Korean firm. In other words, all of the considerations that lead economists to favor allowing the market, free of government interference, to force into bankruptcy firms unable to meet domestic competition, apply with equal force to allowing firms unable to meet foreign competition to fail.

As Figure 1 clearly shows, America's share of the total gross national product of the Organisation for Economic Cooperation and Development countries (OECD) is much lower today than it

FIGURE 1

U.S. SHARE OF TOTAL OECD GROSS NATIONAL PRODUCT

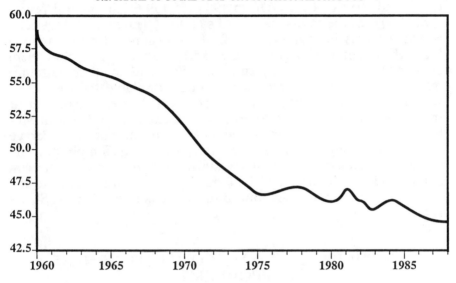

Source: Organisation for Economic Cooperation and Development
          National Accounts, Vol. 1, 1960-1988.

was in 1960, although the American economy remains by far the largest economy in the world.[17] Most economists are unperturbed by this situation, but should the decline in America's *relative* position be of concern? Most economists would say no for two reasons. First, America's share of total OECD GNP has fallen not because the American economy has been growing particularly slowly since 1960, but because the economies of many of the other member countries have been growing more rapidly. Hence, the decline in America's share cannot necessarily be taken as any indication that the American economy has been performing poorly. This very important fact is not generally recognized by the authors of journalistic accounts of the competitiveness problem. Second, the rapid expansion of the economies of many of the other OECD countries in the years since 1960 has greatly increased the range of goods and services available to American consumers. This expansion has also greatly increased the ability of the citizens of other OECD countries to purchase the products of American firms.

The significance of the decline in America's share can be looked at another way. What if the United States possessed the same share of the industrial world's gross domestic product in 1989 as it had in, say, 1950? In other words, what if the widely deplored decline in America's relative economic position had not taken place and the actual level of U.S. GDP in 1989 ($5,199.6 billion) still represented 60% of the industrial world's GDP?[18] The typical American would certainly be much worse off. If, for instance, Japan remained today the country it was in 1950, with Toyota, Sony, and Mitsubishi either very small or nonexistent, the variety and quality of automobiles and consumer electronics products available to Americans would be greatly reduced. If somehow Toyota were to disappear from the face of the earth tomorrow, shareholders of General Motors, Ford, and Chrysler would be overjoyed; but the average American citizen would be perceptibly worse off. Simply put, the economic development of the western European and Pacific rim countries in the years since 1950 has been a boon not only to the citizens of those countries, but to the citizens of the United States as well.

IS THERE, THEN, NO COMPETITIVENESS PROBLEM?

We have argued so far that the tremendous increase in the volume of imports of foreign manufactured goods into the United States during the 1980s has been a benefit to the American people. Undoubtedly this is true. Moreover, many of those who claim to see a competitiveness problem are either special-pleaders, hoping for government protection of their incomes at the expense of the general public, or so ignorant of elementary economic principles as to be incapable of understanding the points at issue. Nevertheless, our discussion to this point might legitimately be held to be overly sanguine for two reasons. First, while it is true that in the long-run society is better off if resources are allocated to their most efficient use, any major reallocation of resources among sectors of the economy may result in short-run problems of unemployment and declining income. Some have argued that this occurred in the United States during the 1970s and 1980s. Second, firms in a number of American industries—most notably, steel, automobiles, and consumer electronics—lost market shares to foreign competitors with extraordinary rapidity during the 1970s and 1980s. The speed and the thoroughness with which foreign firms surged ahead of American firms in these industries raises the question of whether there are some fundamental problems hobbling the ability of

American firms to compete. It is certainly a matter of concern that Toyota has been able to relocate production of its Camry model to a factory in Frankfort, Kentucky and to continue to produce cars of equal quality to those produced in Japan. This is a case of the domestic automobile companies failing to compete even on a perfectly level playing field. Walter Adams and James Brock estimate that the planned capacity of U.S. automobile factories partly or wholly owned by Japanese companies is 1,675,000 vehicles.[19] Annual sales of automobiles in the U.S. during the late 1980s ran in the range of seven to eight million vehicles. If the partly- or wholly-Japanese-owned U.S. automobile factories were to operate at capacity (which they currently are not), they would have a 20% to 25% market share in a year in which automobile sales were seven to eight million. The difficulty that U.S. automobile companies have in selling their products in competition, not just with Japanese cars produced in Japan but also with Japanese cars produced in the United States, is troubling.

It is true, as we have argued, that real income in the United States is higher because Toyota is able to produce automobiles more efficiently than General Motors. In this respect at least, increased imports of Toyotas are no cause for concern. But it is also true that American real income would be higher still if General Motors were able to produce cars in *its* U.S. factories as well as Toyota is doing in *its* U.S. factories. The striking success of Japanese-run automobile plants in the United States indicates a competitiveness problem in the U.S. automobile industry.

Our purpose in this paper, though, is not to explore the reasons for the relative lack of success of General Motors, Ford, and Chrysler in competition with Toyota and Honda. Rather, it is to discuss the reasons why certain definitions of the competitiveness problem are unsatisfactory—which we have done above—and to explore whether the *overall* performance of the U.S. economy has been poor during the period in which the relative importance of imports has increased so dramatically. It is to this latter issue that we now turn.

WAS THE OVERALL PERFORMANCE OF THE AMERICAN ECONOMY PARTICULARLY POOR DURING THE 1970S AND 1980S?

Figure 2 displays movements in the ratio of imports of goods and services into the United States as a fraction of American gross

FIGURE 2

IMPORTS AS A PERCENTAGE OF GROSS NATIONAL PRODUCT

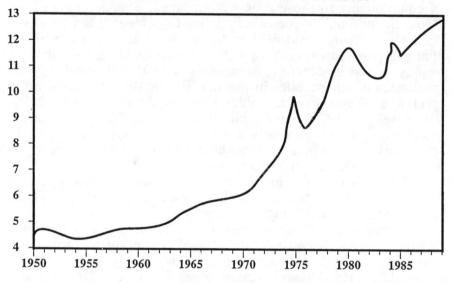

Source: Computed from data in the Economic Report of the President: 1990.

national product for the period since 1950. Table 1 provides an even longer-run perspective by giving figures for selected years back to 1870. The sharp rise in imports after 1965 is evident. Since 1970, imports have become two to three times larger, relative to the economy as a whole, than in earlier periods. The commonly held view is that this rise in imports has harmed the American economy as a whole. As we shall see below, however, there is little evidence that this has been the case.

Table 2 displays average annual growth rates of real gross national product and real gross national product per capita in the United States for each decade since 1870. The table indicates that decade-to-decade variation in the growth of the American economy has been fairly high. Interestingly, growth in per capita real GNP during the 1970s and 1980s, though not as high as during the 1960s, compares favorably with growth in several other decades: the 1880s, 1890s, 1910s, and 1950s in particular. Moreover, as this further breakdown shows, the growth of the U.S. economy since 1965 does not differ appreciably from the growth of the economy from 1950 to 1964, the era of so-called American economic pre-

Table 1

U.S. Imports as a Percentage of Gross National Product

Year	Imports/GNP
1870	7.7%
1880	6.6%
1890	8.4%
1900	6.4%
1910	5.9%
1920	7.3%
1930	4.9%
1940	3.7%
1950	4.3%
1960	4.7%
1965	4.7%
1970	6.0%
1975	8.2%
1980	11.7%
1985	11.2%
1989	12.9%

Sources: U.S. Bureau of the Census, *Historical Statistics of the United States,* Series F1 and U 193 and Executive Office of the President, *Economic Report of the President: 1990,* Table C–1.

dominance. In short, the period of the rapid rise in imports has not been one of particularly slow growth for the American economy.

Nor has the growth rate of the American economy in recent years been slow compared with growth rates in other industrial countries. Table 3 displays average annual growth rates in real gross national product for the United States and Japan for various periods during the last three decades. The table shows that since 1970 the growth rates of the two countries have moved towards convergence, with the difference between the rates having become quite small during the most recent six-year period. Moreover, the table also indicates that Japan's periods of fastest growth came well before it began to export large quantities of sophisticated manufacturing products to the United States. These statistics should dispel the notion that the growth of the Japanese economy has been highly dependent upon exports to the United States, and that Japanese economic growth has somehow been accomplished at the expense of the United States.

If we look at comparative rates of growth of industrial production, then, as Table 4 indicates, the performance of the U.S. econ-

Table 2

Average Annual Growth Rates of
U.S. Real Gross National Product, 1870–1989

Years	Real GNP	Real GNP per capita
1870–1879	5.6%	2.8%
1880–1889	1.7%	−0.4%
1890–1899	3.6%	1.9%
1900–1909	4.2%	2.4%
1910–1919	2.0%	0.7%
1920–1929	3.8%	2.5%
1930–1939	1.3%	0.7%
1940–1949	3.7%	2.4%
1950–1959	3.1%	1.5%
1960–1969	3.8%	2.6%
1970–1979	2.8%	1.9%
1980–1989	2.7%	1.8%

Sources: Calculated from data in Robert J. Gordon, ed., *The American Business Cycle: Continuity and Change,* Appendix B; U.S. Bureau of the Census, *Historical Statistics of the United States,* Series A 6; and Executive Office of the President, *Economic Report of the President,* Tables C–2 and C–31.

Average Annual Growth Rates

	Real GNP	Real GNP per capita
1950–1964	3.4%	1.8%
1965–1989	2.8%	1.8%

Table 3

Average Annual Growth Rates of Real Gross National Product
for the United States and Japan, 1961–1989

	1961–65	1966–70	1971–75	1976–83	1984–89
United States	4.6%	3.0%	2.2%	2.5%	4.0%
Japan	12.4%	11.0%	4.3%	4.4%	4.6%

Source: Executive Office of the President, *Economic Report of the President: 1990,* Table C–110.

Table 4

Average Annual Growth Rates of Industrial Production, 1982–88

Canada	5.9%
United States	4.9%
Japan	4.7%
United Kingdom	3.1%
Italy	2.4%
West Germany	2.3%
France	1.4%

Source: Executive Office of the President, *Economic Report of the President: 1990*, p. 45.

omy in the most recent period has been quite good. During the 1982–1988 period industrial production in the United States grew at a faster rate than in any other major country except Canada.

Conceivably, the rise in imports might have been disruptive in another way: the reallocation of resources necessitated by the loss of sales of some companies to foreign competitors might have had negative consequences for overall employment growth in the

Table 5

Average Annual Growth Rates in Employment, 1982–88

Canada	2.4%
United States	2.4%
United Kingdom	1.4%
Japan	1.1%
Italy	0.5%
West Germany	0.5%
France	−0.1%

Source: Executive Office of the President, *Economic Report of the President: 1990*, p. 45.

United States. Table 5 shows that this was not the case. Over the period 1982–88, employment growth in the United States was well above that in any other major country, again except for Canada. In fact, employment growth in the United States was more than twice that of Japan and more than four times that of West Germany during the period. Advocates of protectionism often allege that the jobs created during these years were low-wage, low-skill jobs largely in the service sector, while the jobs being lost were high-wage, high-skill manufacturing jobs. This claim is at striking variance with the facts. Information available from a study by the Congressional Joint Economic Committee on the wages of jobs created during the early 1980s states that from 1981 to 1985, 46.1% of the jobs created were so-called high-wage jobs paying more than $28,048 per year in 1984 dollars. Only 6% of the jobs created during these years were low-wage jobs paying less than $7,012 per year. Looked at another way, 94% of all jobs created during these years paid more than the minimum wage.[20] Moreover, there was very little absolute decline in manufacturing employment in the United States during the 1980s. In 1980 there were 20,285,000 persons employed in manufacturing; in 1989 19,611,000.[21]

In fact, as the U.S. economy has adjusted to the increased size of the import and export sectors, fewer low-skill jobs and more high-skill jobs have been created. The result is that those workers with few skills and little education have experienced declining relative incomes as the competition for the jobs for which they are qualified has increased because of the decreasing numbers of those jobs.[22]

The Bureau of Labor Statistics has projected that between the years 1986 and 2000 the rate of growth of high-skill jobs, as measured by the educational achievement required, will be significantly greater than the rate of growth of low-skill jobs.[23] There is, therefore, no merit to the assertion made so frequently by advocates of protectionism that the rise in imports into the United States has greatly impeded the ability of the American economy to generate high-skill, high-wage jobs.

While the statistics on employment and output growth considered so far are encouraging with respect to the performance of the U.S. economy in recent years, we need to deal with the objection that comparisons of recent GNP growth rates—total or per capita—with growth rates for prior decades are misleading because GNP growth in the post-1965 period has been sustained in large part by an increase in labor force participation rates, particularly those of women. In other words, growth in measured output has been said to have occurred in a way that is in a sense artificial, and not sustainable, because recent increases in total output have depended more heavily than in the past on increases in the number of workers rather than on increases in output per worker. To the extent that this is the case, it is the growth in GNP per employee rather than in total GNP or in GNP per capita that should be examined in analyzing the performance of the American economy. Statistics on output per worker (or per employee) are also interesting because they comprise one way of measuring productivity.[24]

As it turns out, in fact, increases in measured real GNP per employee have lagged considerably in the post-1965 period:

Average Annual Growth Rates of
Real GNP per Employee

| 1950–1964 | 2.2% |
| 1965–1989 | 0.7% |

The difference between an annual growth rate of 2.2% and a growth rate of 0.7% is quite substantial. At an annual growth rate of 2.2%, real GNP per employee will double in about 32 years; but at a growth rate of 0.7%, real GNP per employee will double only after about ninety-nine years.

There are good reasons, however, for suspecting that the slow-down in the growth rate of real GNP per employee in the post-1965 period is less important than it appears. The first reason concerns an often overlooked consequence of the recent rise in female labor-force participation rates—that is, the fraction of the female population working outside of the home. The female labor force participation rate rose from 33.9% in 1950 to 57.4% in 1989; however, the rise was not uniform over this period. From 1950 to 1965 the rate rose from 33.9% to 39.3%, an average change of 1.0% per year.[25] From 1965 to 1989, however,the female labor force participation rate grew from 39.3% to 57.4%, a rate of growth 60% higher (1.6% per year). In other words, the rate of "feminization" of the labor force has been substantially higher since 1965 than it was earlier. But what is the consequence for productivity growth rates? Because females in the labor force possess on average less experience than males—and experience is one very important determinant of productivity—part of the slowdown in the growth rate of the GNP per employee after 1965 is attributable to an accelerating change in the labor force "mix" during those years. A group with lower average productivity came to comprise a larger proportion of the labor force. However, this process will eventually end because the rate of increase in female labor force participation must eventually slow down and approach zero. When this happens, the growth rate of GNP per employee should return to its long-run trend.

There is a second reason why the post-1965 slowdown in the growth rate of real GNP per employee does not necessarily signify a poor level of performance by the American economy, at least not in the context of the competitiveness debate. As the data below show, the growth performance of the U.S. manufacturing sector since 1965 is not appreciably different from what it was in the previous fifteen years. In other words, the productivity growth slowdown that the American economy has experienced since 1965 has been largely confined to the non-manufacturing sector.

Average Annual Growth Rates of Manufacturing
Output per Manufacturing Employee

| 1950–1964 | 2.5% |
| 1965–1985[26] | 2.2% |

Table 6

Average Annual Rates of Growth in Manufacturing
Output per Manufacturing Employee, 1869–1949

Years	Annual Growth Rates
1869–1879	0.7%
1879–1889	2.0%
1890–1899	0.9%
1900–1909	1.3%
1910–1919	0.3%
1920–1929	4.3%
1930–1939	1.1%
1940–1949	1.2%

Source: Computed from data in John W. Kendrick, *Productivity Trends in the United States,* Table D–II, pp. 465–66.

Table 6 displays more detailed information on average annual growth rates in manufacturing output per manufacturing employee for ten-year periods between 1869 and 1949. A comparison of the data above with that of Table 6 shows that the growth rate during the 1965–1985 period has been higher than for any other period listed, apart from the decade of the 1920s. Overall, then, the period since the beginning of the import surge has seen productivity in the manufacturing sector continue to grow at a rate that is quite high, in historical context.

THE SLOW PRODUCTIVITY GROWTH PUZZLE

If productivity growth in manufacturing has remained strong, why then has overall U.S. productivity growth been so sluggish? In the past few years some researchers have become convinced that measurement problems may be at the heart of the puzzle.[27]

The biggest problem is that output in the service and construction sectors has become increasingly difficult to measure. The widespread use of computers in the service sector has allowed companies to offer a greater variety of services and to offer them more conveniently. Martin Neil Bailey and Robert J. Gordon have listed a few instances of this:[28]

> The transportation sector offers pre-assigned seats and boarding passes, "no-stop" check-in. . . . The retail trade sector offers better inventory control, fewer stock-outs, and most notably the radical increase in the variety of items carried. . . . The finance sector offers all-in-one cash management accounts, costless portfolio diversification for even the smallest investors through no-load mutual funds, . . . and 24-hour money machines. . . . Hotels . . . provide pre-printed registration forms, no-stop check out, and clerks who answer the room-service phone by telling the guest his name and room number, instead of vice versa. (p. 392)

These additional services do not, strictly speaking, constitute more output as output is conventionally measured. However, the provision of these services has certainly raised the quality of the output and the well-being of the customers of the companies providing them. Therefore, it seems reasonable to hold that if a broader measure of output were employed, productivity in the service sector would have risen in recent years much more quickly than the published data indicate.

Measurement of output in the construction sector, where measured productivity has actually fallen since 1967, also seems plagued with problems. The most important involves an upward bias in the government price deflator used to transform the data on construction output from nominal (or current dollar basis) to real (or constant dollar basis) values. Apparently the price index used does not adequately take into account increases in the quality of single-family homes. Many more single-family homes in the 1980s were built with central air conditioning, dishwashers, wooden kitchen cabinets, and so forth.[29]

Measurement problems of this sort, however, almost certainly account for only a part of the decline in measured non-manufacturing productivity growth during the last two decades. Many other factors have been offered by researchers to account for the decline. But often these factors have nothing whatever to do with the surge in foreign imports or with the competitiveness problem. For example, it is sometimes alleged that the quality of American schooling has declined precipitously since the mid-1960s and that this decline has had a deleterious affect on American productivity growth and competitiveness. Although it is true that the performance of U.S. students compares quite unfavorably with students in many other industrialized countries, the matter of how steep the decline has been or, more importantly, what effect it has had on American productivity and competitiveness are still not clear. For example, we know that from 1969–89 verbal scores on the Scholastic Aptitude Test fell from 466 to 424.[30] But can this be taken as evidence that the U.S. educational system is in a state of decline? Not necessarily, if one considers that non-white students are comprising an increasing proportion of all SAT test-takers, 27% in 1990, compared with only 17% ten years earlier, and non-white SAT scores have generally been below those of white students. In fact, this trend—the fact that an increasing percentage of minority students are now attending college—might even be considered as evidence of a favorable development for both society and the competitiveness problem.

Moreover, the link between performance on these tests and the performance of the economy has never been clear. Martin Neil Bailey has estimated that to be solely responsible for the decline in productivity between 1968 and 1979, labor quality would had to have declined by about 50%.[31] This is a much greater decline than that indicated by the test scores. Furthermore, as Gary Burtless has pointed out, because the decline in SAT scores coincided with the decline in rates of productivity growth, the labor quality problems that the SAT score decline may reflect could not have caused the decline in productivity.[32] The reason, of course, is that the decline in productivity began before significant numbers of students in the age group that had been performing poorly on the SATs had entered the work force.

Still it seems reasonable to hold that, at the very least, the quality of the labor force has not been increasing as fast in recent decades as it had previously. Denison, for example, has estimated that of the 1.6% annual rate of increase in U.S. national income per person employed between 1929 and 1957, no less than 0.67 percentage points (approximately 41%) reflected improvements in labor quality due to education.[33] It is very likely that any contributions to productivity growth after 1965 that increases in labor quality due to education have made have not been nearly as high. This fact might well be responsible for some American firms losing sales to foreign competitors. But, again, Bailey's estimates imply that the overall magnitude of such losses is not likely to be large.

POSSIBLE LINKS BETWEEN THE PRODUCTIVITY PUZZLE AND THE COMPETITIVENESS PROBLEM

Two other explanations for the productivity slowdown are more closely linked to issues surrounding competitiveness. Richard Easterlin has been an articulate advocate of the position that demographic factors have been an important source of the problems afflicting the U.S. economy since the mid-1960s.[34] The post-World War II baby boom has given the population of the United States a rather unusual age profile. In particular, beginning in the mid-1960s the U.S. labor market had to absorb an unusually large number of new entrants to the labor market. According to Easterlin, the limited possibilities for substituting new workers for experienced workers and labor for capital have meant that new workers have been competing for entry level jobs, the numbers of which were expanding at a very slow rate. The result has been not only lower incomes for new workers, but an increase in crime rates and suicides together with political alienation. As Easterlin argues: "When young adults find it easier to achieve their lifestyle aspirations, they are more likely to identify with the society in which they live; when they find it difficult, they are more likely to feel rebellious and alienated."[35]

If productivity growth depends to some extent upon the receptivity of the labor force to the introduction of new methods of production, then an alienated segment of the labor force may be a significant obstacle to achieving such growth. If Easterlin is correct, then this alienation may manifest itself in an unwillingness on the part of some workers to do a good job. To the extent that the widely heralded "quality-gap" between American-made and Japanese- and German-made products is at least partially responsible for the erosion of market shares experienced by many U.S. firms— as in the automobile industry, for instance—then alienation of the labor force may be a significant factor in the competitiveness problem. On the other hand, the problem may be a temporary one as the demographic distortions of the baby boom work their way through the labor market over time.

A second explanation for the productivity slowdown that is closely linked to the competitiveness problem can be credited originally to Nobel Laureate Sir John Hicks.[36] This argument also stresses the influence which demographic factors (such as the baby boom) can have on productivity growth rates. Here, though, the focus is on the relationship between wage rate growth and technological innovation. In periods of rapid wage growth, incentives for technological change and other labor-saving productivity improvements cause employers to attempt to economize on the increasingly expensive labor factor of production.[37] On the other hand, in periods of slow wage growth such as the United States experienced during the 1970s and 1980s, the lesser incentive to implement labor-saving technological innovation results in slower growth in labor productivity. As a consequence, the failure to innovate may have left some U.S. companies more vulnerable to competition from foreign competitors operating in economies where wage growth has been more rapid. To a large extent, the slowdown in the rate of growth of wages in the United States during in the 1970s and 1980s has been due to the labor-force-swelling effects of the baby-boom cohort and the substantial rise in female labor force participation rates. Both phenomena have resulted in higher-than-normal rates of growth in labor supply and lower-than-normal rates of growth in wages. But to the extent that the baby-boom cohort is gradually passing through the labor force, and because the female labor force participation rate will not be able to continue its past rise, the rate of growth of wage rates will most likely pick up once again—and with it the pace of technological change.

CONCLUDING REMARKS

Let us recap our arguments. We have noted the various senses in which "competitiveness" has been used and the difficulties associated with the various definitions of the term. In particular, we have argued that:

1) no nation can be noncompetitive in all industries, and
2) a trade deficit is not primarily an indicator of any competitiveness problem that a nation might have.

Most economists agree that productivity growth is the best indicator of how a nation's competitive position is changing—for better or for worse. Though it has no major effect on a nation's balance of trade, high productivity growth increases a nation's *gains* from trade. That is, it increases the amount of imported goods that can be obtained from a given amount of domestic resources devoted to the production of export goods. Over and above its implications for competitiveness, high productivity growth is important to the citizens of a nation because it is the means by which higher living standards are secured. We have found that the overall productivity growth performance of the U.S. economy has been comparable to that of earlier decades and comparable to the recent performance of other economies. Furthermore, even where signs of moderate productivity growth problems exist, these problems were seen to be in large part measurement-related, transitory, or not connected to the most commonly heard issues surrounding the competitiveness debate (poor education, short-sighted management, unfair trade practices, et cetera).

It is clear that our position on the competitiveness issue is not an alarmist one. True, the eroding market shares of many U.S. industries (such as automobiles and steel) and the outright disappearance of certain other industries are sources of concern to many. But we have argued that a natural consequence of the economic development of western Europe and the Pacific Rim has been the rise of companies capable of producing goods and services that are attractive to American consumers and that take sales away from American companies. The standard of living of the typical American is higher, not lower, because of this.

There are those who argue that ensuring the survival of certain industries, even by protectionist policies if need be, is necessary— that, for instance, America cannot survive as an economic power without a strong steel industry or a strong automobile industry. The usual argument is that if the United States does not produce these products, then it is vulnerable to future supply interruptions, price-gouging, and so on. It is also sometimes argued that unless this or that industry remains strong, America's military could be in jeopardy. These arguments have been used for hundreds of years to justify protectionist policies, as one sector of the economy or another has claimed that protection of its products is necessary for national security or to avoid dependency on potentially unreliable trading partners.

In fact, virtually no industry has *ever* asked for protection without invoking the national defense or economic dependency arguments.[38] In the Congressional Hearings on the Trade Expansion Act of 1962, for example, the House Ways and Means Committee heard the following impassioned plea from representatives of the scissors and shears industry:[39]

> H.R. 9900 would give the President unrestricted authority to reduce duties and thereby further reduce the cost of imported scissors and

shears in our market . . . [M]anufacturers would be forced to close their doors and discharge their employees. The United States would then become wholly dependent on imported scissors and shears.

We cannot understand how it could be in the national interest to permit such a loss. . . . In the event of a national emergency and [if] imports [were] cut off, the United States would be without a source of scissors and shears, basic tools for many industries and trades essential to our defense. . . .

Scissors are used to separate us from our mothers at birth; to cut our toenails; to trim the leather in our shoes; to cut and trim the materials used in every piece of clothing that we wear.

They are used to cut our fingernails, to trim our mustaches, the hair in our ears and nose, and to cut the hair on our heads—even down to the end of the road when our best suit or dress is cut down the back so that the undertaker can dress us for the last ride. Scissors are truly used from birth to death. They are essential to our health, education, and general welfare.

I ask you gentlemen, is this an industry that should be permitted to become extinct in this country?

The problems with these arguments in favor of protection are familiar. How does one determine precisely which industries are truly necessary for national security? Just how serious a problem is growing economic dependency in the cases of steel, automobiles, computer chips, or scissors and shears? And, ultimately, because the protection of any industry imposes costs on the nation in the form of lower real incomes, is the insurance that protection provides really worth the costs? These costs are usually underestimated, but in reality they can be very high indeed. For example, Robert Crandall has estimated that the quotas imposed on the importation of Japanese automobiles into the United States during the 1980s did save jobs in the U.S. automobile industry, but at a cost of $160,000 per job per year.[40]

In closing, we should make clear that our refusal to take an alarmist view of the U.S. competitiveness problem does not mean that we believe that there is no competitiveness problem. In particular, it *is* worrisome that in recent years Japanese and other foreign companies have been able to establish production facilities in the United States that turn out products American consumers prefer over those turned out by U.S. companies. This is clear evidence that, on a level playing field, foreign companies in certain industries have been able to outperform U.S. companies. The gist of our argument is that the consequences of the competitiveness problem for the health and future prospects of the U.S. economy have been greatly exaggerated. Moreover, many of the solutions that have been proposed for the problem—particularly those that involve protectionism—are much more likely to reduce the American standard of living than to raise it.

NOTES

The authors would like to thank Colleen Callahan, Steven Goldman, and Frank Gunter for comments on earlier drafts.

1. Martin Feldstein, ed., *The United States in the World Economy* (New York: National Bureau of Economic Research, 1987), 7.

2. See, e.g., Peter Morici, *Reestablishing American Competitiveness* (Washington, D.C.: National Planning Association, 1988).

3. U.S. Bureau of the Census, *Statistical Abstract of the United States: 1990* (Washington, D.C.: USGPO, 1988), 804.

4. International Monetary Fund, *International Financial Statistics* (Washington, D.C.: International Monetary Fund, May 1986), 504, 506.

5. *Statistical Abstract,* 440. These savings rates are computed according to the accounting methods used by the Organization for Economic Cooperation and Development (OECD) and are, therefore, comparable. (See Robert E. Lipsey and Irving B. Kravis, *Saving and Economic Growth: Is the United States Really Falling Behind?* [New York: The Conference Board, 1987], 26.)

6. There has been a great deal of discussion of the supposed fact that years of running large trade deficits have left the United States the world's largest debtor nation. Actually, the figures usually quoted to support this assertion are seriously flawed. Although the net international investment position of the United States as reported by the Department of Commerce stood at −$533 billion in 1988, the actual figure is probably a large positive number. This would mean that the United States remains a large creditor nation rather than a debtor nation. The discrepancy arises from the accounting practice of evaluating foreign fixed investment (such as factories) at historic cost. Because much of U.S. foreign investment was made decades ago, its market value greatly exceeds its historic cost. The bulk of foreign investment in the United States has been made more recently and, hence, its market and historic cost are much closer. (We are indebted to Frank Gunter for bringing this point to our attention.)

Furthermore, even if the United States were soon to become a debtor nation, it remains true that over the greater part of its history (from its beginnings to World War I) the U.S. was a debtor nation. Indeed, the U.S. was the world's largest debtor nation from 1865 on (see, Mira Wilkins, *The History of Foreign Investment in the United States* [Cambridge, Mass.: Harvard University Press, 1989]). Yet during this period U.S. growth rates surpassed those of most other countries.

7. Rachel McCulloch, "Trade Deficits, International Competitiveness, and the Japanese," in Robert E. Baldwin and J. David Richardson, eds., *International Trade and Finance Readings,* 3rd ed. (Boston: Little Brown and Company, 1986), 21.

8. Ibid.

9. U.S. Department of Commerce, International Trade Administration data as reported in *Statistical Abstract,* 1990, Table 1308. The percentage is based on

U.S. exports as a percentage of exports from 14 major trading countries: the U.S., Austria, Belgium-Luxembourg, Canada, Denmark, France, West Germany, Italy, Japan, the Netherlands, Norway, Switzerland, and the United Kingdom.

10. Barry P. Bosworth and Robert Z. Lawrence, "America in the World Economy," *The Brookings Review* (Winter 1988/89): 44.

11. Ibid.

12. Ibid.

13. Canada, Japan, Belgium, Denmark, France, West Germany, Italy, the Netherlands, Norway, Sweden, and the United Kingdom.

14. John W. Kendrick, "Policy Implications of the Slowdown in U.S. Productivity Growth," in Stanley Black, ed., *Productivity Growth and The Competitiveness of the American Economy* (Boston: Kluwer Academic Publishers, 1989), 77.

15. We are not the first to recognize the difficulty in coming to grips with the meaning of competitiveness. As Michael Porter puts it:

> It is far from clear what the term "competitiveness" means when referring to a nation. This is a major difficulty. . . . That there has been intense debate in many nations about whether they have a competitiveness problem in the first place is a sure sign that the subject is not completely understood. (Michael Porter, *The Competitive Advantage of Nations* [New York: The Free Press, 1990], 3)

16. The only important exception is agriculture, where the government has intervened to keep afloat many inefficient businesses.

17. The OECD consists of the former non-Soviet bloc countries of Europe, and the United States, Canada, Japan, Australia, and New Zealand.

18. Because the OECD was not established until 1960, statistics giving the U.S.'s share of the OECD countries' total GNP in 1950 are not available. Bosworth and Lawrence, ("America in the World Economy," 43) estimate that in 1950 the U.S.'s share of the sum of the GDPs of the U.S., Canada, Japan France, West Germany, Italy, and the United Kingdom was 59.3%.

19. Walter Adams and James Brock, "The Automobile Industry," in Walter Adams, ed., *The Structure of American Industry,* 8th ed. (New York: Macmillan, 1990), 106.

20. Warren T. Brookes, "Low-Pay Jobs: The Big Lie," *Wall Street Journal,* 25 March 1987.

21. Executive Office of the President, *Economic Report of the President: 1990* (Washington, D.C.: USGPO, 1990), 342.

22. Gary Burtless, *A Future of Lousy Jobs?* (Washington, D.C.: The Brookings Institution, 1990), 7.

23. Henry M. Levin, "The Economic Consequences of Undereducation" (Paper presented at the Conference on the Consequences of American Education, Lehigh University, 1990).

24. GNP per worker is only one measure of labor productivity. A more common measure would be output per hour worked. Because average hours worked per week have been quite stable in the post-World War II period, ranging from a high of 41.1 hours per week in 1988 to a low of 38.9 in 1982, the difference in growth rates between the two measures is small.

25. The male labor-force participation rate fell from 86.4 percent in 1950 to 76.4 percent in 1989. The total labor force participation rate rose from 59.7 percent in 1950 to 66.8 percent in 1989.

26. The year 1985 is the most recent for which national income account mea-

surements of total manufacturing output are available. See *The Economic Report of the President, 1990,* 306.

27. For a good discussion of the issues involved see Martin Neil Baily and Robert J. Gordon, "The Productivity Slowdown, Measurement Issues, and the Explosion of Computer Power," *Brookings Papers on Economic Activity* 18 (1988): 347–431.

28. Ibid. 392.

29. Ibid. 407.

30. Lee Mitgang, "Verbal SAT Scores Hit 10-year Low," *Allentown Morning Call,* 28 August 1990, A1–A2.

31. Martin Neil Bailey, "Productivity and the Services of Capital and Labor," *Brookings Papers on Economic Activity,* 11 (1981): 13.

32. Gary Burtless, "Current Proposals for School Reform: An Economist's Appraisal" (Paper presented at the Conference on the Economic Consequences of American Education, Lehigh University, 1990), 14.

33. Edward T. Denison, "Education, Economic Growth, and Gaps in Information," *Journal of Political Economy* 70 (1963): 128.

34. Richard A. Easterlin, *Birth and Fortune: The Impact of Numbers on Personal Welfare* (New York: Basic Books, 1980).

35. Ibid. 108.

36. John Hicks, *Theory of Wages* (London: Macmillan, 1963).

37. For a recent discussion of this argument, see Paul M. Romer, "Crazy Explanations for the Productivity Slowdown," *NBER Macroeconomics Annual, 1987,* 163–202.

38. Carl E. Case and Ray C. Fair, *Principles of Economics* (Englewood Cliffs, N.J.: Prentice Hall, 1989), 915.

39. Ibid.

40. Robert W. Crandall, "What Hath Auto-Import Quotas Wrought?" *Challenge* (January-February 1985), 47. These quotas were the so-called voluntary export restraints (VERs).

Stacking the Deck: The European Community's 1992 Single Market Initiative and the Promotion of Europe's Industrial Competitiveness

MICHAEL HODGES

MARKET INTEGRATION, INDUSTRIAL POLICY, AND INTERNATIONAL COMPETITIVENESS

The search for international competitiveness has been a theme, or at least a subtheme, of European integration in the last forty years. At its outset in the 1950s, the main objectives of the statesmen who initiated European integration were to restore the European economies, to prevent war between the member states, and to provide economic growth that would underpin the restoration of democracy to continental Europe. By the time the European Economic Community (EEC) was formed in 1958 (following the signing of the Treaty of Rome the previous year), these objectives were almost fully achieved. Attention now turned to the promotion of further economic growth through the achievement of economies of scale—in other words, emulation of the continental market of the United States.

Although by 1968 the EEC had achieved a customs union, many barriers to the free movement of goods, services, capital, and people remained. At the same time, a wave of investment by foreigners in the EEC (notably by American multinational companies) aroused fears of "the American challenge" and a "technology gap" between Europe and the United States. Nonetheless, the development of common policies, particularly an EEC-wide industrial policy, and the removal of non-tariff barriers between the member states, proved to be especially difficult for the Community. Its enlargement from six to nine members (including that reluctant European, the UK) in 1973 increased these difficulties, in part because the UK objected strongly to the established methods of financing the EEC's Common Agricultural Policy and what the British perceived to be the inequity of its budgetary financing procedures. In addition, the effects of the oil shocks of the 1970s and the subsequent recession of the late 1970s and early 1980s heightened the perception of "Euro-sclerosis": an inability to consummate the common market envisaged by the 1957 Treaty of Rome, let alone progress beyond that to economic and political union.

The EEC initially had no policies intended to increase the competitiveness of European industry through the initiation and coordination of industry-specific, supply-side policies intended to increase the productivity and competitiveness of targeted industrial sectors. Certain member states, such as France and Italy, had identified certain sectors for special treatment (automobiles and petrochemicals, to be followed later by electronics), attempting to "pick winners" by consolidating national capabilities in one or two "national champions."

Although the European Coal and Steel Community (ECSC) Treaty of 1950 gave the ECSC specific industrial policy-making responsibilities for those sectors, the Treaty of Rome that established the EEC in 1958 gave no such powers to the EEC's institutions. The implicit assumption was that the creation of a new, enlarged market for European firms by reducing internal trade barriers would by itself lead to the restructuring of European industry, and that the primary way of ensuring economic well-being was through enforcement of the EEC's fair competition rules and the progressive harmonization of rules governing business organization and conduct in the EEC. The operation of market forces would therefore do the rest of the job, without the need for sector-specific intervention at the EEC level. This assumed that economic integration, through creation of a common market and promotion of competition through enforcement of a supranational anti-trust regime, would lead to structural change and enhanced competitiveness of European industry. As subsequent events showed, such an assumption was not justified.

As Table 1 indicates, the European economies enjoyed significantly increased economic growth rates in the 1950s and 1960s, but this success was overshadowed by the phenomenal growth rates achieved by Japan. The benefits of a large internal market certainly

TABLE 1

Phases of GDP Growth, 1913-1984

(Average annual compound growth rates in %)

	I 1913-50	II 1950-73	Change I to II	III 1973-84	Change II to III
France	1.1	5.1	+4.0	2.2	-2.9
Germany	1.3	5.9	+4.6	1.7	-4.2
Netherlands	2.4	4.7	+2.3	1.6	-3.1
U.K.	1.3	3.0	+1.7	1.1	-1.9
Japan	2.2	9.4	+7.2	3.8	-5.6
U.S.	2.8	3.7	+0.9	2.3	-1.4

Source: *Angus Maddison:* Journal of Economic Literature (June 1987).

did not contribute a great deal to U.S. growth rates in this period, but it should be remembered that the United States remained far ahead of its competitors in gross domestic product per capita in this period and retained its position (if purchasing power parity ratios are used) even in the late 1980s. In the period 1973–1984 all the countries listed suffered a decline in their growth rates, with Japan retaining a comfortable lead over the rest. The concerted industrial policies orchestrated by Japan's Ministry for International Trade and Industry (MITI), in close consultation with the major firms in "Japan Inc," seemed to promote effective and rapid industrial adaptation. The EEC countries were and are diverse in their economic performance, and remain overshadowed by the U.S. in living standards and by Japan in productivity growth. Table 3 shows that the EC is much more dependent on trade as a proportion of its domestic product than either the U.S. or Japan; even after excluding the 60% of EC trade that is carried out between member-states, the degree of EC reliance on world trade is much higher as a percentage of GDP (18.7%) than the comparable figure for Japan (15.9%) or the U.S. (15.7%). This means that the competi-

TABLE 2

Gross Domestic Product Per Head (In US $)

1988 also in PPP [GDP per head adjusted for living costs] as % of US level

	1970	1988	1988 in PPP
U.S.	4,922	19,815	100.0
Japan	1,930	23,325	71.5
Luxembourg	3,468	18,000	79.0
Denmark *	3,215	20,988	74.2
West Germany	3,049	19,743	73.8
France	2,831	17,004	69.3
Belgium	2,669	15,394	64.7
Netherlands	2,585	15,421	68.2
U.K. *	2,209	14,477	66.1
Italy	1,875	14,432	65.6
Ireland *	1,315	9,181	40.9
Greece **	1,170	5,244	36.0
Spain ***	1,117	8,668	46.0
Portugal ***	700	4,017	33.8

Source: *The Economist: Book of Vital World Statistics*
(London: Economist Books/Hutchinson, 1990), pp.32-41.

NOTES: * Joined EEC in 1973
  ** Joined EEC in 1981
  *** Joined EEC in 1986

tiveness of the EC economies, defined in terms of their share of world trade, is of correspondingly greater importance than it is for Japan or the U.S., which import or export a smaller proportion of their GDP. Table 4 shows that in the 1980s the EC has been moderately successful in boosting exports to the U.S. and Japan, while becoming slightly less dependent on imports from its two main rivals.

TABLE 3

% Breakdown of GDP 1988

	Agriculture	Industry	Services	Imports (with EC members)		Exports	
U.S.	2.1	25.6	72.3	6.6	(1.6)	9.1	(1.8)
Japan	2.8	40.4	56.8	9.3	(1.6)	6.6	(0.9)
Denmark	4.5	28.6	66.9	24.5	(12.2)	25.6	(13.7)
West Germany	1.5	39.7	58.8	26.8	(14.5)	20.8	(11.1)
France	3.6	32.1	64.3	17.9	(11.0)	19.5	(12.7)
Belgium/Lux.	2.3	31.2	66.5	58.7	(43.6)	60.8	(42.8)
Netherlands	4.3	33.6	62.1	46.6	(34.8)	46.0	(28.3)
U.K.	1.4	35.7	62.9	17.7	(8.8)	23.7	(11.7)
Italy	3.8	34.5	61.7	15.5	(8.9)	16.6	(9.5)
Ireland	12.0	37.0	51.0	57.4	(42.5)	47.6	(33.9)
Greece	13.2	30.3	56.5	10.4	(6.7)	23.9	(14.9)
Spain	5.1	37.4	57.5	12.6	(7.6)	16.8	(9.5)
Portugal	9.1	39.6	51.3	25.7	(18.4)	40.2	(26.7)
EC AVERAGE	3.1	35.5	61.4	23.0	(13.7)	22.5	(13.1)
OECD AVERAGE	2.8	33.0	64.1	20.6		21.0	

Source: *The Economist: Book of Vital World Statistics*
    (London: Economist Books/Hutchinson, 1990), p. 36.
    Trade data calculated by author from EC statistics.

Although intra-EEC trade increased dramatically in the 1960s, ·
little intra-industry specialization occurred. In many sectors there
was a wave of investment by large American firms seeking to use
their experience of serving a continental domestic market by estab-
lishing operations in the integrating European market, thus threatening the viability of European companies. Some (notably the
French Government) wished to shield indigenous firms from the
"American Challenge" by restricting U.S. investment in the Community, lest American-owned multinationals operating in Europe
extinguish native European capabilities in the future-oriented,
high-technology sectors. Fears that Europeans would be the hew-
ers of wood and drawers of water, with American multinational
corporations in Europe growing to become the third largest indus-

TABLE 4

EC Share in Trade of U.S. and Japan

	% Of Each Country's Exports		% Of Each Country's Imports	
	1980	1988	1980	1988
U.S.	26.7	23.5	15.8	19.3
Japan	14.0	13.4	5.9	12.9

Source: Statistical Office of the European Communities:
BASIC STATISTICS OF THE COMMUNITY (27th ed., 1990), pp. 278-79.

trial power in the world (after the United States itself and the Soviet Union), represented a European "declinist" school that was far more widespread than the similar paranoia and pessimism in the United States in the late 1980s regarding the internationalization of Japanese companies.[1]

The general response of the west European governments to this competitive threat from America was to permit (and in some cases actively assist) the formation of "national champions" in various sectors (mainly in automobiles and electronics/informatics) to promote efficiency and competitiveness through national oligopolies: mostly private sector rather than state-owned enterprises. As early as 1967 the Commission of the EEC, the initiator of EEC-wide policy proposals, had submitted to the Council of Ministers, the policy decision-making body representing the member-states, proposals for EEC medium-term economic policy. These included measures for harmonization of company law in EEC member states and promotion of transnational mergers. This was the first time that the Community had proposed explicit industrial policy objectives. Although some transnational mergers and joint ventures existed in the EEC, such as Agfa-Gevaert in photographic chemicals and Dunlop-Pirelli in tires, the absence of transnational company law and the complexities of integrating different corporate structures and cultures made most of these partnerships unsuccessful. The "national champion" strategy was similarly unsuccessful in meeting the American (and later Japanese) competitive challenge, and in many respects served only to fragment the market.

In 1970 the EEC Commission produced the so-called "Colonna Report" on industrial policy, which pointed out that the development of successful industries in the European Community would require an explicit and coordinated strategy of industrial development, ensuring that all facets of EEC microeconomic policy were following convergent objectives. Implicitly, this was a call for the EEC Commission itself to coordinate regional development policy, identify and sponsor new technologies, and facilitate the creation of a trans-European industrial base. The Colonna Report itself was rather general and non-specific, but it was followed three years later by concrete proposals to endow the Community with the power to promote trans-border mergers through a European Company statute, meaning that merging companies could avoid the often conflicting national regulations that inhibited mergers between firms from different member-states. Up to this time several member states had treated such linkups as a disposal of assets subject to capital gains taxation. The Commission also wanted to establish policies facilitating the targeting of growth-oriented sectors of the economy and easing the adjustment of declining industries through provision of European Community finance to close down uncompetitive plants and retrain redundant workers. These proposals came to naught, since they ran up against a fundamental division between the EEC member states on the role of governmental intervention in the economy. Although France favored industrial intervention, it opposed giving the EC Commission new powers. Germany, on the other hand, objected to sectoral economic intervention, while Britain refused to permit any increases in the EC budget without reform of the Common Agricultural Policy. Given the necessity for unanimity in the EC Council of Ministers for approval of new policies, it is not surprising that the Commission's initiatives were fruitless. It was not until the 1985 Single European Act, which qualified majority voting for measures related to the creation of the Single European Market, that some inroad was made into the member states' power of veto in the EC Council of Ministers, one of the prime causes of stagnation in European Community policy-making in the 1970s and early 1980s. A generalized industrial policy was simply not on the political agenda of the EC member states, which preferred to initiate such matters on the national level, if at all.

Indeed, the reluctance of member states to cede authority to the EC in the field of a common European industrial policy was due to a desire not to be constrained in their own separate efforts to foster the development of indigenous firms. The repeated, and often successful, attempts of the EC Commission (using Articles 92–94 of the EEC Treaty) to prohibit state aids to industry (those that had the effect of distorting trade and competition in the EC) reflect this predilection of the member-states to prefer national solutions rather than EC-wide initiatives, even if they used resources inefficiently and harmed the welfare of the EC as a whole. It is noteworthy that the Council of Ministers did not meet to discuss general industrial policy from May 1973 until December 1990, although in the energy crises and associated recessions from the mid-1970s and early 1980s onward there were a number of significant EC initiatives to deal with surplus capacity in steel, textiles, and coal. In the steel industry, for example, the "Davignon Plan" (named after the EC Commissioner responsible, Etienne Davignon) in the 1980s imposed strict production quotas on EC steel producers, together with transitional import protection, provided that the European steel firms agreed on removal of excess capacity by closure of their least efficient plants. By using its powers under the ECSC Treaty to mandate restructuring of the steel industry, the EC Commission demonstrated that there could be an effective alternative to "beggar-my-neighbor" nationally based policies, with the pain of adjustment shared transnationally and some of the costs of restructuring borne by the successful steelmakers through a levy on their production. In other sectors, automobiles for example, action was taken nationally rather than at Community level: restrictions were imposed on imports of Japanese cars in several EC member states.[2] The advent of the single European market after 1992 will make such national quotas impossible to enforce, however, thus necessitating their abandonment or (more probably) the imposition of an EC-level import quota.

There were also some attempts to promote EC-level technological collaboration, but these usually foundered on arguments about member governments securing a just return for their financial contribution and did not for the most part involve private sector firms as principals. One of the few successful transnational collaboration projects, the four-nation Airbus Industrie consortium to produce commercial aircraft, was not an EC project at all. The Airbus project has also attracted considerable criticism from the United States and others for its extensive use of state subsidies.

In one policy area, that of competition law, the EC has from its inception developed extensive powers to regulate the conduct of firms and thus the course of industrial development. Here it should be noted that, unlike U.S. antitrust law, the EC focuses not on a structuralist approach to monopoly power (witness the breakup of

AT&T in the U.S.) but on eliminating restrictive or abusive behavior by dominant firms. As A. Jacquemin notes, for the EC Commission "the ultimate test of a dominant position is the firm's ability to behave persistently in a manner which would be impossible in a competitive market, and not the structure of the market."[3]

This approach embodies an assumption that to be competitive in world markets European firms may in fact need to command a relatively high market share within the EC in order to achieve the minimum scale efficiency of output. Thus, possession of monopoly power does not of itself constitute a breach of EC competition rules, and (unlike U.S. antitrust laws) there is a predisposition to believe that cooperation between firms is conducive to innovation and technical change.[4] One might therefore regard EC competition policy as a surrogate industrial policy, designed to promote competitiveness in terms of the ability to withstand competitive pressures from firms on the global stage, rather than more narrowly defined competition within the European Community market. In this sense, the Commission has opted for the world rather than the EC as the reference market for evaluating competition and market behavior.

It was in the early 1980s that the rise of Japan as a major player in the world economy and the relative decline of the United States as the hegemonic power in the global economy began to increase European insecurities. Sentiment in the European Community turned from the continued subsidisation of employment in declining industries toward positive adjustment aimed at encouraging competitive industries in growth sectors. The creation in 1984 of ESPRIT (European Strategic Programme for Research in Information Technology) was intended to build up the European capability in what was seen as a strategic metatechnology. The EUREKA program allocated $1.7 billion in EC finance over five years to consortia of European firms working on common technical standards and connectivity/compatibility problems in computer and telecommunications-related technologies.

In 1988 a second five-year phase of ESPRIT commenced, with increased funding of $2.2 billion. The ESPRIT model of providing funds on a cost-sharing basis to groups of firms for precompetitive R&D has also been used by the EC in RACE (Research and Development in Advanced Communications in Europe), BRIDGE (Biotechnology Research for Innovation, Development and Growth in Europe), and BRITE/EURAM (Basic Research in Industrial Technologies for Europe and European Research on Advanced Materials), as well as in the EUREKA R&D program, which is not controlled by the EC but is designed to foster advanced technology collaboration between over 1000 firms and research institutes. EU-

REKA was a French initiative launched in 1985 as a European riposte to the U.S. SDI initiative, which was widely perceived not as a solely defense-related program, but rather as an attempt by the U.S. Government to subsidize the R&D of major American companies and help them withstand Japanese competition. EUREKA has placed more stress than the purely EC projects on market potential as a project selection criterion, and hence quickly attracted a large number of companies (200 projects by mid-1988) with over $6 billion in funding provided by national governments: an amount equal to the European Community's entire R&D budget for 1987–1992.[5]

All these programs aim to identify and support strategic technologies, foster collaboration within industry and between firms and academic researchers on a transnational basis, and promote speedy implementation of the results by industry, with costs shared by industry and the sponsoring governments. This approach to technological collaboration certainly addresses the problem of the escalating costs of participation in some technologies, but it does not necessarily resolve the problem of continuing collaboration when commercially sensitive information or expertise is involved.[6]

It is too early to evaluate the effects of such projects on the international competitiveness of EC firms. The travails of Philips in its semiconductor and information technology businesses in 1990–1991 do not augur well, as Philips was a major participant in several EC collaborative R&D projects, including the High Definition Television Project financed under the EUREKA program. In 1991 France announced a major infusion of state aid to Bull, the principal information technology firm in France, despite warnings from the EC Commission that such aid might be an illegal state subsidy under the terms of the EEC Treaty of Rome (Articles 92–94). It is likely that the main effect of these collaborative R&D programs will be to encourage trans-frontier cooperation between the large "national champions" and to foster links between small- and medium-size firms, as well as encouraging trans-border academic research with commercial applications. One must question whether the social returns of these projects exceed the private returns and thus justify public subsidies, or whether collaborative projects are as efficient as autonomous initiatives.

THE ADVENT OF THE SINGLE EUROPEAN MARKET INITIATIVE

Proponents of what came to be known as the European Community's single market initiative came from two main sources: Euro-

pean-based multinational firms and political elites in many EC
member states. First, and probably most important in terms of
influence, were European industrialists (many of them members of
the Round Table of European Industrialists) such as Wisse Dekker
of Philips, Per Gylenhammer of Volvo and Gianni Agnelli of Fiat.
These captains of European industry wanted to create a large domestic market for their operations, rivaling in scale the American
and Japanese home markets, which could serve as a springboard
for them to gain global market share. The second group were European politicians and statesmen who believed that the era of superpower dominance was over, and that Europe would in the future
have to make greater provision not only for its own security and
foreign policy initiatives, but also for international peace and security in general. In 1985 British Commissioner Lord Cockfield produced his celebrated White Paper for the Commission of the
European Community outlining some three hundred measures that
needed to be taken in order to create a single European market.[7]
What is remarkable about this White Paper is that it was greeted
by member governments with almost unanimous acclaim. Two
years later, in 1987, the member states of the European Community
had all signed and ratified the Single European Act (SEA) which
streamlined decision-making procedures for the measures contained in the White Paper and also included a greater role for the
European Parliament in the decision-making process. The decisive
innovation of the Single European Act was to introduce qualified
majority voting for most measures contained in the White Paper—
with the exception of fiscal and social issues—so that no member-
state would retain and veto over them unless it was joined by at
least two other member-states.

Subsequent economic analyses of the consequences of removing
internal market barriers for the EC's economic performance have
unambiguously shown that the stimulation of cross-border competition will have a strongly positive effect. The EC Commission's
own Cecchini Report[8] estimated that the single market replacing
"Non-Europe" would save business about $460 billion yearly, while
by the end of the century the real national product of the EC
member-states might be some 3 to 6% higher than would otherwise
be the case. Cecchini estimated that some two to five million extra
jobs would be created by unifying the EC's internal market, and
that inflation would be perhaps 6% lower for the EC as a whole
than would otherwise be the case. Although his estimates are undoubtedly optimistic and imprecise, it does seem clear that increased competition deriving from the opening up of national

markets would promote extensive restructuring of European industry and hence improved efficiency and productivity.

As of the end of 1990, all the 281 measures that eventually sprang from the Commission's 1985 White Paper had been drafted by the Commission and submitted to the Council of Ministers, and the Council of Ministers had approved over two-thirds of them. While implementation remains a major problem (less than half of the measures scheduled to be implemented in national law in all member states have in fact been done so) there can be no doubt that the single market initiative is irreversible and that it will indeed be completed, though probably not by the formal deadline of December 1992. The age of "Euro-sclerosis" is therefore over. The dramatic change in superpower relationships, the collapse of the Soviet Union, the epoch-making liberalization of eastern Europe, and the reunification of Germany have all given added impetus to this process. At the same time, due attention should be paid to the changes in behavior of both European companies and their American, Japanese, and other competitors in anticipating and consummating the objectives of the Community's Single Market Initiative. It is business, not member governments, that is making a reality of the single market in Europe. Indeed, it should be noted that American multinationals operating in Europe, such as GM, Ford, and IBM, were among the pioneers in developing Pan-European corporate strategies as long ago as the mid-1960s. The globalization of industry has also meant that the national origins of multinational corporations are increasingly less relevant as a determinant of the location of their most significant and productive activities. After its 1989 acquisition of Zenith Data Systems in the United States, for example, Bull of France (a "national champion" by any standard) transferred virtually all its microcomputer development from France to the United States, while in 1990 IBM moved its worldwide telecommunications R&D program to Britain. When one also considers the efforts of the U.S. Trade Representative to have the EC accept imports of Japanese Honda automobiles assembled in Ohio as being of American origin, it is easy to echo Robert Reich's question: "Who is Us?"[9]

This is not to say that there is agreement on what the European single market should look like. Some see the initiative as the greatest exercise in deregulation ever undertaken. Others see it as an opportunity to replace conflicting, or non-existent national regulation with a coherent and consistent system of regulation at the Community level. Business leaders see in the creation of a single market an opportunity to escape the rigidities caused by national regulation. Trade unions are concerned to maintain at the European Community level the social welfare provisions that many of them had gained at the national level; and to prevent "social dumping" as provisions for social welfare were pushed down to the level of the lowest common denominator among the twelve member-states of the European Community. Still others feared the creation of a huge bureaucracy in Brussels that would smother the firm-based initiatives of business and produce a European socialist state in which regulation would stifle market forces.

The very ambiguity of the single market concept, the fact that it meant all things to all men, undoubtedly contributed to the success of the 1992 concept and strengthened its role as a catalyst for change. It is not yet clear whether 1992 will produce a deregulatory chain reaction that sweeps away all barriers between the member states of the European Community and lowers the level of regulation on business, or whether it will result in the reregulation of markets at the European Community level. Moreover, the use of a "competition among rules" approach to economic integration in preference to harmonization of national regulations may mean that the weaker member-states, such as Britain, will be obliged to adopt the rules of the economically stronger countries, such as Germany.

Although there is now no doubt that the single European market will be achieved, it will not be a homogeneous market, devoid of local characteristics and entrenched informal barriers to trade. Some of these barriers, notably in the field of public procurement, will persist long after the December 1992 deadline for the creation of the single market. In the telecommunications sector, for example, long-standing relationships between public network operators and their "national champion" equipment suppliers make it difficult for outsiders to obtain contracts. Performance of the EC member states' economies will also continue to diverge. This is one of the factors that complicates EC attempts to create economic and monetary union in the Community.

THE DYNAMICS OF 1992

The European Community's 1992 single market program has been driven by two forces. First, by the market-led dynamic of the globalization of competition and the escalating cost of technological innovation. Second, by the policy-led factors that have a micro-economic impact at the level of the individual firm, notably the application of the "new approach" to regulation in the EC, based on home-country control and mutual recognition of standards. The steady globalization of business has made it impossible for European companies largely dependent on their domestic national market to remain internationally competitive. Most European national markets, even if not subject to external competition from imports, are too small to generate the economies of scale necessary to fund product research and development, especially in high-technology fields. In the case of telecommunications switching equipment, for example, the development of the next generation of digital switches will cost over \$1.2 billion to develop, requiring an 8% share of the world market for a firm to break even. No EC national market accounts for more than 6% of world switchgear demand. This means that the EC market in digital switchgear, which represents approximately one-quarter of world demand, can only support two or three systems developers, as compared to the six firms now making such systems in the EC. Thus, either two or three multinational consortia must be created, or two or three "national champions" must be encouraged to expand by acquiring companies in other EC member-states.[10] The 1989 AT&T linkup (through a minority shareholding) with Italtel, Italy's national supplier of telecommunications equipment, is an example of an outsider firm attempting to gain insider status. An example of a "national champion" expanding across borders within the EC is Alcatel of France's acquisition of Standard Elektrik Lorenz (SEL), Germany's second largest supplier of telecommunications equipment. This Alcatel acquisition of SEL created a more credible competitor against the entrenched market position of Siemens and is a good example of cross-border mergers enhancing rather than reducing competition.

ESTABLISHING THE SINGLE MARKET: REGULATION, DEREGULATION AND REREGULATION

Nonetheless, the importance of the policy-led dynamic behind the EC's single market proposals should not be underestimated. The pressures of global competition and the rising minimum scale of efficient globally competitive production would not of themselves have galvanised some of the more entrenched national champions into venturing beyond their home territory. What has happened is that they have been obliged to do so. In some cases, competitors have broken ranks from within established oligopolistic market structures in order to gain a competitive advantage by building a Pan-European market presence. In others, outside firms have been lured into the market by the promise of 1992. Even so, it was the momentum achieved by the Community's policy-makers, the "box-score" of single market directives and regulations drafted, passed, and implemented, that forced the pace and direction of corporate strategy reappraisal. Probably the most important element in the policy-led dynamic is the application of the principles of mutual recognition of national standards and of home-country regulatory control, which means that the firm's home government bears prime responsibility for regulating its activities and ensuring compliance with EC rules. Products meeting the standards of one EC member state will, after 1992, be able to be sold in all other member states, subject to minimum EC-wide safeguards for public welfare: Germany must therefore let the cereal-laden Great British Sausage do its worst! Taken together, these two principles have replaced the agonizingly slow attempts of the EC Commission in the 1970s and 1980s to harmonize national regulations on an EC-wide basis, a process that was often fruitless and never rapid. This attempt at homogeneity through harmonization has now been superseded by a competition among rules, creating a form of deregulatory dynamic.

Just as American corporations flocked to Delaware because it had the most hospitable regulatory environment, so the post-1992 EC firms will tend to gravitate to the most liberal member state and from that base attack the markets of more restrictive countries. Thus the more restrictive countries, faced with the prospect of corporate migration and import-induced competition, will tend not to block, but rather to moderate, common EC rules, preferring half a loaf rather than no bread at all. Indeed, common EC rules may be the only way to prevent unrepentantly liberal states from achieving the advantages of a regime reminiscent of the Liberian/Panamanian shipping registry within the EC as the haven for footloose corporations.

In this way, the 1992 policy process has set off a national deregulatory chain reaction, accompanied by a certain degree of reregulation at the EC level. The Single European Act's provision for qualified majority voting on all measures covered by the Commission's 1985 White Paper (save for fiscal harmonization, abolition of border controls, and passage of social welfare measures) means that legislation can only be blocked by the opposition of at least three of the twelve EC member-states. States in a minority on some issue therefore have an incentive to negotiate a compromise.

The evidence thus far[11] indicates that, although there will be some erosion of national regulatory regimes, there are limits to competitive deregulation. Just as national, or even regional, differences in consumer preferences or market practices will remain long after December 1992, so the architecture of regulation in each EC member-state represents a form of social contract reflecting a particular domestic consensus or a balance between competing interests. EC member-states are reluctant to unravel these settlements, whatever form they take. They are even more reluctant to remove regulation without at least some agreed-upon common minimum standards at the EC level.

Deregulation at national levels, therefore, will almost invariably be accompanied by some measure of reregulation by the institutions of the EC. This in turn can have repercussions outside the EC. The 1989 Second Banking Coordination Directive, which effectively created a single banking passport enabling banks established in one EC member state to conduct business in any other member state without further authorization, brought pressure on the U.S. to liberalize its banking regime and precipitated a series of similar measures in Scandinavia.

This process of national deregulation and supranational reregulation is by no means a smooth and linear one. The demarcation between national and EC competence, and reluctance to abandon national sacred cows—an example is the long tradition in France of extensive state subsidies to industry—mean that EC member states frequently are unable to agree on what degree of regulatory power to transfer to the European Community's institutions. The EC's merger-screening regulation, which came into force in 1990, is a case in point. Only mergers between firms with a combined turnover of $6.2 billion (5 billion ECU) would be controlled by the EC Commission, while all mergers below that level will be screened by national authorities.[12]

However, Article 9 of the Merger Control Regulation, known as the "German Clause," provides that national competition authorities may request that the EC Commission refer the case to them if they desire to investigate the impact on national markets, even if the Commission would otherwise allow the merger to proceed. This procedure, which contains an element of double jeopardy, was included at the insistence of Germany, which wanted to maintain some form of parallel national control and threatened to block the Merger Regulation without it.[13] Thus the regulation, which was intended to encourage cross-border corporate restructuring by reducing multiple and possibly conflicting merger controls at national level, in fact perpetuated the risks of double jeopardy and uncertainty. The ultimately successful Siemens-GEC bid for Plessey Electronics in 1989, for example, had to be cleared by the UK and German competition authorities and the EC Commission: it also required notification to the relevant authorities in Australia, South Africa, Canada, and the United States thereby involving seven different law firms in preparing the necessary papers.

It is nevertheless clear that the merger control regulation is a significant step toward creating a coherent merger control policy for the single EC market, and demonstrates a way of reconciling differing regulatory approaches that might be used in the United States to reduce jurisdictional disputes in the case of hostile corporate takeover bids. The existence of some common regime inhibits or prevents individual EC member states from adopting discretionary approaches that deviate too far from the EC norm. Reregulation at the EC level is therefore a bulwark against excessive intervention by national regulators.

Clearly, some measure of EC-level regulation or reregulation is necessary to ensure that liberalization is achieved. Even so, EC member-states have been very reluctant to cede discretionary authority to the EC Commission. In March 1991 four national governments lost their suit in the European Court of Justice to block the Commission from introducing measures to liberalize the supply of telecommunications equipment by introducing rules under Article 90 of the EEC Treaty. EC laws introduced in this way do not require prior assent of the Council of Ministers, a procedure that most member governments opposed, even though they generally supported the Commission's objectives in the case concerned.

WILL NATIONAL APPROACHES TO MARKET REGULATION CONVERGE?

The twelve member states of the EC each have distinctive (and frequently nonconvergent) approaches to market regulation, based on their respective domestic consensuses on desired objectives and acceptable outcomes. These national regulatory accords are subject to change—witness the marked swing toward liberalization of the French Socialist administration after 1983, following the failure of its attempt at an autonomous dash for growth due to countervailing economic trends in the international economy. Such changes are hard to predict in terms of direction, speed, and overall magnitude. Which of the various types of approach toward market regulation will prevail in the European Community, if any? Will the future (inevitable) enlargement of the EC to fifteen, or even twenty, member-states from its current twelve result in more or less convergence toward a common approach to industrial change and market competition? Certainly the EC member-states have moved away from "picking winners," targeted national champion firms. The preference now is for an industrial policy focused on infrastructure development and encouragement of greater linkages between EC firms for such things as research and development. The objective is to have participant firms bearing most of the cost and all of the responsibility for coordination and control. That there are fundamental differences between the member-states in levels of economic performance, conceptions of the role of the state in the economy, and the degree and extent of regulation necessary and desirable, means that the emergence of a Pan-EC regulatory regime to govern the architecture of the single market after 1992 will not be a rapid or automatic process. The difficulty is compounded by the different methods of consultation and consensus formation in each member-state: there is no universal pattern in the European Community for framing regulations and enforcing them, but rather twelve different national procedures, some more corporatist than others.

France, for example, has a long tradition of state direction of industrial development and a somewhat adversarial dialectic between government, unions, and industrialists. This is moderated by extensive state ownership of major industrial enterprises and much of the banking system. Nonetheless, the French model of a relatively centralized, statist economy has become more and more dysfunctional as the French economy has become increasingly enmeshed with the EC market and the world economy at large. As a result, the French government has begun to adopt a more liberal, internationalist, approach—including active encouragement for the internationalization of state enterprises, even at the risk of some dilution of state control. This process of liberalization is being conducted cautiously, in order to avoid a protectionist backlash from adversely affected groups. Although the French government is executing this policy in a paternalist (rather than a corporatist or consensual) fashion, without much consultation with industry or trade unions, it does perhaps mark the beginning of the end for Colbertiste industrial policy and French neo-mercantilism. The French state retreats, perhaps the better to advance.

Germany has a legalistic approach to regulation, limiting discretionary and day-to-day government intervention in favor of consistent long-term policy objectives formulated after wide consultation with industry, workers, and government departments. Regulation is administered by independent regulatory bodies that are accountable to the Bundestag, but are insulated by public law from direct political interference. The Bundesbank is obliged to support the German government's economic policy objectives, but carries out its constitutional duty to maintain a sound currency free from government intervention. This model is, like the Japanese process of consensual decision-making, slow to produce results and somewhat impervious to change. Although Germany has a reputation as a liberal, market-oriented economy, it still maintains a number of sectors that are highly regulated. Insurance is a notable example of a sector that is protected from cross-border competition to a significant degree. In the German "social market economy" the definition of market failure is much broader than it is in the United States or in Britain, with a correspondingly more extensive network of consultation and regulation. The degree of public ownership of enterprises is higher in Germany than it is in Britain (after the privatization of the Thatcher years) and unification is unlikely to accelerate the movement toward privatization of important sectors such as telecommunications and air transport.

Britain, by contrast, has an approach to regulation based, not on public law or constitutional foundations, but on the political and economic objectives of the government of the day, translating its interpretation of the public interest into law. This regulatory process is derived from minimal formal consultation with trade unions or industry associations, translated into statutory form through the government's control over the majority in Parliament. After Mrs. Thatcher became Prime Minister in 1979, Britain quite rapidly became one of the most liberal economies in the EC, with an extensive amount of deregulation—a dramatic reversal of the interventionist policies of the preceding Labour Party administration of Prime Ministers Wilson and Callaghan. This deregulatory initiative was most evident in the telecommunications and financial services sectors, and was accompanied by far-reaching privatization policies. Privatizations took place not only of state-owned industries, such as British Petroleum and British Gas, but also of functions that long had been considered the preserve of the state, such as cleaning services in state-run hospitals. Thus the British government, whatever its political complexion, has much more discretionary power than the German government, although probably not as much as the President of the Fifth French Republic. Although regulatory policies are translated into statutes and achieve consistency thereby, they continue to be susceptible to policy U-turns. The rapid abandonment of a number of Mrs. Thatcher's policies by Mr. Major, when he succeeded her as Prime Minister in late 1990, is an example of this flexibility. So, too, is the history of policy reversals accompanying changes of government over the last fifty years. The successive nationalization, denationalization, renationalization and, most recently, privatization of the British steel industry is an example of the inconsistency in industrial policy which perhaps explains some of the reasons for Britain's poor economic performance in relation to her EC competitors in the last forty years.

"Tot patriae, quot sententiae" [as many opinions as there are countries] might be the best way of describing the different approaches to market regulation in the European Community. Nonetheless, the forces of global competition, the fears of European technological helotry, and the allure of an internal market with almost as many consumers (337 million) as the United States and Japan combined, will be powerful forces acting to promote convergence. Given the diversity of the European Community and the relative weakness (in terms of power and legitimacy) of its institutions, it seems likely that such convergence will be slow. National market structures are being undermined, but local market characteristics will persist. The process for achieving consensus and limiting the discretionary power of the EC to intervene will probably be closer to the German model than the British one. Germany's *Ordnungspolitik,* meaning procedures for consultation with affected groups, in order to develop a regulatory framework governed and circumscribed by public law, is better suited for the diversity of the European Community. Member-states of the European Community are unlikely to transfer to EC institutions the extensive discretionary power that the British political system seems content to grant to the central government in Westminster and Whitehall.

Although Germany's economic strength will reinforce the EC's convergence toward this *ordnungspolitik* paradigm, the main reason for its adoption will not be German dominance, but the refusal of EC member-states to cede discretionary power to the EC Commission. Simply put, the German model of the "social market economy" will prevail not because Germany dominates the EC, but because it has manifestly enhanced the international competitiveness of German industry. In regulatory regimes, as in other human endeavours, nothing succeeds like success.

Whatever the final outcome, it is clear that the attainment of the European Single Market is both inevitable and irreversible, and that there will be convergence (if not integration) of the member-states' approaches toward market regulation and the promotion of competitiveness. The end result will probably not be a zero-sum game in which member states lose power and the EC institutions gain it, but rather a division of labor based upon a prolonged and continuous dialogue between the relevant economic actors, member governments, and the EC Commission. Such a division of functional responsibility, based not on separation of powers or division of labor (in any fixed sense) will probably be based on the principle of "subsidiarity." That is, it will be based on the idea that functions should be carried out at the lowest and least remote level (local, national, EC) consistent with efficiency and effectiveness. Doubtless the choice of level will seldom be self-evident, but the European Community is sufficiently conscious of its economic vulnerability to prefer hanging together rather than being hanged separately in the global economy. In this sense, then, the New Europe that is emerging in the 1990s is condemned to succeed.

NOTES

1. See J. J. Servan-Screiber, *The American Challenge* (New York: Atheneum, 1968) and M. and S. Tolchin, *Buying into America* (New York: Times Books, 1989).
2. M. Hodges, "Industrial Policy: Hard Times or Great Expectations?" in H. and W. Wallace and C. Webb, eds., *Policy-Making in the European Community* (New York: Wiley, 1983).
3. A. Jacquemin, *European Industrial Strategy* (Oxford: Oxford University Press, 1975), 132.
4. D. B. Audretsch, *The Market and The State* (New York: Harvester/Wheatsheaf, 1989), chapter 3.
5. J. Grahl & P. Teague, *1992—The Big Market: The Future of the European Community* (London: Lawrence & Wishart, 1990), 154–56.
6. J. S. Alic, "Cooperation in R&D", *Technovation* 10, no. 5 (1990): 319–32.
7. Commission of the European Communities, *Completing the Internal Market,* COM(85)310 (Brussels: 1985).
8. P. Cecchini, *The European Market—1992* (London: Gower, 1988).
9. R. Reich, *The Work of Nations* (New York: Knopf, 1991).
10. *The Economist* (25 February 1989); H. Ungerer & N. Costello, *Telecommunications in Europe* (European Perspectives Series) (Brussels: Commission of the European Communities, 1988), 113–14.
11. See S. Woolcock, M. Hodges, and K. Schreiber, *Britain, Germany and 1992,* (RIIA/Pinter, 1991).
12. See *Frankfurter Allgemeine Zeitung* (21 December 1989).
13. Woolcock, Hodges, and Schreiber, *Britain, Germany, and 1992,* chapter 3.

Cross-Border Mergers and Acquisitions and International Capital Flows: U.S.–Japan

GERALDO M. VASCONCELLOS AND
RICHARD J. KISH

ISSUES IN AMERICAN COMPETITIVENESS VIS-A-VIS JAPAN

One of the most visible aspects of the discussion of American competitiveness in recent years has been motivated by the marked increase in cross-border mergers and acquisitions involving American firms. When a Japanese company is the acquirer, the transaction tends to attract an unusual amount of attention, especially if very large sums are involved. Yet these cross-border mergers and acquisitions are only one aspect of a vast spectrum of international capital flows that encompass both financial asset and international direct investment (IDI).

The purpose of the research presented here is to examine these cross-border mergers and acquisitions involving American and Japanese firms within the context of this broad movement toward the internationalization of business and finance that has taken place at an unabated pace since the end of World War II, although its origins can be found much earlier.[1] We start by looking into certain basic issues that recur in most discussions concerning international capital flows. This will be the focus of our attention in the remainder of this section. The bulk of the paper is organized as follows:

In Section 2, we examine several aspects of international direct investment (IDI) in the context of international capital flows. The discussion will proceed from an examination of international direct investment, which is one important component of international capital flows, to the study of cross-border acquisitions, an important component of international direct investment. Section 3, in turn, focuses on cross-border mergers and acquisitions as a form of IDI, as oppposed to de novo entry, that is, to the establishment of a foreign subsidiary "from scratch." In other words, our approach is to start with the general phenomenon of international capital flows and to narrow the scope progressively first to IDI, and then to cross-border mergers and acquisitions. In addition, in this section we look into certain factors that seem to act as a positive inducement to cross-border acquisitions, as well as into others that appear to discourage them.

Section 4 contains our empirical research in the United States-Japan case. We examine these cross-border mergers and acquisitions in the period 1982–1989, a period that witnessed a surge of this type of international direct investment between the United States and Japan. Our aim is to identify certain variables that help to explain why, during most of the last decade, Japanese companies were more likely to acquire American companies than vice-versa. In Section 5, the final section, we restate some of the major issues that concerned us in this study, review the major empirical findings, and present our conclusions. We also venture suggestions for future studies.

Analyses of the present state of competitiveness of the American economy in general, and of cross-border mergers and acquisitions in particular, have appeared with increasing frequency in recent years in academic publications, the specialized press, and the general press. The tone, depth, and quality of these analyses varies considerably. Yet there are a few recurring themes that seem to attract the attention of most writers. These issues are related to the attractiveness of American markets to foreign investors and companies, to fears of protectionism or of a more generally diffuse backlash directed against foreign ownership of business, to the political stability offered by the American government, as evidenced by a well-known set of rules and regulations, and to the matters of corporate restructuring and technology transfer. In the case of international business transactions where the other party is a Japanese company, issues of corporate culture and labor relations, as well as the investment horizon, evidenced by the popular notion of Japanese companies as "patient investors," frequently come to the foreground.

Attractiveness of American Markets

The size of the American economy, the largest in the world, with its vast consumer markets, presents a powerful attraction to would-be foreign investors. In a discussion of motives for Japanese foreign direct investment, Chernotsky singles out "the size, importance and accessibility of the U.S. market" as one of the major "pull" factors attracting Japanese investment.[2] This powerful pull attracts other investors as well. Despite the recent surge—and publicity—of Japanese investment in the United States, until recently the United Kingdom and the Netherlands, combined, had about four times as much invested in the United States as Japan, as noted by Pitman and Choe.[3] Nor is this pull restricted to large companies, at least in the Japanese case. Yoshida found that a majority of large *and* small firms in his sample rated the large size of the U.S. market as the "primary reason" for their investments. In particular, Yoshida reports that "some small companies opted for assembly and technical service operations locally in order to increase their market presence in the United States."[4]

Yet size alone cannot explain this extraordinary attraction of U.S. markets to foreign investors. After all, there are other large economies and consumer markets. Additional explanations must be sought in the investment climate offered to foreign investment, which has traditionally been very hospitable in the United States. In the last decade, however, analysts have begun to refer ominously to a "Japanese economic assault on the American market." This change in attitudes concerns foreign investors, and Japanese in particular, who make comparisons with the "European debate of the 1960s over a flood of direct American investment into European industry."[5] Fears of a surge in protectionism in the United States, then, become another common theme in the debate concerning foreign investment.

Fears of Protectionism

If a slice of the American markets is so attractive to foreign companies, then it follows that a partial or total loss of these vast markets must be a serious concern to them. It is not surprising, then, that foreign businesses took actions to protect themselves from the threat represented by protectionist demands that surfaced in the 1980s. Thus, Hiraoka states that "Japan has decided to internationalize its industrial base by systematically planting its red and white, sun-dotted flag in backyards throughout the world."[6] The establishment of subsidiaries of major Japanese automobile manufacturers in the United States during the 1980s is a visible example of this strategy. Other strategies involve cross-border acquisitions, the main topic of this paper, and joint ventures. The latter has attracted attention of late as a strategy that combines access to technologies and engineering, as well as to U.S. distribution markets and supplier networks, with a hedge against protectionism and exchange rate fluctuations.[7] Therefore, "to overcome trade restrictions—both existing and anticipated trade barriers" has been, not surprisingly, a high priority for Japanese companies, as well as for the Ministry of International Trade and Industry (MITI) and the Federation of Economic Organizations (Keidanren), as Yoshida (1987) reports.[8]

The threat of a protectionist tide in the United States has not materialized, some legislation and voluntary restraint agreements (VRAs) notwithstanding. One should not, however, discount the continuing pressure exerted by those who demand a levelling of the playing field. Some analysts continue to insist that "Japan will come to dominate many of the world's industries, in particular, high technology," that ". . . the U.S. will become increasingly poorer compared to Japan," and ". . . [the U.S.] *relative* standard of living will decline."[9] Despite some mollifying analyses that profess to show that Japan and the United States may be finally "wrangling toward reciprocity,"[10] there is plenty of talk about the "Japanization of America" and other similar militant positions.[11] For Japanese companies, in particular, the threat of U.S. protectionism is likely to exist for most of the coming decade, due to "fundamental issues" which still divide the two economic superpowers.[12]

However, for foreign investors as a whole, the political stability offered by the U.S. marketplace, evidenced by a generally benign set of rules and regulations concerning foreign businesses, is a factor of attraction that ranks second only to the sheer size of the U.S. economy.

Political Stability

The term "political stability," when applied in the context of international capital flows, and international direct investment in particular, generally means that the government tends to adopt a non-interventionist stance toward business and to adhere to the concept of "national treatment," that is, to submit foreign-owned businesses to the same set of laws and regulations that apply to their domestic counterparts. The absence of discriminatory practices directed against foreign businesses or investors can only enhance the appeal of a particular host country, quite independently from other factors.[13]

As stated above, the United States has consistently offered a very hospitable climate for foreign investment. This distinction holds even in comparison with other advanced industrial countries a point not missed by analysts of different persuasions. Thus, Kelman notes that ". . . [T]he United States allows free capital outflows as well as free inflows, and the same things that might make foreigners wary of holding American paper would presumably also apply to sophisticated American purchasers." Moreover, continues Kelman, "[I]n the final analysis, the most interesting issues raised by the internationalization of America and the growing sense of dependence that it has produced are cultural."[14] Rosendahl goes one step further to contend that "the U.S. should avoid the developing country outlook, which it has fought for so many years from the side of the investors."[15] In addition, Yoshida reports that "to look for the political stability" is one of the main reasons for Japanese manufacturing investment in the United States; furthermore "special tax incentives" and other state and local government incentives" rank among the most important factors influencing location decisions *within* the United States.[16] The *Japan Report* drives the point home by noting that ". . . until the [budget] deficit is reduced, and the domestic U.S. savings rate is increased, foreign financing of the deficit is likely to continue for as long as foreign investors believe that long-term U.S. economic prospects are essentially sound, that global trade will continue to expand, and that *protectionism will be kept at bay.*"[17]

In the final analysis, the conflict between the traditionally open and stable business environment in the United States and the fears and suspicions aroused by the ever-increasing internationalization of business and finance is likely to remain an active topic of debate, fueled by broad coverage in the press, which likes to raise questions such as "Will Japanese money change the face of America, and will the U.S. thereby lose control over its own destiny and its influence abroad?"[18] Whereas questions like these seem a bit overstated, the concerns that give rise to them are all too real.

In sum, the attractiveness of the large U.S. markets, the traditionally liberal U.S. business environment, and pervasive fears of a rising tide of protectionism have figured predominantly as issues to be carefully considered by current and prospective foreign investors, especially by companies contemplating a merger with or acquisition of a U.S. concern. There are, however, other major factors in this complex decision, which have received increased attention. They relate to corporate restructuring, technology transfers, corporate culture, and the investment horizon.

Corporate Restructuring

The 1980s witnessed extensive corporate restructuring, both in the United States and abroad. Multibillion dollar mergers and acquisitions, previously almost unheard of, have become one of the

business icons of a decade marked by the longest period of uninter-
rupted growth on record in peacetime. What motivates this restructuring? More to the point of this study, what factors seem to trigger
multinational corporate restructuring?

Enderwick attempted to address these questions. He pointed to
"the breakdown of international monetary stability, the slowness
and variability of economic growth rates, and the sharp commodity
price changes of the 1970s" as major triggering factors over the
last fifteen years. Enderwick's major conclusion is that there is no
single pattern of corporate restructuring; instead, this pattern
seems to vary considerably in different nations, due to the domestic focus of restructuring strategies and, in particular, their sensitiv-
ity to labor market characteristics.[19]

Perhaps inevitably, a good deal of attention has been focused on
the participation of Japanese firms in cross-border corporate restructuring. Observers are telling us that "Japan learns the takeover
game," that the Japanese may "nibble, not devour" their corporate
targets, that U.S. companies are "Japan's new goal" and that Japanese banks are ready to join into this "global M&A assault," because
[Japanese banks] are finally "shed[ding] their corporate inhibi-
tions."[20] Public opinion and some voices on Capitol Hill seem to believe that it is "so much easier for Japanese companies to buy U.S.
ones than the other way round."[21] Holloway suggests that this imbalance may be explained, at least in part, by the "complex web of inter-
locking shareholdings that makes it almost impossible for an
outsider, foreign or Japanese, to take control of a company without
the full support of the insiders." Yet the winds of change apparently
reached the Japanese corporate restructuring arena. Some analysts
now believe that the Japanese environment for mergers and acquisitions will become closer to the European model, which, albeit not as
liberal as its American counterpart, "is substantially more conducive
to corporate restructuring than the traditional Japanese system."[22]

The pursuit of cross-border acquisitions or mergers presents a
special attraction to companies in technologically advanced industries, insofar as such combinations represent the quickest way to
obtain access to critical technologies that will impact on future
growth and market share. It is to this dimension of restructuring
that we now turn.

Technology Transfers

The Organization for Economic Cooperation and Development
(OECD), in a recent publication titled *International Direct Invest-*

ment and the New Economic Environment, reckons that "invest-ment has conventionally been regarded as a combination of capital, technology, management and commercial expertise. International direct investment can be seen as a well balanced package enabling technology to be implanted. . . ."[23] Yet the control of emerging frontier technologies poses particular economic and political ques-tions. A few pages later, the same OECD report concedes that "if the technology is fundamentally new, the host country has diffi-culties in negotiating with the small number of firms possessing the technology and creating the conditions to protect it, such as a high level of R&D, product differentiation and *barriers to entry.*"[24] Moreover, says the OECD, "in a situation . . . where the new tech-nologies and the know-how concerning them represent a major competitive asset for the enterprises concerned, the latter have no desire to lose any advantage. . . ."[25]

As a result, one would not be surprised by the fact that interna-tional direct investment (and cross-border acquisitions in particu-lar) in industries where frontier technologies are crucial to competitive advantage tends to attract unusual attention and to give rise to concerns in the political, as well as in the business, arena.[26] For example, in his analysis of pluses and minuses of joint venturing with the Japanese in the United States, Brandt notes that "another disadvantage of joint venturing is that one partner seldom retains total ownership rights for new products or innovative de-signs." This would seem to be a fairly general observation about joint ventures, but a stronger word of caution follows: "Where the U.S. partner does obtain proprietary rights, the value of ownership is highly diluted because the Japanese partner has intimate knowl-edge of the product design, composition, production, and distribu-tion."[27] Similar concerns arise from the foreign investor's standpoint, however. Rosendahl states forcefully that "one of the first steps to be undertaken in connection with the establishment of manufacturing facilities in the U.S. would be to secure protection of any intellectual property to be utilized in connection with the facility including patent, trademark, and know-how protection as well as arrangements for intercompany licensing agreements be-tween the Japanese investor and the U.S. operation."[28]

In any event, securing access to technology appears to be high on the agenda of companies involved in one form or another of international direct investment, especially in the advanced indus-trial countries. This motive ranks fourth in Yoshida's 1987 survey of reasons for Japanese manufacturing investments in the United States.[29] Herr, surveying U.S. companies acquired or established by foreign direct investors in 1988, contends that foreign multinationals generally look for U.S. companies that can "round out their global market position, add manufacturing capability, *provide access to new technology,* or furnish a well-known brand name."[30] The quest for know-how is moving to the service industries as well. For example, although Japanese commercial banks are predominant in the ranks of the largest banks worldwide, investment banking and the acquisitions business itself is still dominated by American firms. This very specialized, highly profitable niche market has started to generate strong interest in Japanese securities firms, as Smith reports.[31] Similarly, Dowsley reports the emerging presence of Japanese life insurance companies in North America, and Canada in particular.[32]

It seems appropriate that, in concluding this introduction to major issues concerning international direct investment and competitiveness, we discuss two aspects of IDI that are uniquely associated with Japanese foreign direct investment, as oppposed to other traditional foreign investors in the United States. These aspects concern corporate culture and labor relations, and the so-called long-term investment horizon of the Japanese investor.

Corporate Culture and Labor Relations

There is a perception that most Japanese manufacturing and service companies conform to certain modes of operation or have "corporate cultures" with traits that are thought to be uniquely Japanese. Among them are more harmonious labor relations, loyalty to the firm, and long-term employment horizons and prospects. This is not to say that Japanese firms shy away from Western, in particular American, management methods. In fact, quite the opposite is true. No small part of the path of full competitiveness of the Japanese economy after World War II was due to its ability to adopt not only the latest Western technology, but also managerial expertise. In the process, however, the Japanese companies appear to have adapted these techniques and blended them with certain national traits, gaining one more competitive advantage as a result.

For example, Rosendahl credits "the strong preference of Japanese society for harmony in all aspects of life" with the "harmonious team play relationship of government and business, employer and employee, and . . . the strong preference for harmonious resolution of disputes."[33] Moreover, these perceptions lead to beliefs that these Japanese corporate mores are likely to be a source of strength. Not surprisingly, a recent survey of attitudes toward Japanese investment in the United States found that "the presence of Japanese companies in America helps us to be more productive as a nation." In addition, respondents with a higher level of education were more likely to believe that Japanese presence in America helps American business to become more productive.[34]

In any event, the intensification of Japanese direct investment in the United States brought about a keen awareness of this distinct corporate culture and set off a lively debate of its relative merits vis-a-vis Western, in particular American, practices. Some observers believe that Japanese-style management, or some aspects of it, will be absorbed into the American mainstream and become part of the "American business culture," in much the same way as happened in Japan itself one generation ago.[35] Others contend that "corporate immigrants from Japan are having a particularly strong impact on managerial techniques used from the plant floor to the executive suite."[36] While this seems a bit overstated, the public sees Japanese transplant companies as "winning over U.S. workers" with promises of higher job security and better benefits than their American counterparts.[37] These improvements have come usually with strings attached, in this case with strenuous attempts to avoid the unionization of the work force, or by locating new facilities in places where unions are traditionally weak. This strategy has earned Japanese companies some powerful adversaries in the American organized labor movement.

Long Term Investment Horizon

By the same token, Japanese corporations are perceived to be substantially more inclined than their American counterparts to consider a long-term investment horizon, that is, to make decisions regarding products and processes with a view on returns that may only materialize in a few years' time. American corporations, on the other hand, are perceived to be affected by, if not entirely subject to, the "quarterly reports syndrome." This syndrome manifests itself in decisions that may not be optimal at best, or seem irrational at worst, when looked upon from a long-term perspective, but have a favorable impact on the following quarterly reports and, by implication, on the community of security analysts.

Accordingly, Metzger and Ginsberg reckon that "the Japanese strategy of taking the longer-term view toward markets and market share before profits has produced several of the most successful companies in this century, Sony, Mitsubishi and Nissan among them."[38] Prestowitz, examining the sources of United States-Japan trade frictions, identifies a fundamental difference of views with regard to the workings of markets. The United States, claims Prestowitz, being well-endowed with natural wealth, believes that "comparative advantage in trade arises from factor endowment more or less automatically," whereas for Japan, which is not naturally wealthy, "comparative advantage is something to be conquered through the concerted efforts of all elements of society—and, once achieved, defended. This gives rise to extensive industrial policies aimed at fostering infant industries and restructuring aging ones."[39] A long-term investment horizon, one might add, follows naturally from these views.

In the cross-border merger and acquisitions arena, these views have translated into a combination of a "quest for value with traditional caution in moving into new territories."[40] Hector, on the other hand, believes that Japanese companies still think long term, but they may be catching on in the "takeover game," insofar as they seem to be making faster decisions with respect to acquisitions and have even learned to walk away when a prospective acquiree seems overpriced.[41] All in all, no less an authoritative source than *The Economist* credits Japan for using "financial power to extraordinarily benign effect," claiming that this "has been one of the main sources of stability for the world economy in the 1980s."[42]

This uneasy mix of praise, mistrust, awe, respect, resentment, and, yes, continuous change is likely to permeate the issues of American competitiveness vis-a-vis Japan in the 1990s. Having highlighted some major points of the debate in this section, we now examine the evolution of international capital flows, and international direct investment in particular, since the heyday of American hegemony in the global economy following World War II, with a focus on the last decade.

INTERNATIONAL DIRECT INVESTMENT IN THE CONTEXT OF INTERNATIONAL CAPITAL FLOWS

One of the remarkable developments that accompanied the vigorous growth in international trade in the post-World War II era has been an unabated increase in international direct investment. According to recent estimates, foreign direct investment in the United States increased by $72 billion in 1989 alone, a 22% increase over 1988. International direct investment in the U.S. continues to be led by British investors, followed by the Japanese, Dutch,

Canadians, Germans and French. The stock of foreign direct investment outstanding at the end of 1989 amounted to $122.1 billion for British investment (20% higher than the total at the end of 1988) and $70.6 billion for Japanese investment (a 32.4% increase over the 1988 total). British investors controlled 30.5% of all foreign direct investment in the United States by the end of 1989, followed by the Japanese with 17.6% of the total.[43]

The phenomenon of international direct investment, including its theoretical underpinnings, benefits, and costs, has been the subject of voluminous research. In addition, many studies have examined the attendant questions of host country attitudes toward international direct investment.[44] The extant research suggests that some of the main benefits of international direct investment can be found in the avoidance of tariffs and non-tariff barriers to arms-length international trade, in tax incentives usually associated with efforts to attract foreign investment to a particular country or region within a country, in the ability to tap different markets for short-term and long-term capital, and in the possibility of obtaining quicker and cheaper access to superior technology, as well as the ability to spread out the output of a multinational corporation's own research and development efforts over a broader market base. On the other hand, risks and constraints affecting international direct investment include closed sectors or industries, limitations on the acquisition of a controlling interest in a foreign company, limitations on remittances of profits and dividends, limitations on cross-border mergers and acquisitions and, in some extreme cases, the possibility of expropriation.

The growth in international direct investment has been impressive, with the countries affiliated with the Organization for Economic Cooperation and Development (OECD includes all the major advanced market economies) leading the way. Tables 2.1 and 2.2 show the flows of outward and inward direct investment of OECD member countries for most of the last three decades. Notice that both the annual and the cumulative outward direct investment flows are, in general, larger than the inward flows. The reason is that OECD countries invest in non-OECD countries, generally less developed ones, but the inward flows of foreign direct investment in OECD countries come almost exclusively from other OECD countries, that is to say, other major industrial countries.

Tables 2.3 and 2.4 present more disaggregated information on inward and outward direct investment flows for seven OECD countries: The United States, Japan, Canada, France, Germany, Italy and the United Kingdom. The flows for the United States and Japan

Table 2.1. Outward direct investment flows of OECD member countries
(Including reinvested earnings)

$ million

Cumulative flows			Annual flows					
1961/70	1971/80	1981/86	1981	1982	1983	1984	1985	1986
70576	301106	294403	49740	23193	29545	38441	60464	93080
Source: OECD								

Table 2.2 Inward direct investment flows of OECD member countries
(Including reinvested earnings)

$ million

Cumulative flows			Annual flows					
1961/70	1971/80	1981/86	1981	1982	1983	1984	1985	1986
42060	187873	218392	40821	30006	31398	34347	35367	47153
Source: OECD								

are particularly relevant for this study; however, presenting the flows for all the seven largest market economies helps to put the differences between the United States and Japan in perspective. A closer look at the outward flows of direct investment (Table 2.3) shows a marked increase for Japan in the last decade, coupled with a slowdown in American outward investment. By 1988, Japan invested $34 billion abroad, compared with $20.4 billion for the United States. This increase in outward investment is also present for Canada, France, Germany and Italy, albeit in more modest amounts. The growth in outward British direct investment was also impressive in the 1980s, with the exception of 1988, where it declined, but not quite as dramatically as the U.S. flows.

The disaggregated flows of inward direct investment, shown in Table 2.4, tell a different story, In particular, while the magnitude of U.S. outward flows is matched by large inward flows, in the case of Japan the inward flows of direct investment are a mere fraction of the outward flows. This preponderance of outward over inward flows is also the case, but less markedly so, for the major European economies and Canada. The conclusion is clear: during the 1980s,

Table 2.3. Outward direct investment for selected OECD countries[1]

U.S. $ millions

| | Cumulative flows of direct investment | | | | | | Flows of direct investment | | | | | | | |
	1961/70	%²[2]	1971/80	%²[2]	1981/88	%²[2]	1981	1982	1983	1984	1985	1986	1987³[3]	1988⁴[4]
Canada	1483	2.1	11335	3.7	29437	5.2	5756	709	2758	2277	3515	3257	4752	6413
a.a.	148		1134		3680									
France	2641	3.7	13940	4.6	40556	7.2	4615	3063	1841	2126	2226	5230	8704	12751
a.a.	264		1394		5070									
Germany	4091	5.8	23130	7.7	47745	8.5	3862	2481	3170	4389	4804	9610	9036	10393
a.a.	409		2313		5968									
Italy	1667	2.4	3597	1.2	18805	2.4	1404	1025	2126	1995	1818	2661	2326	5450
a.a.	167		360		1908									
Japan	1438	2.0	18052	6.0	93672	16.7	4894	4540	3612	5965	6452	14480	19519	34210
a.a.	144		1805		11709									
United Kingdom	7398	10.5	55112	18.2	120520	21.4	12065	7145	8211	7988	11293	16551	30699	26569
a.a.	740		5511		15065									
United States	46822	66.3	134354	44.4	121230	21.6	9620	-2360	380	2820	18070	27810	44470	20420
a.a.	468		13435		15154									

a.a. Annual average.

1. Including reinvested earnings.
2. Share of OECD total outward flows of direct investment.
3. Revised figures.
4. Provisional figures.

Source: Department of Economics and Statistics, OECD.

the United States was the major recipient of flows of international direct investment, followed by Europe and Canada in more modest terms. Japan was the main source of flows of international direct investment. This turnabout helps to explain why the United States gave up its position as the world's largest creditor nation to become the world's largest debtor in less than a decade. In the same period of time, Japan became one of the largest creditors. The direct investment flows, however, explain only one part of these transformations. The rest of the explanation will be found in portfolio investments and their reallocations.

The international direct investment position of the United States vis-à-vis Japan is presented in Table 2.5. Notice that this table shows stocks of direct investment at a point in time, as opposed to flows over a period of time. This information is important because it highlights the magnitude of Japanese and American stakes in each other's economy. The data show that, for most of the past decade, the dollar magnitude of the Japanese presence in the United States has been nearly twice as large as the American direct investment position in Japan. Insofar as the size of the American economy, as measured by GNP, is more than twice that of Japan's, the *relative* stakes are not too different. However, as discussed in the previous section, the buildup of Japanese assets in the United States continues unabated, whereas the reverse is not true. This difference helps to explain some of the uneasiness of the critics who contend that Japanese control of assets in the United States is increasing "too fast."

In order to put the Japanese and American stakes in each other's economy in perspective, it is helpful to look into how important Japanese flows of direct investment into the United States are compared to flows directed to other countries or regions and, by the same token, how large the inflows of American direct investment into the Japanese economy are, compared with inflows from other sources. This information is provided in Tables 2.6 and 2.7. Whereas these figures are not strictly comparable with Balance of Payments data contained in the previous tables (see the explanatory notes), they provide some additional insights. For example, we see in Table 2.6 that the Japanese direct flows to the United States have been the largest of any foreign destination during the last decade, but there are significant flows directed towards Europe (especially the U.K.), Asia, and Latin America. Only small portions of Japanese direct investment flows, however, are directed to African countries and the Middle East.

In addition, Table 2.7 shows the inflows of foreign direct invest-

Table 2.4. Inward direct investment for selected OECD countries[1]

U.S. $ millions

	Cumulative flows of direct investment						Flows of direct investment							
	1961/70	%[2]	1971/80	%[2]	1981/88	%[2]	1981	1982	1983	1984	1985	1986	1987[3]	1988[4]
Canada	5489	13.1	5534	2.9	3665	0.9	-3670	-831	243	1313	-2050	1115	3581	3964
a.a.	549		553		458									
France	2804	6.7	16908	9.0	24127	6.1	2426	1563	1631	2198	2210	2749	4621	6729
a.a.	280		1690		3016									
Germany	6270	15.0	13957	7.4	8716	2.2	340	819	1775	553	587	1086	1933	1623
a.a.	627		1396		1089									
Italy	3634	8.6	5698	3.0	16148	2.3	1146	636	1190	1290	1003	-15	4059	6839
a.a.	363		570		1330									
Japan	624	1.5	1424	0.8	2582	0.7	189	439	416	-10	642	226	1165	-485
a.a.	62		142		323									
United Kingdom	4310	10.2	40503	21.6	53940	13.6	5891	5286	5132	-241	4856	7104	13258	12654
a.a.	431		4050		6742									
United States	6282	14.9	56276	30.0	213690	53.8	25190	13800	11960	25390	19030	34090	42000	42230
a.a.	628		5628		26711									

a.a. Annual average.

1. Including reinvested earnings.
2. Shares of OECD total inward flow of direct investment.
3. Revised figures.
4. Provisional figures.

Source: Department of Economics and Statistics, OECD.

Table 2.5.   Direct investment position

U.S. $ millions								
	1980	1981	1982	1983	1984	1985	1986	1987
U.S. position in Japan	6243	6755	6928	8063	7920	9246	11332	14270
Japan's position in U.S.	4225	7697	9677	11336	16044	19313	26824	33361

NOTE: The position is the book value of the direct investors' equity in, and net
outstanding loans to their foreign affiliates at year's end.   Includes reinvested
earnings.

Source: U.S. Department of Commerce, Survey of Current Business; OECD.

ment in Japan for most of the last decade, and in particular the contributions of selected OECD countries and Hong Kong. One can see that U.S companies are by far the largest investors in the Japanese economy. In fact, the cumulative flows of American direct investment in Japan over the last decade are twice as large as those of five major European economies—France, Germany, the Netherlands, Switzerland, and the United Kingdom—*combined*. Therefore, one can hardly make a case that American companies are being singled out as far as barriers from investing in Japan are concerned. The Japanese economy, however, given its size, appears to have been far less receptive to foreign direct investment in the last decade—regardless of the source—compared to the American and European economies.

Finally, it needs to be pointed out that the data in Tables 2.5 and 2.7 probably underestimate the participation of U.S. companies in the Japanese economy, as compared to the stake of Japanese companies in the U.S economy. The reason is that foreign direct investment data are reported at historical cost, not replacement value. This means that the investment by U.S. companies in Japan is underestimated, since these companies have established themselves in that country much earlier, on average, than most of Japanese direct investment in the United States. A more accurate comparison would involve market value or replacement cost data on both sides. Unfortunately, we are not aware of the availability of such figures.

International direct investment takes place in basically two forms: de novo entry or mergers and acquisitions. Whereas the establishment of new affiliates or subsidiaries in foreign countries

Table 2.6. Japan: flows of direct investment abroad by country

U.S.$ millions

	Cumulative Flows End of Fiscal Year 03/31/89	Flows								
		1980	1981	1982	1983	1984	1985	1986	1987	1988
Europe, total	30164	511	650	761	883	1937	1930	3469	6576	9116
Belgium	1027	67	107	64	126	71	84	50	70	164
France	1764	83	54	102	93	117	67	152	330	463
Germany	2364	110	116	194	117	245	172	210	403	409
Italy	370	8	28	19	13	22	23	59	109	N.A.
Luxembourg	4729	10	104	127	265	315	300	1092	1764	657
Netherlands	5525	41	138	73	113	452	613	651	829	2359
Spain	1045	22	39	19	52	140	91	86	283	161
Switzerland	1432	28	67	79	37	229	60	91	224	454
United Kingdom	10554	186	110	176	153	318	375	984	2473	3956
Other OECD countries										
Canada	3231	112	167	167	136	184	100	276	653	626
United States	71860	1484	2329	2738	2565	3360	5395	10165	14704	21701
Latin America										
Inc. offshore banking	31617	588	1181	1503	1878	2290	2616	4737	4816	6428
Middle East	3388	158	96	124	175	4273	45	44	62	259
Inc. OPEC										
Asia	32227	1186	3338	1384	1847	1628	1435	2327	4868	5569
Africa	4604	139	573	489	364	326	172	309	272	653

NOTE: These figures are collected on an approval or notification basis and are not strictly comparable to balance-of-payments data. Moreover, there is a divergence between the methods used to measure inward and outward direct investment. Reinvestment to acquire equity is generally included.

Source: Japanese Ministry of Finance; OECD.

Table 2.7. Japan: flows of foreign direct investment by country

U.S.$ millions

	Cumulative flows End of Fiscal Year 03/31/89	Flows							
		1981	1982	1983	1984	1985	1986	1987	1988
Europe	3013	150	90	107	117	334	235	448	817
France	202	19	16	7	7	21	16	20	27
Germany	546	37	18	16	20	23	47	53	195
Netherlands	482	15	7	31	26	47	19	78	157
Switzerland	928	N.A.	1.4	10	10	68	89	169	273
United Kingdom	518	30	77	24	46	58	35	49	112
Other OECD countries									
Canada	152	2	N.A.	31	N.A.	13	2	4	22
United States	6288	149	449	772	214	385	488	938	1774
Hong Kong	390	6.8	25.4	67	42.3	39	57	36	44

NOTE: These figures are collected on an approval or notification basis and are not strictly comparable to balance-of-payments data. Moreover, there is a divergence between the methods used to measure inward and outward direct investment. Reinvestment to acquire equity is generally included.

Source: Japanese Ministry of Finance; OECD.

is a topic that has received a substantial amount of attention in the literature, in this study our main interest concerns cross-border mergers and acquisitions, their financial and economic underpinnings, and the factors or relevant variables that affect their direction and magnitude. This is the subject of our discussion in the next section.

CROSS-BORDER MERGERS AND ACQUISITIONS AS A FORM OF INTERNATIONAL DIRECT INVESTMENT

Since the 1981–1982 recession in the United States, there has been a marked increase in domestic and cross-border merger and acquisition activity. Cross-border acquisitions involving U.S. firms increased from 364 in 1982 to 553 in 1987. During 1988, the number of cross-border acquisitions involving U.S. firms reached 605.

Moreover, the composition of cross-border acquisition activity has shifted abruptly over the same period. For example, U.S. firm acquisitions of non-U.S. firms increased modestly from 149 in 1983 to 177 in 1987, while foreign acquisitions of U.S. firms rose substantially. In 1983, there were 116 foreign acquisitions of U.S. firms, valued at about $22 billion; this increased to 363 foreign acquisitions of U.S. firms in 1987, with an approximate value of $42 billion. To put it another way, U.S. firms acted as acquiring firms in about

56% of the cross-border acquisitions involving U.S. firms in 1983, versus only about 26% in 1987. In some of the more publicized foreign acquisitions of U.S. firms, a Japanese company acted as the acquiring firm, including Sony's acquisition of CBS Records Group and Bridgestone's acquisition of Firestone Tire & Rubber Co.

It seems important to examine the variables that a company considers when contemplating a cross-border acquisition or merger. The extant literature lacks a framework within which different cases of cross-border mergers and acquisitions can be analyzed. In this section we consider the positive as well as the unfavorable factors affecting cross-border mergers and acquisitions, with a focus on recent experience. In addition, using a capital budgeting framework, we illustrate how the feasibility of a proposed foreign acquisition can be measured. This framework is then applied to explain the recent trends of increasing acquisitions of U.S. firms by foreign firms and reduced acquisitions of non-U.S. firms by U.S. firms. In the following section, we examine the empirical evidence on cross-border acquisitions between firms in the United States and Japan.

Factors Affecting Cross-Border Acquisitions and Mergers

A larger, diverse, and sometimes conflicting collection of factors affecting cross-border acquisitions is found scattered throughout the literature in this subject area. What follows is a summary of these factors, keeping in mind the objectives of this study.[45]

(1) Positive Merger Factors Factors that encourage cross-border acquisitions and mergers are those that offer the acquiring firm an advantage not available within its home market.

• Exchange rates. According to much of the literature, exchange rates play a major role in the decision-making process concerning a foreign acquisition. If the U.S. dollar is strong with respect to foreign currencies, we should see an upward trend in the acquisitions of foreign firms by U.S. firms and a downward trend in the acquisitions of American firms by foreign firms. The opposite should hold in periods where the dollar weakens against major foreign currencies.

However, there is an opposite argument with respect to the importance of the value of the dollar at the time of the acquisition. As the dollar strengthens, the future profits to be remitted from the prospective subsidiary will have a lower discounted value when measured in dollars. Thus, the direction of the exchange rate effect is not as clear-cut as the previous view implies and becomes ultimately an empirical question.

• Diversification. Given a firm's preferred risk-return position, international diversification by way of acquisitions or mergers improves the trade-off, because the covariance of returns across economies, even within the same industry, is likely to be smaller than within a single economy. The prospective acquiring company must first decide on its desired levels of risk and return. Only then should it attempt to identify countries, industries, and specific firms which fall within this "risk class."

• Current economic conditions in the home country. Adverse economic conditions in the home country, such as a slump, recession, or capital constraint, may cause firms to concentrate on their domestic business while temporarily delaying strategic international moves. Once the economy rebounds, cross-border acquisitions are likely to become again a means for increasing demand and diversification.

•Acquisition of modern technology. As discussed in the introductory section, there are cases in which firms fall behind the level of technological knowledge necessary to compete efficiently in the industry in the domestic and/or international market. If a firm is unable or unwilling to develop the required technology through research and development, it may try to acquire a foreign firm that is technologically more advanced. Such an acquisition allows the firm a foothold in the foreign country's market, and it may transfer the acquired technological advantages back home in order to strengthen its position in the domestic market.

(2) Unfavorable Merger Factors   These are factors which seem to restrain the cross-border merger movement. They include information effects, inefficiencies, monopolistic power, and regulations.

• Availability of information. Information about a prospective target firm is crucial in the decision-making process of the acquiring firm. For example, areas in which timely and accurate information is necessary include current market share figures, comparisons with the competition, current sales, cash flow forecasts, and company-specific strengths and weaknesses. Yet foreign firms might not disclose these and other relevant figures. If the necessary information to make an accurate analysis is not available, the prospective acquiring firm may be forced to delay or discontinue its plans, even though the foreign firm appears to be a very attractive target on the surface. Otherwise, failure to come up with an accurate analysis may prove to be devastating for the acquiring firm.

However, information effects are not always harmful. Arguments based upon asymmetry of information claim that the acquirer is able to obtain information not available to other market participants.

• Inefficiencies. Inefficiency arguments center on the acquiring firm's ability to replace incompetent or inefficient management within the acquired firm in order to better utilize the acquired firm's assets. The hope is that new management will be able to increase the efficiency of the acquired firm and thus generate a higher rate of return. A drawback of this action is the cost of replacing the inefficient management. The negative aspects of the inefficiencies argument apply to the resistance that may materialize from the foreign managers who are left in place after the shake-up, which takes the form of negative attitudes directed to the outsiders taking over the firm.

• Monopolistic powers. Synergy arguments in defense of domestic or cross-border acquisitions are based upon the economies of scale supposedly derived from horizontal mergers, economies of scope associated with vertical mergers, or the gains from acquiring monopolistic power. However, if monopolistic power is attained by one firm (a difficult proposition in the United States, because of the threat of antitrust action), then entry into the industry becomes much more difficult for any competitor, domestic or foreign. In addition, a monopolist is much more likely to resist a foreign take-over. Among the entry barriers that will make a cross-border acquisition difficult (or even de novo entry, for that matter) one finds product differentiation, which is tied to huge advertising expenditures and R&D outlays, and the capital necessary to establish a plant of minimally efficient size.

• Government restrictions and/or regulations. Most governments have some form of takeover regulation in place. In many instances, government approval is mandatory before acquisition by foreign businesses can take place. In addition, government restrictions may exist on capital repatriations, dividend payouts, intracompany interest payments, and other remittances. These restrictions seem to be more prevalent in less-developed countries.

Moreover, international transactions may raise antitrust issues, as discussed above. Mergers with foreign firms certainly belong to this category, but so do distributorship contracts, patent and trademark licenses, overseas distribution arrangements, raw material procurement agreements and concessions, and overseas joint ventures for manufacturing, research, and distribution. Antitrust considerations, then, will probably have some bearing on a firm's decision to merge with or acquire a foreign firm, to the extent that uncertainty about the foreign government's reaction to cross-border acquisitions may cause some companies to limit or discontinue their acquisition plans.

The Cross-Border Acquisition in a Capital Budgeting Framework[46]

A merger or acquisition, domestic or foreign, may be looked at as an investment decision made by the acquiring firm. As with other successful investment decisions, the expected benefits must outweigh the expected costs. Within the acquisition framework, the incremental cash flows generated by the combination of the previously independent firms or by the achievement of control over the operations of the target firm must be greater than the expenses incurred, on a present value basis. These expenses include both the search and negotiating costs plus the actual dollar amount paid (or the equivalent dollar amount of the securities issues) to the shareholders of the target firm. The net present value (NPV) of the decision represents the expected dollar gain to the shareholders of the acquiring firm.

This line of reasoning implies that the feasibility of a foreign acquisition can be evaluated like any other project, with specific attention to its peculiar characteristics. It follows that capital budgeting analysis can be applied to determine whether the NPV of the acquisition is positive. Consider the following capital budgeting framework, as applied to a foreign acquisition:
where

$$NPV_{FA} = -I_{FA} + \sum_{t=1}^{n} \frac{CF_{FA},t}{(1+k_{FA})^t} + \frac{SV_{FA},n}{(1+k_{FA})^n} \qquad (3.1)$$

NPV_{FA} = net present value of a foreign acquisition;
I_{FA} = initial outlay of a foreign acquisition;
k_{FA} = required return on the foreign acquisition;
CF_{FA} = cash flows to the acquirer;
SV_{FA} = salvage value to the acquirer:
    t = time period; and
    n = expected economic life of the project.

As with any project, the variables above should incorporate any tax implications so that the net present value reflects after-tax cash flows. In addition, all cash flows should be measured from the acquirer's perspective and in the acquirer's home currency.

The factors that influence a firm's attraction to a prospective foreign acquirer can be identified by breaking the general NPV equation (3.1) into its components. The following discussion identifies the specific factors that affect a foreign acquisition's initial outlay, periodic cash flows, salvage value, and required rate of return.

(1) Factors Affecting the Initial Outlay   The initial outlay (I_{FA}) can be broken down into three components, as shown below:
where

$$I_{FA} = E_h + D_h + D_f (ER_f) \qquad (3.2)$$

E_h = equity funds in the home currency;
D_h = borrowed funds in the home currency;
D_f = borrowed funds in the foreign currency; and
ER_f = exchange rate at the time the foreign funds are borrowed.

In order to measure the entire initial outlay in terms of the home currency, any foreign funds borrowed by the acquiring firm must be translated into the home currency. Moreover, some firms may cover the entire initial outlay from any of the above components.

Any factors that can reduce the initial outlay will make a foreign acquisition more attractive. The existing exchange rate at the time of the planned acquisition is important because it affects the amount of home currency funds needed to make the acquisition.

(2) Factors Affecting the Periodic Cash Flows   The relevant cash flows in the analysis of cross-border mergers and acquisitions are those flows received by the acquiring firm. They are determined by: (a) the after-tax foreign cash flows generated; (b) the percentage of those after-tax cash flows to be remitted to the acquirer; and (c) the exchange rate at the times that the after-tax foreign cash flows are remitted. Then, the after-tax cash flows received by the acquiring firm can be described as:
where

$$CF_{FA,t} = (CF_{f,t}) (1 - R_{f,t}) (ER_{f,t}) \qquad (3.3)$$

$CF_{f,t}$ = foreign cash flows generated during period t;

$R_{f,t}$ = proportion of cash flows retained by the (then) foreign subsidiary to support future operations; and

$ER_{f,t}$ = exchange rate at the time the cash flows are remitted.

The feasibility of a foreign acquisition is highly influenced by the estimated cash flows to the acquirer (CF_{FA}), which are dependent on several factors. Among the factors affecting the foreign cash flow ($CF_{f,t}$) are the foreign country's rate of economic growth and the cost of consumer credit. In addition, a strategy of retaining more funds abroad lowers the CF_{FA} over the short run but allows for more growth in the foreign business. It follows that CF_{FA} may be higher in the future if this growth creates sufficiently more foreign cash flows (CF_f) to offset the higher cash flow retention percentage (R_f). As a result, the market value of the foreign business could increase. The prevailing exchange rates at the time cash flows are remitted will also affect CF_{FA} directly. That is, if the foreign currency appreciates, CF_{FA} increases and vice-versa, other things equal.

(3) Factors Affecting the Salvage Value   The salvage value from the acquirer's perspective as of time n or terminal time ($SV_{FA,n}$) is determined by the anticipated foreign market value of the acquired business at time $n(MV_{f,n})$ and the prevailing exchange rate at the time of the planned sale, as described below:

$$SV_{FA,n} = (MV_{f,n}) (ER_{f,n}) \qquad (3.4)$$

Note that the foreign value may represent a liquidation value or a going concern value, whichever is likely to be higher. Accordingly, the salvage value to the acquirer can be affected by any factors that influence the market value of the foreign concern ($MV_{f,n}$) at the end of the investment horizon. In general, the market value of any business at terminal time (n) is determined by the anticipated cash flows from that point on. In addition, from the foreign acquirer's perspective, the future salvage value of the acquired firm or project is also affected by the exchange rate at which the proceeds from the sale of the foreign business can be converted to its home currency.

(4) Factors Affecting the Required Rate of Return   The required return on a foreign business is dependent on the cost of financing the business, which in turn is influenced by: (a) the risk-free interest rate; and (b) the business risk. The lower the risk-free interest rate and the lower the perceived risk of business, the higher the market value assigned to a business, other things equal. When assessing a foreign business, however, two risk-free rates are important. First, the home risk-free rate influences the home cost of equity funds and borrowed funds. Second, the foreign risk-free rate influences the cost of borrowing foreign funds. When foreign borrowing costs are relatively low, foreign acquisitions that can be partially financed with foreign funds may become more attractive.

The perceived business risk of acquiring a foreign firm emanates from the uncertain components that affect its value to the acquirer, such as the periodic cash flows, the proportion of cash flows retained in the foreign country, the periodic exchange rate, and the future market value of the business.

Relevant Variables in Cross-Border Mergers and Acquisitions Involving U.S. Firms

Because firms vary by industry, risk, size, and international expertise, their interest in foreign acquisitions varies. Our previous discussion implies that some macroeconomic variables (for example, the exchange rate) may be used to explain general foreign acquisition trends involving firms of a particular country, whereas other industry or firm-specific variables help to explain whether cross-border mergers and acquisitions are more common for certain industries, or for firms with particular characteristics.

In the particular case of cross-border mergers and acquisitions involving U.S. firms, several relevant microeconomic variables can be identified. The initial outlay necessary for non-U.S. firms to acquire a U.S. business was relatively lower during the 1985–1988 period because of a downward trend of the foreign exchange value of the dollar since 1985. In addition, while U.S. stock prices have generally increased in recent years (except for the crash of October 1987), U.S. businesses have still been perceived as bargains by non-U.S. firms that can obtain dollars cheaply.

Moreover, the estimated periodic cash flows of a U.S. business from a non-U.S. firm's perspective has been generally high, other things equal, insofar as the economic conditions in the U.S. have been generally favorable since 1982. Finally, the cost of capital for foreign firms appears to have been low in recent years due to a relatively plentiful supply of equity and borrowed funds, both in the United States and in other major industrial countries.

The combined impact of these macro- and micro-economic variables has resulted in a flurry of activity in the cross-border mergers and acquisitions arena in the last decade, with U.S. firms finding themselves more frequently in the position of acquirees rather than acquirers. Of particular interest to this study is the foreign merger and acquisition activities between U.S. and Japanese firms. In the next section, we examine the empirical record of this activity, using a statistical model derived from the relevant variables studied above.

EMPIRICAL EVIDENCE ON CROSS-BORDER MERGERS AND ACQUISITIONS: U.S.-JAPAN

Our approach in this section is to introduce a statistical model to assess the impact of the relevant variables identified by the capital budgeting approach to foreign acquisition activity. This model is then applied to foreign acquisitions involving U.S. and Japanese firms over the period 1982–1989.

Table 4.1 shows the magnitude of the U.S.-Japan cross-border acquisitions on a quarterly basis. We can see that, over the eight-year period investigated in this study, Japanese firms were acting predominantly as acquirers, and that this trend intensified after 1984. Although it is not possible to obtain dollar amounts for the total value of the cross-border mergers and acquisitions, insofar as many transactions go on record with their values undisclosed, it is safe to say that these dollar amounts rose substantially during the last decade in both nominal and real terms.

The Model

The following model, which evolved from the capital budgeting framework developed in the previous section, was specified:

$$ACQ_t = f(EXRATE_{t-n'}\ BYDIF_{t-n'}\ STKUS_{t-n'}\ STKJ_{t-n}) + e_t \qquad (4.1)$$

where

        ACQ = difference between the number of Japanese acquisitions of American firms and the number of American acquisition of Japanese firms;

        EXRATE = the exchange rate, measured in ¥/$;

Table 4.1. U.S.-Japan Cross-Border Mergers and Acquisitions, 1982-1989

		(Number of Transactions)	
YEAR	QUARTER	Japanese Acquisitions of U.S. Firms	American Acquisitions of Japanese Firms
1982	I	2	5
	II	1	2
	III	3	0
	IV	0	0
1983	I	1	0
	II	0	0
	III	1	2
	IV	2	2
1984	I	3	1
	II	0	0
	III	2	0
	IV	4	3
1985	I	7	0
	II	1	1
	III	2	1
	IV	2	0
1986	I	4	1
	II	1	0
	III	5	1
	IV	14	2
1987	I	4	0
	II	5	0
	III	3	1
	IV	7	0
1988	I	7	0
	II	12	1
	III	14	1
	IV	7	1
1989	I	21	2
	II	1	0
	III	16	1
	IV	24	0

Sources: *Mergers and Acquisitions*, several issues. The total dollar values for acquisitions are generally not available. These values are disclosed for some acquisitions but not for all of them.

BYDIF = bond yield differential between comparable debt securities in the U.S. and Japan;

STKUS = stock market index in the U.S.;

STKJ = stock market index in Japan.

The corresponding statistical model was hypothesized as a linear

$$ACQ_t = b_0 + b_1\,EXRATE_{t-n} + b_2\,BYDIF_{t-n} + b_3\,STKUS_{t-n} + b_4\,STKJ_{t-n} + e_t \quad (4.2)$$

model as follows:
where n = 0 for the contemporaneous model and n = 0, 2 or 3 for the lagged models below. The error process was assumed to be $e \sim N(0, \sigma^2 I_T)$. In line with these assumptions, the proposed empirical relationships were estimated by ordinary least squares (OLS). A more detailed description of the data is provided below.

The Data

All variables were measured on a monthly basis, from January of 1982 through December of 1989. This period encompasses most of the current expansion, which is the longest on record in peacetime. Therefore, this is a period of growth in both the United States and Japan. In addition, this time frame for the analysis encompasses both a cycle when the U.S. dollar appreciated against major foreign currencies (January 1982–Spring 1985) and the subsequent cycle of depreciation of the U.S. dollar (Spring 1985–December 1989).

Data for the dependent variable (ACQ) were obtained from *Mergers and Acquisitions.* These data were obtained separately for Japanese acquisitions of U.S. firms (AJ) and U.S. acquisitions of Japanese firms (AU). Then, the latter figures were subtracted from the former. Data for the exchange rate variable (EXRATE) were compiled from the IMF's *International Financial Statistics.* Again, we obtained separate series for the Y/SDR exchange rate (EJ) and the $/SDR exchange rate (EU). The series for the variable EXRATE results from dividing the former by the latter.

By the same token, the series for the bond yield differential variable (BYDIF) results from subtracting Japanese bond yields (BJ) from the U.S. bond yields (BU). These yields were obtained from *World Financial Markets,* published by Morgan Guaranty Trust Co. The stock prices for the U.S. (STKUS) are the monthly averages of the S&P 500 Composite, published by S&P's *Security Price Index Record.* Finally, the stock prices for Japan (STKJ) are monthly averages of the Tokyo Stock Exchange Index, published in the *Moody's International Manual.* The results of our empirical analysis are presented next.

Empirical Results

Table 4.2 presents some descriptive statistics: the mean, standard deviation, and minimum and maximum values for the dependent and independent variables. A positive integer value for ACQ means that the number of Japanese acquisitions of U.S. firms exceeded the number of U.S. acquisitions of Japanese firms in a given month. The mean value (1.3) for the ACQ variable suggests that Japanese acquisitions of U.S. firms exceeded American acquisitions of Japanese firms on average. For comparable debt securities, U.S. annualized yields exceeded Japanese yields by 4.79% (479 basis points) on average during the period 1982–1989. The remainder of Table 4.2 lends itself to similar interpretations.

The main results of our empirical analysis are presented in Tables 4.3–4.6. The statistical model (4.2) was estimated with comtemporaneous variables.[47] In addition, three other models were estimated, with the explanatory variables lagged one, two, and three months, as follows:

Table 4.2. Descriptive Statistics

VARIABLE	MEAN	STD DEV	MINIMUM	MAXIMUM
AJ	1.598	1.989	0	10
AU	0.293	0.638	0	4
ACQ	1.304	2.010	-3	9
EU	1.160	0.126	0.959	1.419
EJ	219.562	37.992	166.360	294.600
EXRATE	194.448	50.778	121.751	277.297
BU	11.085	2.028	7.920	15.750
BJ	6.296	1.039	4.620	8.100
BYDIF	4.789	1.320	2.520	8.040
STKUS	211.826	64.485	109.400	346.610
STKJ	1315.315	675.770	523.300	2631.400

NOTE: Number of monthly observations n=92 (January 1982 to December 1989)

$$ACQ_t = b_0 + b_1 \, EXRATE_{t-1} + b_2 \, BYDIF_{t-1} + b_3 \, STKUS_{t-1} + b_4 \, STKJ_{t-1} + e_t \quad (4.2a)$$

$$ACQ_t = b_0 + b_1 \, EXRATE_{t-2} + b_2 \, BYDIF_{t-2} + b_3 \, STKUS_{t-2} + b_4 \, STKJ_{t-2} + e_t \quad (4.2b)$$

$$ACQ_t = b_0 + b_1 \, EXRATE_{t-3} + b_2 \, BYDIF_{t-3} + b_3 \, STKUS_{t-3} + b_4 \, STKJ_{t-3} + e_t \quad (4.2c)$$

Table 4.3 presents the results for the basic model (4.2). This table (and subsequent tables 4.4–4.6) shows the parameters estimates of the model, as well as tests of significance for the explanatory variables, and goodness-of-fit tests for the model. The results in Table 4.3 suggest that, although the model as a whole performs quite well, as indicated by the F-value, only the stock prices in the United States and Japan are significant at the 5% level or better, and the bond yield differential is significant at the 10% level. The signs of the coefficients are as expected: the higher the stock prices in Japan and the lower the stock prices in the United States, the more favorable are the conditions for Japanese firms to acquire U.S. firms (the converse statement also holds). By the same token, the larger the bond yield differential, that is, the higher interest rates are in the United States compared to Japan's, the less favorable it is for Japanese companies to acquire U.S. firms. The reason is that debt financing for such an acquisition is obtained in the U.S. markets, by and large; also, much lower costs of debt at home encourage Japanese companies to reinvest domestically. This domestic investment is an alternative to foreign acquisitions. The exchange rate variable (EXRATE) is not significant. This somewhat surprising result may be explained by the presence of multi-collinearity. As Kennedy explains, although the OLS estimator retains its desirable properties in the presence of multicollinearity, the variances of the OLS estimates may turn out to be quite large.[48] For our purposes, however, it is important to notice that the combined impact of the exchange rate, cost of debt (that is, bond yields), and equity prices explains quite well the trends of U.S.-Japan cross-border acquisitions.

Table 4.3. Regression Results - Contemporaneous Variables

Parameter Estimates and Tests of Significance

Model: $ACQ_t = b_0 + b_1 \, EXRATE_t + b_2 \, BYDIF_t + b_3 \, STKUS_t + b_4 \, STKJ_t + e_t$

VARIABLE	INTERCEPT	EXRATE	BYDIF	STKUS	STKJ
Coefficient	b_0	b_1	b_2	b_3	b_4
Estimated value	3.487	0.0002	−0.335	−0.028	0.004
(t-value)[1]	(1.084)	(0.024)	(1.730)	(2.441)	(3.647)
Prob >t[2]	.282	.981	.087	.017	.001

$R^2 = 0.404$ F Value = 14.770

Adjusted $R^2 = 0.377$[3]   Prob>F = .0001[4]

NOTES: (1) t for H_0: $b_i = 0$;

     (2) Probability of obtaining the observed t-value or one larger in absolute value in a T distribution with the appropriate DF's (two-tailed test);

     (3) R^2 adjusted for degrees of freedom;

     Adj. $R^2 = R^2 - \dfrac{m}{n-m-1} (1-R^2)$

     where m = 4 (# of DF's) and n = 96 (# of observations);

     (4) Probability that an F distribution will take on values greater than the observed F-value.

The results for the models (4.2a), (4.2b), and (4.2c), with the explanatory variables lagged one, two, and three periods, respectively, are presented in Tables 4.4, 4.5, and 4.6. In general, the lagged models do not explain the U.S.-Japan cross-border acquisitions better than the contemporaneous models. From a predictive standpoint, however, note that the significance of the stock prices and bond yields fades and that the exchange rate increases with the size of the lag. In a previous study with quarterly data, Vasconcellos, Madura and Kish found the exchange rate to be significant in cross-border acquisitions involving U.S. and British firms.[49] Thus, it is conceivable that the exchange rate performs the role of predictor of trends in cross-border acquisitions, with the costs of debt and, in particular, the stock prices being the deciding factors on a contemporaneous basis.

SUMMARY AND CONCLUSIONS

The motivations involved in the complex web of international capital flows represent an important dimension of competitiveness. The globalization of business and finance is one of the most im-

Table 4.4. Regression Results - Lagged One Month

Parameter Estimates and Tests of Significance

Model: $ACQ_t = b_0 + b_1 EXRATE_{t-1} + b_2 BYDIF_{t-1} + b_3 STKUS_{t-1} + b_4 STKJ_{t-1} + e_t$

VARIABLE	INTERCEPT	EXRATE	BYDIF	STKUS	STKJ
Coefficient	b_0	b_1	b_2	b_3	b_4
Estimated value	3.618	-0.003	-0.269	-0.024	0.004
(t-value)[1]	(1.068)	(0.294)	(1.367)	(2.051)	(3.130)
Prob.t[2]	0.288	.770	.175	.043	.002

$R^2 = 0.389$ F Value = 13.689

Adjusted $R^2 = 0.361$[3]   Prob>F = .0001[4]

NOTES: See Table 4.3.

portant economic phenomena to surface in the post-World War II
era. This globalization takes two major forms: international portfolio investment and foreign direct investment. To be sure, both
forms have existed for much longer, with portfolio investment generally dominating foreign direct investment. The magnitudes involved have soared in the last 45 years, however. In addition,
foreign direct investment has become even more important, to such
an extent that it is now an integral part of discussions and policy
analyses of U.S. competitiveness vis-a-vis other major industrial

Table 4.5.   Regression Results - Lagged Two Months

Parameter Estimates and Tests of Significance

Model: $ACQ_t = b_0 + b_1 \ EXRATE_{t-2} + b_2 \ BYDIF_{t-2} + b_3 \ STKUS_{t-2} + b_4 \ STKJ_{t-2} + e_t$

VARIABLE	INTERCEPT	EXRATE	BYDIF	STKUS	STKJ
Coefficient	b_0	b_1	b_2	b_3	b_4
Estimated value	2.210	−0.001	−0.223	−0.017	0.003
(t-value)[1]	(0.629)	(0.122)	(1.112)	(1.379)	(2.604)
Prob.t[2]	.531	.903	.270	.171	.011

$$R^2 = 0.368 \qquad F \text{ Value} = 11.358$$

$$\text{Adjusted } R^2 = 0.338^{[3]} \qquad \text{Prob>F} = .0001^{[4]}$$

NOTES: See Table 4.3

nations. In the context of foreign direct investment, cross-border
acquisitions have become even more visible. Accordingly, the study
of this form of foreign direct investment has received detailed attention here, complementing and illustrating the several angles from
which the competitiveness question is examined in this volume.
This study has investigated cross-border mergers and acquisitions
involving American and Japanese firms in the context of international capital flows, with a focus on the developments in the last
decade.

Several major issues surfaced in our examination of the motiva-

Table 4.6. Regression Results - Lagged Three Months

Parameter Estimates and Tests of Significance

Model: $ACQ_t = b_0 + b_1 \, EXRATE_{t-3} + b_2 \, BYDIF_{t-3} + b_3 \, STKUS_{t-3} + b_4 \, STKJ_{t-3} + e_t$

VARIABLE	INTERCEPT	EXRATE	BYDIF	STKUS	STKJ
Coefficient	b_0	b_1	b_2	b_3	b_4
Estimated value	4.254	−0.010	−0.132	−0.015	0.002
(t−value)[1]	(1.221)	(1.022)	(0.665)	(1.292)	(1.994)
Prob.t[2]	0.225	.310	.508	.200	.099

$R^2 = 0.371$ F Value = 12.368

Adjusted $R^2 = 0.341$[3]   Prob>F = .0001[4]

NOTES: See Table 4.3

tions for international capital flows in the U.S.-Japan experience: the attractiveness of the American market, fears of protectionism, political stability, corporate restructuring, technology transfers, corporate culture and labor relations, and the investment horizon, among others. Moreover, a detailed examination of international direct investment in the context of international capital flows showed that, during the last decade, the U.S. acted as the major recipient of those flows, with Japan being one of the major providers. In addition, our analysis shows that, although there is no evidence of discrimination against U.S. firms, the Japanese economy has absorbed a much smaller proportion of foreign direct investment, given its size, than the American and European economies.

Cross-border mergers and acquisitions are a major component of international direct investment. This study examined some of the favorable as well as the unfavorable factors which, on a priori grounds, may be expected to affect these transactions. In addition, a model of cross-border acquisitions in a capital budgeting framework provided the theoretical underpinnings for the relevant variables in cross-border acquisitions involving U.S. firms.

Finally, an empirical analysis of the cross-border acquisitions between American and Japanese firms was performed for the period 1982–1989, using both contemporaneous and lagged statistical models. The results suggest that, in the U.S.-Japan case, stock prices and the costs of debt financing are major contemporaneous causal factors, whereas the exchange rate acquires significance only as a predictor of trends in acquisitions.

At the outset of the 1990s, the trends in international capital flows continue to show the Japanese economy as a major source of foreign investment, either direct or on a portfolio basis. The imbalances present in the American economy, evidenced by the budget and current account deficits, have not been resolved. Therefore, it seems that the preponderance of Japanese acquisitions of U.S. firms, with the attendant irritations in the bilateral economic and political relations of the two economic superpowers, is likely to continue as the century draws to a close.

NOTES

1. One needs only to note the role of monopolies such as the East India Company in the European colonial exploits, as well as some of the older multinational corporations in the agricultural, mining, and oil industries. In addition, international financial flows are not new, as evidenced by loans to finance wars in Europe, foreign bonds, and the like.

2. Harry I. Chernotsky, "The American Connection: Motives for Japanese Foreign Direct Investment," *Columbia Journal of World Business* (Winter 1987): 47.

3. Glenn A. Pitman and Sang T. Choe, "Attitudinal Variations Toward Japanese Investment in the United States," *SAM Advanced Management Journal* 54 (Summer 1989): 15.

4. M. Yoshida, "Micro-Macro Analyses of Japanese Manufacturing Investments in the United States," *Management International Review* 27:4 (1987): 25–26.

5. Michael B. Smith, "U.S.-Japan Economic Relations in the 1990s: A Crossroads?" in William Brock and Robert Hormats, eds., *The Global Economy: America's Role in the Decade Ahead* (New York: W. W. Norton, 1990), 72–91.

6. Leslie S. Hiraoka, "Japan's Increasing Investments Abroad," *Futures* 17 (October 1985): 495.

7. Note that the alternative, i.e., the outright acquisition of U.S. companies, would probably be substantially more expensive. These points are discussed in detail in Scott A. Brandt, "Perspectives on Joint Venturing with the Japanese in the United States," *SAM Advanced Management Journal* 55 (Winter 1990): 34–36, 47–48.

8. M. Yoshida, "Micro-Macro Analyses of Japanese Manufacturing Investments in the United States," *Management International Review* 27:4 (1987): 19, 27.

9. Clyde V. Prestowitz, Jr., "U.S.–Japan Trade Friction: Creating a New Relationship," *California Management Review* 41:2 (Winter 1989): 9.

10. See, for example, Kazuo Nukazawa, "Japan & the USA: Wrangling Toward Reciprocity," *Harvard Business Review* (May-June 1988): 42.

11. Contrary to what its provocative title might appear to suggest Kelman wrote a balanced essay, concluding that "we must complete the transition from a period in which Americans tended to consider our culture as better than the cultures of other nations to one in which we accept that we have things to learn as well as to teach." Steven Kelman, "The 'Japanization' of America?" *The Public Interest* (Winter 1990): 83.

12. See Michael Smith, "U.S.-Japan Economic Relations in the 1990s," 72, 73 for a discussion.

13. One needs only to note that high expected rates of return do not seem to encourage more foreign investment in certain less developed countries. The pervasive and restrictive regulations concerning profit and dividend remittances, as well as an environment where those regulations change frequently, goes a long way toward explaining the caution of foreign investors.

14. Steven Kelman, "The 'Japanization' of America?," 82.

15. Roger W. Rosendahl, "Japanese Investment in the U.S.," *International Financial Law Review* 7 (September 1988): 29.

16. M. Yoshida, "Micro-Macro Analyses of Japanese Manufacturing Investments in the United States," 26, 29. Emphasis added.

17. Japan Information Center, "Controversy Over Foreign Investment," *Japan Report* 34:6 (June 1988): 1. Emphasis added.

18. Urban C. Lehner and Alan Murray, "'Selling of America' to Japanese Touches Some Very Raw Nerves," *The Wall Street Journal* (19 June 1990): A1.

19. For a complete discussion see Enderwick, *California Management* (1989): 45, 57.

20. See related discussions in Gary Hector, "Japan Learns the Takeover Game," *Fortune* (31 July 1989); Susan Chira, "Japan's New Goal: U.S. Companies," *The New York Times* (27 April 1988): D1, D5; Henry Sender, "Japanese Banks' Global M&A Assault," *Institutional Investor* 22 (August 1988): 167–72; and David Lake, "A Prized Link to the Takeover Market," *Asian Finance* (15 February 1990): 42–44, 79.

21. Nigel Holloway, "How Japan Takes Over," *Far Eastern Economic Review* (11 January 1990): 40.

22. Ibid., 40, 44.

23. Organization for Economic Co-operation and Development, *International Direct Investment and the New Economic Environment* (Paris, France: OECD, 1989). Emphasis added.

24. Ibid., 118.

25. Ibid.

26. It is not too uncommon that a company will attempt to move these levers to ward off an unwanted foreign suitor.

27. Scott A. Brandt, "Perspectives on Joint Venturing with the Japanese in the United States," *SAM Advanced Management Journal* 55 (Winter 1990): 36.

28. Roger W. Rosendahl, "Japanese Investment in the U.S.," 27.

29. Table 4 in M. Yoshida, "Micro-Macro Analyses of Japanese Manufacturing Investments in the United States," 26.

30. Ellen M. Herr, "U.S. Business Enterprises Acquired or Established by

Foreign Direct Investors in 1988," *Survey of Current Business* (May 1989): 22. Emphasis added.

31. Charles Smith, "A Taste for Takeovers," *Far Eastern Economic Review* (18 August 1988): 72–73.

32. Gordon K. Dowsley, "Here Comes Japan!" *Canadian Insurance/Agent & Broker* 93 (July 1988): 14, 20.

33. Roger W. Rosendahl, "Japanese Investment in the U.S.," 28.

34. Pitman and Choe, "Attitudinal Variations Toward Japanese Investment in the United States," 17; Figures 2 and 3.

35. See this point in Kazuo Nukazawa, "Japan & the USA," 42.

36. Henry Eason, "The Corporate Immigrants," *Nation's Business* 75 (April 1987): 14.

37. See the series of stories under the heading "Strained Alliance," recently published by *The Wall Street Journal*. In particular, see Lehner and Murray, "'Selling of America' to Japanese Touches Some Very Raw Nerves," A1, A14.

38. Robert O. Metzger and Ari Ginsberg, "Lessons From Japanese Global Acquisitions," *The Journal of Business Strategy* (May/June 1989): 35.

39. Prestowitz, "U.S.–Japan Trade Friction," 11.

40. Gary Viner and Neil Cohen, "The Allure of Small Firms to Japanese Acquirers," *Mergers & Acquisitions* 23 (March/April 1989): 51.

41. Gary Hector, "Japan Learns the Takeover Game," *Fortune* (31 July 1989): 12.

42. "Thank You, Japan," *The Economist* (23 December 1989): 12.

43. See Martin Tolchin, "Foreign Investors Held $2 Trillion in U.S. in '89," *The New York Times* (13 June 1990): D2.

44. For a thorough discussion of the many issues concerning international direct investment, see Stefan H. Robock and Kenneth Simmonds, *International Business and Multinational Enterprises*. 4th ed. (Homewood, Ill,: Irwin, 1989), especially Part One—"The Nature and Scope of International Business;" Part Three—"Global Business Strategy" and Part Four—"The Nation-State and International Business." For the Japanese case, see Noritake Kobayashi, "Japanese Intervention with Respect to Direct Foreign Investment," in Richard D. Robinson, ed., *Direct Foreign Investment: Costs and Benefits* (New York: Praeger, 1987).

45. For an extended discussion of these factors, see Geraldo M. Vasconcellos, Jeff Madura, and Richard J. Kish, "An Empirical Investigation of Factors affecting Cross-Border Acquisitions: The U.S./U.K. Experience," *Global Finance Journal*, (forthcoming) and the references cited therein.

46. The view of cross-border acquisitions as capital investment projects is fully developed in Jeff Madura, Geraldo M. Vasconcellos, and Richard J. Kish, "A Valuation Model for International Acquisitions," unpublished manuscript, July 1990. The following discussion draws heavily from that study.

47. This implies that, in the basic model (4.2), $n = 0$.

48. See Peter Kennedy, *A Guide to Econometrics*, 2d ed. (Cambridge, Mass.: MIT Press, 1985), 146.

49. See Note 45.

Part II
Competitiveness and Institutional Values

Ecology, Efficiency, Equity, and Competitiveness

JOHN B. GATEWOOD

Historically, marine fish of the United States have been regarded as an open-access resource. Fish belong to whoever catches them, and there are no legal restrictions on entrance into the fisheries. These conditions have led to repeated overexploitation and overcapitalization, prompting Garrett Hardin to use ocean fisheries as a classic example of what he called "the tragedy of the commons."[1]

Over the past thirty years, economists and other social scientists have proposed a variety of regulatory mechanisms that would prevent the competition among fishermen in an open-access fishery from resulting in overexploitation of their resources and overcapitalization of their vessels. Some of these mechanisms are monopolistic ownership, fleet quotas, limited entry licensing, and individually transferable catch quotas. Virtually all of these regulatory devices run counter to American ideals of equal opportunity, social equity, and distributive justice, though in varying degrees. In consequence, America's fisheries show a wide range of management policies reflecting local compromises between the goals of resource conservation, economic efficiency, and social equity. These same fisheries are now faced with yet another challenge: international competition.

This paper reviews select examples of fisheries management in the United States, outlining the trade-offs inherent in alternative regulatory regimes in the face of international price competition. For example, should the United States continue management policies congenial with large fleets of small vessels, or should policies favor consolidation of our fleets to achieve greater harvesting efficiency? The lessons of competition and cooperation from the particular case of fisheries are then transposed to America's competitiveness situation more generally. There, too, unrestrained exploitation of an open-access resource (the international market-place in a free trade environment) threatens to be ruinous in the long run. The fisheries model is a miniature of the contending forces, policy options, and likely outcomes of national industrial competition.

The first section of the paper describes abstract, theoretical frameworks that explain why commercial fisheries around the world tend to be overexploited and overcapitalized. The second section discusses the various interventionist responses proposed to solve these problems. The third section examines how the new factor of international price competition can undermine even care-fully crafted management plans. The final section draws some general lessons from the case of fisheries to larger-scale discussions of competitiveness.

THEORETICAL FRAMEWORKS FOR UNDERSTANDING FISHERY DYNAMICS

The very expression "fishery" is somewhat ambiguous. An un-utilized fish resource is not a fishery. Similarly, a group of humans who claim they are "fishing" but catch no fish does not constitute a fishery. At a minimum, then, a fishery refers to an exploitative relation between some population of humans and some population of fish (finfish, mollusks, crustaceans, et cetera). Technical defini-tions also take account of the fact that the human population usu-ally shows a gradation in terms of involvement in direct exploitation: fishermen (primary harvesters), processors, distribu-tors, consumers, and managers. It should be no surprise, therefore, that fisheries research is highly interdisciplinary, involving not only biologists but also a variety of social scientists (economists, anthro-pologists, political scientists).

This section reviews the basic theoretical frameworks that guide much fisheries research. For convenience, the presentation is orga-nized somewhat along disciplinary lines. Beginning with the under-lying mathematical models of population biology, we will move to economic perspectives on fisheries, then consider the more com-plex human motivations and behaviors that are part and parcel of commercial fishing.

Biological Perspectives

From the biologist's perspective, there are two basic mathemati-cal frameworks for understanding population dynamics in fisheries.[2] The more complex of these two is the Volterra-Lotka model, which describes the population dynamics generated by a predator-prey interaction. This formulation explicitly recognizes that the population size of the predator group (fishermen) will causally affect the population size of the prey group (fish), and vice versa, as expressed in Equation (1) below:

$$(1) \qquad dx/dt = bx(1-(x/N)) - sxy$$
$$dy/dt = sxy - my$$

where

bx :	a density dependent "birth" term for the prey,
1–(x/N) :	a saturation level determined by the maximum niche size, N,
sxy :	conversion of prey into predator, and
my :	natural predator mortality.

Note that if the niche size, N, is infinite, then these equations produce never-ending oscillations in the population sizes of both predator and prey. If, however, N is finite, which is much more plausible empirically, then the oscillations are damped and will converge around a stable stationary state. In this latter case, the model requires some sort of additional input for the system to exhibit ongoing oscillatory behavior.[3]

Human predatory interactions with fish differ, however, in some interesting ways from the classic cases of wolves with caribou or anteaters with ants. First, humans are a very generalized and omnivorous species. We seldom depend on any single prey species for a large proportion of our diet. Second, the bulk of human sustenance today comes from *domesticated* plants and animals rather than from hunted or gathered wild species. Through our food-producing technologies, we dramatically increase and stabilize the population level of our prey species, whether plant or animal. Third, in most fishing communities of the world, and especially in the commercial fisheries, only a small segment of the human populations engages in fishing. For example, whereas adult wolves either hunt or die, less than one percent of Americans fish for a living. Fourth, the immediate human motivation responsible for most of the world's catch is profit rather than hunger. Price rather than poundage drives fishing effort. These complicating factors undermine the tight causal dependency between predator and prey populations described in the Volterra-Lotka model. Perhaps for these reasons, the Volterra-Lotka model has *not* been used much in fisheries management.

The dominant mathematical formulation for fisheries management has been the logistic equation, which describes the growth of a single species in a limited environment. Milner Schaefer reviews the history of this ecological model and is commonly given credit for its application to fishery dynamics.[4] The logistic equation can be made more complicated— by incorporating competition among species for the same resource or building in age-cohort calibrations for determining the breeding population—but its basic form is:

$$(2) \qquad dx/dt = bx(1 - (x/N)) - mx - Fx$$

where

bx :	a density dependent "birth" term;	
$1-(x/N)$:	a saturation level determined by the maximum niche size, N;	
mx :	natural fish mortality; and	
Fx :	fish mortality due to fishing (i.e., the yield).	

The equilibrium solution for yield, Fx, is a parabola with a maximum value at that point of total fishing effort where $F = (b-m)/2$. This defines the fishery's *maximum sustainable yield* (MSY)—that level of catch at which fish mortality (both natural and human-caused) equals the population's increase rate. The fish population will decline if exploitation goes beyond this level, and for this reason, conservation-minded managers usually target the "total allowable catch" (TAC) for a fishery at slightly less than its calculated MSY.

The fundamental logic of these biological models is to determine the maximum production level a given wild fishery resource can sustain. Thus, to espouse MSY as the proper management target is to focus strictly on how much biomass (protein, calories, etc.) can be harvested from a wild fishery without depleting the resource. There are other factors to be considered, as discussed below, which is why MSY is no longer the pillar of fisheries management it once was.[5]

Economic Perspectives

The same year that Schaefer published his formulations of the MSY idea, H. Scott Gordon, an economist, published his seminal article on the economic theory of common property resources.[6]

His ideas and arguments map onto a Schaefer production function quite easily, by simply renaming the vertical axis "value of catch" instead of "number of fish" (see Figure 1).

Gordon was concerned with optimal economic utilization of fishery resources. Thus, instead of focusing on how much biomass can be harvested on a sustainable basis, he developed the notion of *maximum economic yield* (MEY)—that level of catch at which the difference between the fleet's total revenue and total cost is greatest.[7] Obtaining the most "rent from the sea," rather than the most "food from the sea," should be the manager's objective, and the fact that MEY is always less than MSY ensures resource conservation (see Figure 1).

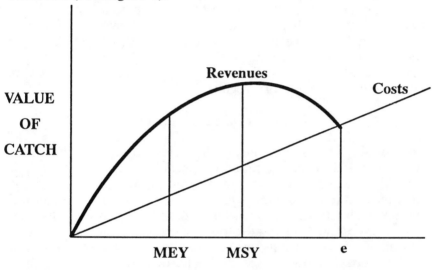

FISHING EFFORT OF FLEET

Figure 1

He then addressed the question of why this economically optimal level of exploitation is so seldom achieved in the world's major fisheries. The reason, according to Gordon, lies in the common property nature of our marine fisheries. When individuals cannot exert property rights over a resource or exclude others from entering the fishery, they are caught up in a prisoner's dilemma between short-term self-interest and the long-term collective good. This situation undermines internal restraint, because, unless everyone cooperates, the long-term savings produced by individuals who refrain from intensifying their fishing effort only benefit their competitors. In consequence, fishing fleets tend to become overcapitalized, whether through more vessels entering the fishery or through upgrading of existing vessels. Indeed, unless the fundamental political economy of the fishery is altered or subjected to external regulation, the fleet's fishing effort will increase to the equilibrium point where revenue equals cost (*e* in Figure 1). The end result is Hardin's "tragedy of the commons," namely, resource depletion and profit loss.

Gordon's economic formulation of both the proper policy objective (MEY) and his analysis of why fisheries tend to be overexploited and overcapitalized are central pillars of contemporary fisheries management. Whether the tragedy of the commons scenario is an inevitable and inherent aspect of all fisheries is an issue receiving considerable attention, but the conceptual framework itself guides virtually all current discussions. Following the implications of Gordon's argument, economists today tend to favor economic efficiency ("rationalization") as the proper management target and champion "privatization" of rights over the resource as the most efficient regulatory regime.

Sociocultural Perspectives

Anthropological case studies of fisheries throughout the world have contributed to the "common property" theoretical framework in several ways. For example, the very notion of optimal yield has been expanded to include the *non*-monetary rewards (sociocultural values) as well as the economic benefits obtained through fishing. Lee Anderson and Courtland Smith's notion of "worker satisfaction bonus" is a promising sociocultural elaboration of the Schaefer-Gordon model.[8] Because fishermen tend to enjoy their work—fishing is not only a means to an end, but also an end in itself—the exploitation level producing the greatest total rewards (at least to the harvesting sector) will generally lie between ME and MSY, at the point OY in Figure 2.

There are tactical problems, glossed over in Figure 2, that impede applying this conceptualization of *socially optimal yield* (OY) to actual cases. For the Anderson-Smith model to be more than just a useful abstraction, there must be some reasonable way to convert job satisfaction into dollar values, and this is problematic.[9] Still, the Magnuson Fishery Conservation and Management Act requires regional management councils to consider all "relevant social, economic, and ecological factors" when developing management plans, and the Anderson-Smith conceptualization of OY offers one vision of how this might be achieved.

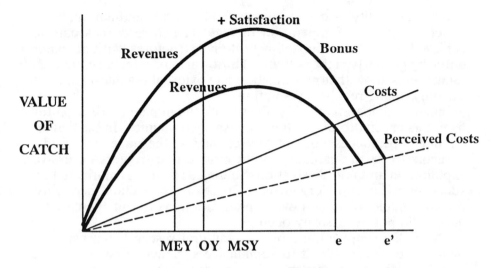

MEY OY MSY

FISHING EFFORT OF FLEET

Because fishing tends to be positively valued as a way of life, the "Optimal Yield" occurs at that level of fishing effort where the net returns, including satisfaction bonus, to the factors of production is greatest.

Assumptions : **Costs are proportional to effort.**
Satisfaction bonus is proportional to revenues.
Price per unit of catch is constant.

Figure 2

Relatively greater effort has gone into ascertaining the conditions under which tragedies of the commons might or might not occur. Detailed studies of fisheries around the world have revealed a wider spectrum of possible solutions to the so-called "commons problem" than were considered by Gordon and Hardin.[10] For example, in coastal Japan, many places in Micronesia and Polynesia, and among most Northwest Coast Indians, fish resources were subject to property rights vested in kin groups or local communities that controlled access to, and exploitation levels in, their territorial waters. Such studies show that the relation between property regimes and sustainability of fish resources is not simple and automatic in effect.[11] Similarly, cooperation to regulate fish resources can be achieved through a variety of institutional structures working under differing property right systems. These various comanagement arrangements show that privatization and external regulation are not the only viable regulatory solutions.[12]

Finally, comparative study shows that the human motivation for fishing is crucial to understanding fishery dynamics. In particular, although open access to the resource may set the stage for tragedy, it seems to be the capitalist profit motive that triggers excessive exploitation and rent dissipation. So long as fishing is motivated by subsistence needs or organized as part of a household economy, resource depletion and/or overcapitalization in even an open access fishery do not necessarily occur.[13]

The policy implications of sociocultural research for fisheries management are difficult to summarize succinctly.[14] Whereas the biological and economic models consider relatively few variables and lead to quantifiable management targets, anthropologists typically consider a multitude of qualitative issues on a case-by-case basis with the end product being descriptions of how fisheries are situated within broader social contexts. In their emphasis on the relevance of such factors as fishermen's job satisfaction, the microeconomic organization of production, relations of the fishery to community life, the social consequences of displacing fishing laborers, and other economic opportunities, anthropologists are endorsing the idea of socially optimal yield and elaborating on the range of human values it should incorporate. Generally speaking, these social scientists tend to champion social equity as a criterion to be used along with resource conservation and economic efficiency when evaluating specific management plans.

Combining the biological, economic, and sociocultural perspecives on fisheries, we see the complexity of the "commons problem" in wild marine fisheries. While this review has been necessarily brief and the precise conditions that trigger the tragedy scenario are still subject to scholarly debate, we may summarize the emerging understanding as follows. Unrestricted access to a wild fish resource sets up a conflict between short-term self-interest and the long-term collective good, which, if exploitation is motivated by profit returned to capital, seems to result in (a) overexploitation of the resource, and (b) overcapitalization of the fleet. The question is, What can we do about it?

THE REPERTOIRE OF SOLUTIONS

To succeed in a competitive arena generally requires strategies that look beyond the immediate situation to longer-term objectives. Napoleon won the battles but lost his war with Russia. Today's prosperous industries, if they neglect research and development, are forfeiting the future. And, short-sightedness is an element of the commons problem in fisheries, as well.

There are two fundamentally different attitudes countries and fleets may adopt towards commercial fishing. On the one hand, people may recognize the commons problem but elect to do nothing about it. In high-capacity fleets, this orientation generally leads to "pulse fishing," that is, intensive exploitation of a given fish stock until it becomes unprofitable, then shifting to another fish stock or species, during which time the first stock may recuperate. So long as the fleet's market has eclectic tastes for fish products and the fleet can move to new locations easily, this shifting pattern of exploitation will work, at least in the short term (several decades). The Japanese and (former) Soviet distant-waters fleets are examples of this. MSY, ME, and OY are non sequiturs in such systems, for the explicit logic driving exploitation is short-term profitability utilizing a broad spectrum of fish resources rather than long-term sustainability of each resource considered separately.

Alternatively, people may subscribe to the idea of "scientific management," that is, management of a given fish stock to achieve long-term sustainability of the resource and to stabilize the human values realized from it. Scott identifies four, more specific reasons to regulate fisheries: (a) to achieve "X"-efficiency, usually done by effort restrictions such as limited entry or gear/temporal restrictions; (b) to increase the quality, weight, or size of individual fish in the catch; (c) to achieve redistribution of income; and/or (d) to prevent waste of labor and capital.[15]

Most coastal fisheries in the world operate, nominally at least, under the second policy attitude. Virtually all United States marine fisheries are subject to governmental management, and this practice is mandated by the Magnuson Fisheries Management and Conservation Act, which established a system of regional councils charged with developing fisheries management plans (FMPs) for the marine resources in their areas. Sharing this common underlying value, however, does not guarantee agreement regarding specific management policies and tactics. As reviewed above, there are at least three plausible conceptualizations of the proper management target—MSY, MEY, and OY—and there are a wide variety of management tools for achieving them.

The key to any fisheries management program lies in gaining the cooperation, willingly given or coerced, of the exploiters. There are examples of international cooperation for the purpose of fisheries management, such as the Pacific Halibut Commission and the Inter-American Tropical Tuna Association, but scientific management is more easily implemented when a fishery is under the jurisdiction of a single state. Thus, following Peru's lead, most countries in the world today claim the waters within 200 miles of their coasts as exclusive economic zones. The United States expanded its territorial claim from 12 to 200 miles in 1977 as part of the Magnuson Act. This expansion of the state's legal jurisdiction can also be used to exclude foreign fleets, thereby reducing the level of fishing effort within coastal waters.

Currently, there are six basic kinds of regulatory tactics in the tool kit of fisheries managers in the United States. A necessarily brief review is provided, below, in which each tactic is also evaluated in terms of its consequences with respect to the goals of resource conservation, economic efficiency, and social equity.

Regulatory Tactics

1. Fleet Quotas. Fleet quotas are the most direct and obvious mechanisms to curb over-fishing. The key data for this form of regulation are biologists' estimates of the maximal exploitation level for a given fish stock, during a specified season, using some variant of MSY reasoning. Regulators review this scientific advice, decide on the season's legal TAC for the fleet as a whole, and monitor the catch (usually as recorded by processors) as the season progresses. Once the TAC has been landed, the season ends.

This sort of regulatory regime is an elegantly simple solution to the problem of fish stock conservation. If properly calculated and enforced, TACs are clearly capable of preventing overexploitation. There is nothing in the logic of fleet quotas, however, that addresses issues of efficiency in how the harvesting is done or equity in the disbursement of the captured rent. Fundamentally, a TAC regulation simply says, "The fleet can fish until X fish are landed; the number and type of vessels are up to the industry." Economic and equity concerns can and often do enter into the picture, but only insofar as the announced TAC may deviate from the scientific advisors' MSY estimates. This sort of "fudge factor," because it is informal and inexplicit, subjects regulators to considerable political pressures. For these reasons, TACs, by themselves, constitute an inadequate regulatory regime. They remain, however, a fundamental and generally presupposed component in more complex management plans.

2. Gear and Temporal Restrictions. Gear restrictions can be used to address three sorts of management objectives. First, they are sometimes instituted as a means of resource conservation. By limiting the exploitative efficiency of harvesters one unit at a time, one hopes to reduce or at least retard the growth of the fleet's overall catch. Second, fine points of gear (mesh size, vessel storage facilities) can be regulated to improve the quality of the catch. Finally, gear restrictions can be used to address, rather directly, issues of income redistribution, for example, banning the use of specific gear types for a given fish stock.

Temporal restrictions follow a logic similar to gear restrictions. Officials can simply close fishing grounds for spans of time as a means of preventing overexploitation of the spawning stock. Income redistribution among different kinds of harvesters can be achieved by closing areas only to some gear types.

While gear and temporal restrictions can be successful in terms of conserving fish stocks and achieving income redistribution among user groups, they are simply at odds with the goal of economic efficiency.[16] The fundamental reasoning behind these regulatory tactics is sequential consideration of only two management objectives: first and foremost achieve MSY, then worry about allocation or social equity issues. The root of the problem is that gear restrictions control the cost of fishing only for each harvesting unit taken singly, but not for the fleet collectively. In consequence, if these are the only forms of regulation in force, the fleet tends to be highly overcapitalized in the sense of a large number of small vessels that fish only occasionally instead of a small number of highly efficient and busy vessels.

3. License Fees and Landing Taxes. Unlike gear/temporal restrictions and TACs, license fees and landing taxes, if sufficiently large, are means to limit the inputs to the fishery rather than restrict its output. The difference between fees and taxes is largely a matter of when payments to the government (the public) are received. Fees are paid up front for the opportunity to engage in a fishery, whereas landing taxes are levied ex post facto on a vessel's catch. Both mechanisms have the desirable aspect of returning a goodly portion of a fisher's rent to the public at large.

Most U.S. fisheries require commercial fishermen to purchase a license. Currently, these are cheap relative to the income derived from fishing (typically, $50 per person) and exist principally to defray the costs of fisheries administration. The price could be considerably higher, however, and in this way discourage the more marginal fishermen from participation. Similarly, the government could impose rather substantial taxes on landed catch to discourage inefficient vessels from participation.

Aside from the practical problem of calibrating the fee or tax structure, this regulatory logic is generally criticized on three grounds. First, the power to impose taxes, at least in the United States and Canada, is vested in legislative bodies rather than given over to bureaucratic agencies. Thus, were fisheries managers to institute fees or taxes large enough to reduce participation in a fishery, their action would almost certainly encounter constitutional objections.[17] Second, imposing severe fees or landing taxes would be politically naive, for it would amount to assessing a new charge on people who already suffer low incomes and underemployment.[18] Finally, a fee or tax system cannot be manipulated rapidly enough to deal with year-to-year, season-to-season fluctuations in fish stocks.[19]

4. Limited Entry Licenses. Limited entry licensing is the most direct and dramatic way to restrict inputs to a fishery. As the name implies, limited entry systems restrict the fishing power of a fleet by limiting the number of harvesting units (and, thereby, the capital investment) allowed in a fishery. Ideally, managers would determine the number of vessel licenses to be issued by estimating the TAC for the fish stock in question and dividing that by the catching power of vessels of a given type. In this way, each vessel could work at its maximum efficiency and still not overfish the resource.

The difficult issue in limited entry systems, of course, is how the licenses are to be distributed initially. One disbursement scheme is to auction off the licenses, for example, by selling them to the highest bidders. More commonly, licenses are distributed to all vessel owners who meet specified qualifications regarding historic participation. A third possibility is a random lottery. There are also questions of whether licenses should be issued for a fixed or indefinite duration, whether they could be bought or sold during their term, and so on.

Another problem with limited entry is that, by itself, it is only a temporary solution to overfishing and overcapitalization, for it does not eliminate the motivation of each vessel owner to increase his or her vessel's catching power. Thus, to be effective, limited entry must be part of a management plan that includes gear restrictions or other means of inhibiting vessel enhancements. In such configurations, limited entry systems are, in principle at least, an effective way to achieve conservation and efficiency goals (provided the system has not simply grandfathered an already overcapitalized and overly powerful fleet). They are objectionable, however, in terms of excluding marginal people, especially native populations, who have few other economic opportunities than fishing.[20] Also, they run counter to deeply held cultural values that see fishing in the special category of a "God-given right of citizenship."

5. Individual Vessel Quotas. Individual vessel quotas are a form of privatization achieved by managers allocating a given TAC among a fixed number of vessels participating in a fishery. The advantages of vessel quotas are (a) they accomplish resource conservation as effectively as a fleet quota system; (b) they can be recalibrated quickly to respond to short-term or seasonal fluctuations; (c) they do not increase the costs incurred by fishermen; and (d) they restrict capital inputs much more effectively than a limited entry system. This last point is especially significant in arguments favoring vessel quotas. Because vessel owners know in advance their quotas, and these are guaranteed independent of what other fishermen do, they are freed from the "prisoner's dilemma" situation and will be motivated to configure their vessels in the most economically optimal fashion capable of catching their quotas.[21]

On the negative side, individual vessel quotas, which logically presuppose some sort of limited entry system, are subject to the same debates regarding equity that apply to limited entry. Additional problems revolve around how the vessel quotas are to be determined—that is, whether quotas should be equal among participating vessels, variable based on historical performance of the vessels, variable based on the catching power of the vessels, or variable based on capital value of the vessels. Further, the rights vested in vessel quotas could be transferable, of fixed duration, and/or priced (hence marketable). Finally, as Gatewood and McCay argue, precisely because vessel quotas eliminate the competitive aspects of fishing, they may diminish the nonmonetary rewards (aspects of "social benefits") derived from some fisheries.[22]

6. Sole Ownership of Fishing Rights. Scott argued in favor of sole ownership of fishing rights as the most satisfactory long-term solution to the commons problem. (Sole owners differ from monopolistic owners in that they cannot control price.) He noted that the simple existence of private property is insufficient to assure economic rationalization of a fishery: privatization of the resource had to be "on a *scale* sufficient to insure that one management had

complete control of the asset."[23] The essential differences between sole ownership at the proper scale and a competitive regime are that the sole owner can (a) maximize short-terms gains by reorganizing production to take advantage of economies of integration and of scale; and (b) maximize long-term gains by fixing current output at that level where marginal current net revenue is equal to marginal user cost.[24] While sole ownership does not guarantee resource conservation, it should foster greater efficiency in production.

The first problem with this regulatory scheme is how to establish the exclusive property rights. A common way of allocating state-owned property is for the state to auction exclusive leases to highest bidders, such as is done for offshore oil tracts. An auction of this sort would return some rent directly to the general public and reward those who can organize efficient exploitation of the resource, but it ignores several social considerations. There are social costs when labor is displaced from an economic sector, which is a principal way sole owners can establish more efficient operations. This issue will loom large in regions of the country where few other economic opportunities exist (for example, Alaska, Maine, much of the Gulf Coast). Also, the share system of payment for crew members, which is customary in fishing, means that the entrepreneurs who will enjoy the benefits of the property rights do *not* hazard the usual business risks. If fishing is bad, it is the laborers who have had no say in the matter who absorb a large proportion of the consequences.

None of the various regulatory alternatives is perfect. Each is capable of achieving some management objectives, but none addresses completely the triadic goals of conservation, efficiency, and equity.[25] Because the schemes have differential social impacts, they are also highly political. Different groups of people enjoy the benefits and endure the costs depending upon which plan is in force. The six basic regulatory alternatives grade along a continuum from those preserving open access (nonexclusionary) to those creating property rights (privatization), as illustrated in Figure 3.

In broad terms, fleet quotas, gear and temporal restrictions, and license fees and landing taxes, because they preserve the right of any citizen to exploit marine resources, favor equity concerns (equal opportunity) over economic efficiency. By contrast, limited entry licenses, individual vessel quotas, and sole ownership are forms of economic protectionism in that they establish state-sanctioned private property rights, either to fishing opportunities or

Schematic of the Trade-Offs Inherent in the Six Major Regulatory Alternatives

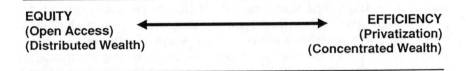

EQUITY   ⟵⟶   EFFICIENCY
(Open Access)   (Privatization)
(Distributed Wealth)   (Concentrated Wealth)

Fleet Quotas

  Gear and Temporal Restrictions

    License Fees and Landing Taxes

        Limited Entry Licenses

          Individual Vessel Quotas

           Sole Ownership

Figure 3

specified fish resources, where none previously existed. As social policies, they explicitly favor efficiency over equity and hope to achieve efficiency by creating property regimes that will induce fishermen to restrict their own capital and effort investments.

The current rage in scientific and managerial literature is for individual vessel quotas. The first large-scale implementation of this kind of system occurred in New Zealand a few years ago. A similar system has just been instituted in Mid-Atlantic surf clam fishery. But these management regimes have not been in place long enough for anyone to ascertain their full consequences.[26]

Because no management panacea exists and because each regulatory alternative has different ecological, economic, and social consequences, there are a wide range of management plans in effect in the United States. In regions where fisheries are one of very few economic opportunities for the population, we tend to find non-exclusionary management regimes such as fleet quotas in conjunction with gear and temporal restrictions. In other regions, where a variety of other economic opportunities exist, we find more concern with economic efficiency; hence, their management regimes often include individual vessel quotas or other privatization strategies.

The larger point, which bears upon the subsequent discussions of competitiveness, is that each fishery management plan reflects *locally appropriate compromises* among conservation, efficiency, and equity concerns. Regulatory agencies usually insist on conservation objectives, but they resolve efficiency versus equity tradeoffs through involuted political processes as well as through consultation with social science advisors. Not surprisingly, then, debates concerning proper management policies are ongoing as managers respond to pressures from the various interest groups. In principle and in law, managers are supposed to optimize the social benefit derived from the publicly-owned resource. Pursuit of this diffuse objective may or may not result in lower fish prices.

THE "COMPETITIVENESS" PROBLEM IN FISHERIES

The complex management compromises that exist in several major U.S. fisheries are now being confronted by another kind of challenge: international price competition. While our management schemes were being worked out under the political-legal umbrella of the United States to achieve locally appropriate definitions of "socially optimal yield," people in other countries have gradually increased their shares in the international market and in some of our domestic markets.

Growth in the market shares of foreign fish does not necessarily indicate a competitiveness problem, however, for there are two ways countries can increase their share of the international and U.S. domestic markets. These should be clearly distinguished at the outset.

Firstly, markets for fish can expand, either through (a) increases in the size of human populations, that is, growth in the sheer number of human consumers; and/or (b) increases in the per capita consumption of fish. This second source of increased demand is particularly relevant to the U.S. market, where the recent diet and health craze has substantially increased the domestic demand for fish. The U.S. per capita consumption of fish during the 1960s averaged 10.73 pounds, essentially the same as that during previous decades back to 1910. This average rose to 12.49 pounds per person during the 1970s and to 14.07 pounds during the 1980s. For 1989, the per capita consumption was 15.9 pounds, a record high.[27] America's wild marine fisheries, because of the sorts of ecological limits discussed previously, cannot simply increase production to

supply this increased demand without overexploiting our resources. Thus, in these cases, foreign fish is required to satisfy
increased demand, and the competitiveness of our domestic fisheries is not at issue.

Alternatively, the percentage of foreign fish in world and U.S.
domestic markets can increase because foreign fish is cheaper and/
or is considered to be of better quality than fish produced domestically. In these cases, the "competitiveness" of U.S. domestic fisheries is at issue and could affect management policies.

For many years, despite its abundant fish harvest, the United
States has run a trade deficit with respect to fish imports and exports. In 1989, the most recent year for which statistics are available, the United States imported 3.2 billion pounds of edible fishery
products valued at $5.5 billion, plus another $4.1 billion of imported nonedible fishery products (primarily fish meal used in animal feed). Offsetting this, we exported 1.4 billion pounds of edible
fishery products valued at $2.3 billion, plus $2.4 billion of nonedible
fishery products.[28]

In terms of dollar value, the general pattern of U.S. foreign trade
in edible fishery products has been stable for at least a decade.
Shrimp and tuna are our major imports; salmon is our major export. Given the importance of the U.S. salmon industry with respect to offsetting our foreign trade deficit in fish, and the fact that
it is currently losing ground in the world market, salmon illustrates
very nicely the general problems "competitiveness" poses for fisheries management in the United States. And, because most of the
U.S. salmon catch comes from Alaska, it is appropriate to focus
attention on the Alaskan salmon fisheries for our principal case.

The remainder of this section first describes the productive and
regulatory history of Alaskan salmon fisheries, particularly in the
southeast region, which was the first to be developed. Then, recent
trends in the world market for salmon are reviewed to show that a
genuine competitiveness problem exists for the U.S. salmon industry. The section concludes by sketching out and evaluating alternative ways the U.S. salmon industry might respond to its
competitiveness problem.

Historical Overview of the Alaskan Salmon Fisheries

Salmon are caught as they return from wide-ranging ocean mi-
grations to spawn in fresh water streams and rivers. The indigenous
peoples of Alaska who lived along the coastlines and rivers looked
forward to the annual salmon runs as a time of bounty. They em-

ployed a variety of fishing techniques, such as traps, nets, angling devices, and harpoons, and built up food surpluses from the summer season by preserving their catch through drying or smoking. In many regions, ownership rights over specific fishing stations or territories were vested in corporate kin groups.[29] It was only toward the latter part of the nineteenth century, however, that Alaska's salmon resources became subject to commercial, profit-motive exploitation, and within a short time, the native property-right system was ignored in favor of an open-access regime that benefited immigrant Whites.

In 1878 the first cannery appeared in Alaska (village of Klawock), and within a few decades, an influx of non-native fishermen and cannery workers had developed a booming commercial industry based on canning.[30] During the early years of this commercial fishery, the principal catchment technique was scooping up salmon schools with beach seines at barricaded stream mouths, but by the mid-1890s, the mobile purse seine began to be used in southeastern Alaska. Around the turn of the century, both the stationary and the floating fish trap were in use, and between 1905 and 1920 the floating trap was responsible for about a third of the total southeastern salmon catch.[31] In the mid-1920s, the first regulatory intervention in salmon harvesting was imposed. The U.S. Bureau of Fisheries (now defunct) imposed a gear restriction on vessels working in the Alaska purse seine fisheries: vessels could not be greater than 58 feet in overall length.[32]

From around 1920 to 1941, salmon production reached its peak levels in the southeast region of Alaska. In the ten years 1915–1924, for example, the southeast region produced an annual average of 40,720,000 fish, and production continued at nearly that level through 1941.[33] During the years 1915–1944, between 61.8% and 84.2% of southeastern Alaska's salmon was caught by traps.[34] These devices, generally owned by the canning companies, were located at stream mouths. Traps cost relatively little to build and maintain, at least in comparison to today's vessel costs, and involved no labor costs other than a trap-watcher and the occasional visit by crews to bring the entrapped fish back to the cannery. Without doubt, traps were (and still are) the best salmon harvesting technology to be devised, at least from the viewpoint of economic efficiency. And, although it was not much of a concern before the 1950s, traps make resource conservation relatively simple, because the number of salmon allowed to escape upstream for spawning is easily controlled.

During the first half of the twentieth century, then, the pattern of salmon exploitation was quite similar to what was happening in other industrial sectors across America. There was a steady displacement of labor-intensive (wealth distributing) techniques by capital-intensive (wealth consolidating) techniques. Economic efficiency, pure and simple, seems to have been the driving consideration. Canning companies—whose owners might live in Seattle, San Francisco, Boston, or New York—got most of the salmon pack from their own traps, and relatively little of the resource's value was paid to primary harvesters. Thus, as over-exploitation of the resource led to declines in the salmon catch during the 1940s and 1950s, the fish trap became symbolic of the rampant absentee capitalism that had drained away Alaska's wealth in natural resources with little or no return to residents.[35] The antagonism between small-scale, independent vessel owners and company-owned, passive-gear traps often led to "fish pirating"—vessels coming alongside traps at night and stealing the fish. More than once, these clandestine encounters involved physical violence between boat-fishermen and the company trap-watchers.

Given this political climate, as Alaska prepared for statehood, the Secretary of the Interior declared fish traps illegal in 1959. This decision was an endorsement of social equity over economic efficiency with respect to how Alaska's salmon wealth should be harnessed to achieve the greatest social benefit. In declaring traps illegal, the government deliberately reallocated the entire salmon catch to small-vessel harvesters, that is, to the purse seine, gillnet, and trolling fleets. The hope was that by restricting the catch to small-vessel harvesters, Alaska's fishery resources would attract and support a growing resident population and, in this way, a more secure economic foundation for the new state would develop.[36]

Subsequent regulation of the salmon fisheries has maintained this general policy. For example, as purse seining became more efficient, additional gear restrictions were imposed. Seines cannot exceed 250 fathoms in length, and drum-seining is not allowed. Similarly, in the rich Bristol Bay drift gillnet fishery, vessels cannot exceed thirty-two feet in overall length, and until 1952, they could not be powered by engines.[37] The basic logic of these restrictions is to prevent both overexploitation of the resource and overcapitalization of the vessels by controlling the catching power of individual vessels. Such a regulatory regime gives rise to large fleets of small boats, which is a way to distribute wealth generated from the natural resource as widely as possible. Conservation objectives are achieved through temporal closures in specified areas until "escapement" targets (specified numbers of fish allowed upstream to spawn) have been met.

Unfortunately, even though traps were no longer in use, salmon production continued to decline through the 1960s. The catching power of each vessel was being restricted, but the catching power of the fleet was not, because additional vessels could enter the fisheries freely. In the southeast region, during the interval 1965–1974, the average annual catch dropped to a record low of 15,166,000 fish. Also, the fleet's catching power had increased to the point that the 1975 southeastern purse seine season consisted of only eighteen days of legal fishing.

Responding to declines in the resource and to the fleet's overcapitalization, state officials instituted a limited entry license system in 1973. By 1979, there was a total of 9,861 commercial permits distributed to individuals throughout the state.[38] Permits belonged to individual vessel owners (or, in the case of set gillnets or fish wheels, to gear owners) who could demonstrate specified levels of historical participation in the fishery.

The last major ingredient in Alaska's overall management regime for salmon occurred in the mid-1970s. The state enacted legislation allowing private non-profit salmon hatcheries to commence operation. Fry from these hatcheries are released into the wild; hence, this is technically an enhancement program rather than full-blown aquaculture or fish-farming. The hatchery program differs philosophically from regulation in that the objective is to increase the abundance of salmon directly, rather than to trust in natural population increases as a result of restricting exploitation.

Today the management regime for the Alaskan salmon fisheries includes the following ingredients: (a) escapement targets for specific streams and regions enforced by temporal closures; (b) a variety of gear restrictions; (c) limited entry licenses; and (d) a growing hatchery program. The combination of these measures has curtailed the decades-long decline, and Alaskan salmon production is slowly recovering, although it is unlikely to achieve a sustainable yield at the 1920–1941 levels. From 1975–1984, for example, the average annual catch in the southeast region was 21,538,000 fish.

Improvements in the technology for fish-processing have also had a felicitous effect on the salmon industry. For the industry's first fifty to sixty years, the vast majority of Alaskan salmon ended up in cans. With the development of fish-freezing technology, which began in the early 1900s, the high volume of salmon caught between August and July could be preserved for subsequent canning. In the last few decades, however, frozen Alaskan salmon has increasingly been diverted to the fresh (frozen) market, particularly as an export product to Japan.

In summary, the Alaskan salmon fishery has run full cycle. One of the world's most abundant fish resources went from subsistence fishing to unrestrained capitalistic exploitation (salmon traps) resulting in resource decline, to regulated inefficiency (gear and temporal restrictions) as a means of achieving greater social equity, to modest privatization (limited entry), to aquacultural enhancement. What appeared to be Alaska's "fading future" in 1960[39] is now on the rebound. But just as the industry appears to have weathered the storm successfully a new cloud has appeared on the horizon. Foreign developments in salmon-farming technology are eroding the United States's market share and calling into question the "competitiveness" of Alaska's rejuvenated salmon industry. Whereas fellow citizens may tolerate the higher prices that result from management policies favoring social equity over economic efficiency, consumers in the international marketplace seem less inclined to subsidize American fishermen.

The World Market in Salmon

In the decade of the 1980s, the landed weight of the U.S. Pacific salmon catch has been relatively stable, fluctuating from a low of 562 million pounds in 1987 to a high of 786 million pounds in 1989. During that same interval, the percentage of the catch exported has grown from about a third to a half (see Figure 4).

The pattern of U.S. salmon exports by product type has also changed substantially during the 1980s. There are three main types of edible salmon products distinguished in U.S. government statistics: canned, whole or eviscerated, and fillets or steaks. The percentage of exported canned versus fresh salmon (including both frozen whole/eviscerated and frozen fillets/steaks) reflects the changes in consumer taste noted previously, that is, preference for fresh rather than canned products. In 1980, canned salmon comprised 37% of the U.S. export by weight, whereas by 1989, it had declined to only 11% (see Figure 5).

The world market in fresh (frozen or chilled) salmon is dominated by a handful of countries. Japan, France, and ironically, the United States are the major importing nations. The United States, Norway, and Canada are the major exporting nations. The import-export patterns of trade for the year 1987 are shown in Figures 6 and 7.

The three majors suppliers of fresh salmon—United States, Nor-

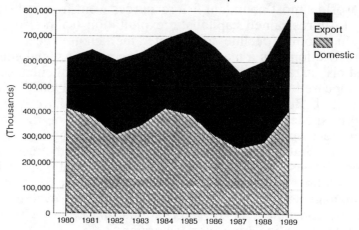

U.S. Pacific Salmon Catch
(Pounds for Domestic vs. Export Market)

Source: Fisheries of the United States, 1980–1989. Department of Commerce, NOAA, NMFS.

Figure 4

way, and Canada—differ substantially in their production technologies and the particular markets they supply. Both the United States and Canada rely on intricately managed, wild-harvested salmon, whereas the Norwegians have developed a technology for salmon-farming.[40] Further, virtually all of Norway's exported salmon is for the high-quality chilled salmon market, whereas Canada exports mainly frozen salmon, and all of the United States' "fresh" salmon exports are actually frozen. Figure 8 shows the total export values of the world fresh salmon market from 1980 to 1987, as well as the those for each of the three major exporting countries. Figure 9 shows the market shares of the United States, Norway, and Canada expressed as percentages of total salmon export values.

The clear point from Figures 8 and 9 is that Norway's new salmon-farming technology has been successful in increasing Norway's market share, with this at the expense of the United States and Canada. The United States retains the huge Japanese market in frozen salmon, but Norwegian chilled salmon (higher-quality, more expensive than frozen) now dominates the European market. Indeed, the United States itself imports a substantial amount of chilled salmon from Norway. Thus there is, in fact, a "competitive-

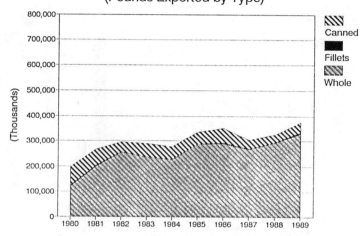

Source: Fisheries of the United States, 1980–1989. Department of Commerce, NOAA, NMFS.

Figure 5

ness" problem developing for the U.S. salmon industry vis-a-vis Norway. Further, the problem will only intensify as Norwegian production increases and as other countries, such as Iceland, Chile, and New Zealand, adopt the new salmon-farming technologies.

Possible Responses to the Competitiveness Problem in Fisheries

There are several ways that the U.S. salmon industry might respond to its growing competitiveness problem:

1. develop processing and transportation capabilities to compete in the chilled salmon market;
2. develop salmon-farming programs comparable to Norway's;
3. launch a marketing/advertising campaign stressing the product superiority of "natural" salmon vis-a-vis farmed salmon;
4. launch a marketing/advertising campaign stressing patriotic consumerism ("Buy American");
5. protect the domestic market by raising the price of foreign salmon via tariffs or other import restrictions;
6. achieve greater competitiveness in the world market by reducing the price of U.S. salmon products.

Imports of "Fresh" Salmon: 1987

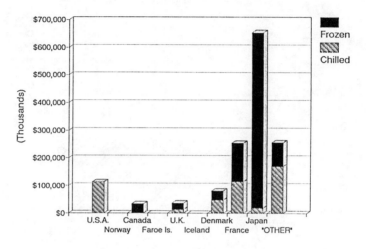

Source: F.A.O. Yearbook of Fishery Statistics, v. 67, 1988.

Figure 6

The first and second responses involve capital-intensive restructuring of the U.S. salmon industry to compete in the world market using the newest technologies of production and food-processing. Basically, these would be attempts to catch up with the Norwegians. Efforts in this direction would almost certainly be additional to, rather than substitutive for, wild salmon harvesting and, in the political-legal context of the United States, developments of this sort would most likely be left to private firms.

The third and fourth strategies would attempt to manipulate consumer attitudes without really modifying the structure of the U.S. industry. Such efforts may or may not be successful. Encouraging patriotic consumerism, however, even if successful, would work only to protect the U.S. domestic market; it would not help the United States in the larger world market.

The fifth response represents a common political solution to economic problems. Unfortunately, tariffs, like efforts to engender patriotic consumerism, work only to protect the domestic market and do virtually nothing to improve the position of U.S. products in the world market.

Exports of "Fresh" Salmon: 1987

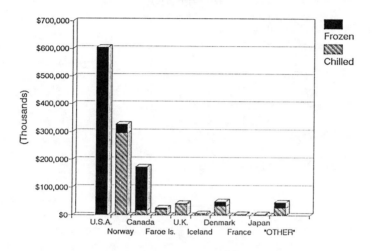

Source: F.A.O. Yearbook of Fishery Statistics, v. 67, 1988.

Figure 7

The sixth strategy, reducing the price of U.S. salmon products, is the most direct way to regain competitive advantage in both the domestic and world markets. Further, it is the cheapest solution, because it does not require large-scale capital investments in a new salmon-farming technology. Price, however, can be reduced in four very different ways, and it is the differences among these that highlight the fundamentally political nature of "competitiveness" problems:

(a) In the short run, prices could be lowered by increasing the size of the catch. Because of the ecological limits discussed previously, however, the industry would pay for these short-term gains with years, and perhaps decades, of poor fishing; hence, this is not a serious alternative.

(b) Fish-processing firms could reduce their prices by paying harvesters less for wild-caught salmon. This would make primary producers bear the burden of international price competition, but it would not modify the basic social policy implicit in the current management regime (income redistribution via small-vessel harvesters).

World "Fresh" Salmon Exports
(Export Value)

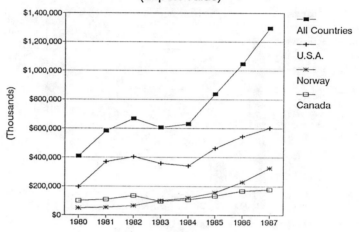

Source: F.A.O. Yearbook of Fishery Statistics, v. 65, 1987.

Figure 8

(c) Fish-processing firms could reduce their prices by reducing their profit margins. In this scenario processors, instead of producers, would bear the burden of international price competition. This is an unlikely turn of events in a capitalist political economy, but it could be accomplished relatively easily if processing firms were state-owned, non-profit, or fisherman-cooperative enterprises.

(d) Prices could be reduced by altering the current management regime to realize greater economic efficiency in wild-salmon harvesting. This would reduce the operating costs of firms, and the means of achieving this sort of efficiency is well known, that is, repeal the ban on salmon traps. However, the reasons traps were banned in 1959 remain true today: traps consolidate salmon revenues into very few hands, whereas other catching technologies result in a more equitable distribution of income, which is deemed essential if Alaska is to gain the economic vitality and long-term stability appropriate to a state of the union rather than an internal colony.

In summary, competitiveness problems in the international market conflict with issues of social equity at home. This is the lesson from fishing, and it seems to be true of many other industries as

World "Fresh" Salmon Exports
(Market Share in terms of Value)

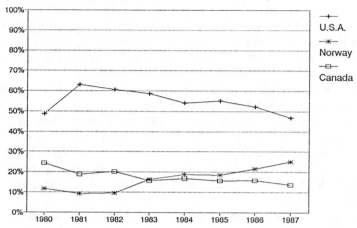

Source: F.A.O. Yearbook of Fishery Statistics, v. 65, 1987.

Figure 9

well. Whether and how we choose to modify our modes and relations of production to become more competitive will always be a highly political issue because different decisions benefit different groups of people; but, to the extent that it is the business of governments to be concerned about the welfare of their citizens, rich and poor, it is clear there will always be a need to accept the political challenge and formulate explicit fisheries policies. The notion that fisheries should be deregulated and left to laissez-faire market forces (such as Presidents Reagan and Bush have championed for most American industries) would most certainly lead to ruination. On the other hand, each policy option has its pitfalls. Policies maintaining fisheries as open-access public resources may spread the wealth to more people, but they lead to inefficient (less competitive) configurations of capital and labor. The various privatization solutions may improve the cost efficiency of our fisheries (and thereby restore their competitiveness), but they would do so by displacing large numbers of already marginal laborers to the benefit of a few individuals who are already relatively well-to-do. This is the social dilemma that competitiveness issues raise. Let me now extrapolate from the particulars of fishing to America's industrial competitiveness problems more generally.

AMERICAN COMPETITIVENESS: SPECULATIONS ON ALTERNATIVE FUTURES

There are three conditions that seem to underlie and give rise to economic competitiveness: abundant and/or cheap natural resources, abundant and/or cheap labor, and a technological advantage in the mode of production.

Throughout most of its brief history, the United States has been fortunate to have all three conditions working to its advantage. The early European settlers came into a continent whose natural resources were not only diverse, but virtually untapped. Cheap labor arrived with each boatload of immigrants, indentured servants, and slaves. And the latest industrial technologies were put into place de novo, without having to calculate the cost-efficiency of replacing older and superseded modes of production.

In this most felicitous environment, capital and labor alike prospered without need of a far-flung colonial empire. Especially with the passing of income redistributive laws (anti-trust, income tax, social security) in the early decades of the 20th century, the average American's standard of living soared to new heights. In the wake of such prosperity, and especially in the political aftermath of World War II, ideologies new to the American people began to guide national policy and everyday life. On the one hand, long-standing isolationist tendencies gave way to a view of America as "leader of the free world" and "world policeman." The military-industrial complex burgeoned in an arms race with the Soviet Union, diverting much of America's economic resources into military capabilities. On the other hand, fueled by Madison Avenue marketing, conspicuous consumption and built-in obsolescence became the order of the day. Conservation, thrift, and delayed gratification gave way to wastefulness, buying on credit, and indulgence. Compounding matters, we carelessly imagine that economic growth can continue without bumping up against ecological limits.

The puzzling aspect of contemporary American values and ideology is that we cling to our belief in the benefits of free trade, but also believe we are somehow entitled to a higher standard of living than the rest of the world. Thus, the growing realization that other countries now make many consumer products superior in quality as well as cheaper in price than we do represents a fundamental challenge to our sense of manifest destiny. We are addicted to consumerism—buying sustains our private sense of self-worth—but increasingly we consume other people's products instead of our own. Our cultivated optimism and complacency (or, as Herodotus would have called it, our "hubris") have resulted in massive trade deficits, factory closures, and lost jobs. Our national pride is offended.

Given the current state of affairs, it would appear there are basically two roads we may follow: (a) go for domestic equity, that is, protect our domestic industries from foreign competition, at least in the U.S. market; or (b) go for efficiency, that is, compete in a free trade global market. This choice presents a perennial and familiar tension in fisheries management, but it seems less well recognized in other industries. Each view has its proponents and detractors. What I would like to consider is the large-scale, long-term consequences of each response.

The most ethically compelling argument for protectionism is that free trade is not always fair trade. Nations differ in the extent to which fiscal cooperation is allowed between public and private sectors. So long as foreign industries are not on a comparable legal-fiscal footing with U.S. industries, tariffs or import quotas are "fair" ways to "level the playing field." Alternatively, politicans and business leaders can stir up protectionist consumer sentiment without imposing formal trade barriers. Indeed, this desired effect seems to underlie much of the current rhetoric about American competitiveness (see Morgan and Rosenwein, this volume). The problem with protectionism, of course, is that other countries usually reciprocate with their own trade barriers. Thus, the long-term consequence of protectionism is global economic stagnation.

If, on the other hand, we continue to operate in a free trade environment, there are three plausible scenarios for America's future. First, many American industries may simply lose ground to foreign competitors, such as has been happening with salmon, shoes, and steel. Second, American industries may become more competitive (improve the quality of products and make them cheaper) by lowering labor costs, whether through reducing wages paid to American citizens or by moving production facilities abroad, such as has happened with the San Diego-based tuna processing, General Motors factories, and "Made in America" television sets. Third, American industries may become more competitive by developing new and more efficient modes of production, as the Norwegians have done with their new methods of salmon-farming. This last scenario is the hope of those who believe in technological fixes to social system problems, but it is a short-term solution because other countries invariably catch up and competitiveness problems reappear (see Smith, this volume). Thus, although they may initially appear to differ, the three scenarios lead to the same global system outcome: eventually, free trade will diminish the differences among national standards of living, countries will become specialized in the kinds of products they export, and return to capital will become increasingly multi-national. The differences among the three scenarios is a matter of how long Americans (and other First World countries) can sustain inflated lifestyles vis-a-vis Third World countries.

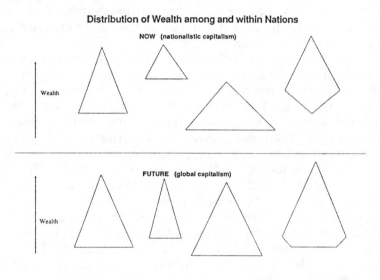

Figure 10

Currently, although there are vast differentials of wealth in America, the variance in wealth *among* nations is still greater than the variance *within* nations. The long-term effect of free trade in a capitalist global market, however, will be reduction in the difference among nations and an increase in the wealth differentials within them. (see Figure 10). When that happens, the stage will be properly set for a true, world-wide class struggle.

Thus, looking ahead to the twenty-first century, or perhaps the twenty-second, when capitalism seems likely to complete its transformation to global scale, the rhetoric of competitiveness will be seen as anachronistic, for it makes sense only on the presumption that there must be a correspondence between sovereign nations and economic systems. In this future light, all the late twentieth-century hoopla about "competitiveness" will be seen as only the last gasp of nationalistic capitalism, when owners tried one more time to subdue and exploit workers by fanning patriotic fervor.

NOTES

1. G. Hardin, "The Tragedy of the Commons," *Science* 162 (1968): 1243–1248.
2. P. M. Allen and J. M. McGlade, "Dynamics of Discovery and Exploitation: The Case of the Scotian Shelf Groundfish Fisheries," *Canadian Journal of Fisheries and Aquatic Sciences* 43 (1986): 1187–1200.
3. Ibid., 1189.
4. M. B. Schaefer, "Fisheries Dynamics and the Concept of Maximum Equilibrium Catch," in *Proceedings of the Gulf and Caribbean Fisheries Institute, Sixth Annual Session, Miami, Florida, November 1953*, ed. C. P. Idyll (Coral Gables, FL: University of Miami Marine Laboratory, 1954), 53–64; M. B. Schaefer, "Some Aspects of the Dynamics of Populations Important to the Management of the Commercial Marine Fisheries," *Inter-American Tropical Tuna Commission Bulletin* 1 (1954): 25–56.
5. P. A. Larkin, "An Epitaph for the Concept of Maximum Sustainable Yield," *Transactions of the American Fisheries Society* 106 (1977): 1–11.
6. H. S. Gordon, "The Economic Theory of a Common-Property Resource: The Fishery," *Journal of Political Economy* 62 (1954): 124–142.
7. Ibid., 129.
8. L. G. Anderson, "Necessary Components of Economic Surplus in Fisheries Economics," *Canadian Journal of Fisheries and Aquatic Sciences* 37 (1980): 858–70; C. L. Smith, "Satisfaction Bonus from Salmon Fishing: Implications for Management," *Land Economics* 57 (1981): 181–96.
9. R. B. Pollnac and J. J. Poggie, Jr., "The Structure of Job Satisfaction among New England Fishermen and Its Application to Fisheries Management," *American Anthropologist* 90 (1988): 888–901; J. B. Gatewood and B. J. McCay, "Comparison of Job Satisfaction in Six New Jersey Fisheries: Implications for Management," *Human Organization* 49 (1990): 14–25.
10. K. Ruddle and T. Akimichi, eds., *Maritime Institutions in the Western Pacific*, Senri Ethnological Studies No. 17 (Osaka: National Museum of Ethnology, 1984); B. J. McCay and J. M. Acheson, eds., *The Question of the Commons: The Culture and Ecology of Communal Resources* (Tucson: University of Arizona Press, 1987); F. Berkes, ed., *Common Property Resources: Ecology and Community-Based Sustainable Development* (London: Belhaven, 1989); J. Cordell, ed., *A Sea of Small Boats* (Cambridge, MA: Cultural Survival, Inc., 1989).
11. D. Feeny et al., "The Tragedy of the Commons: Twenty-Two Years Later," *Human Ecology* 18 (1990): 1–19.
12. E. Pinkerton, ed., *Co-Operative Management of Local Fisheries: New Directions for Improved Management and Community Development* (Vancouver: University of British Columbia Press, 1989).
13. O. Brox, "The Common Property Theory: Epistemological Status and Analytical Utility," *Human Organization* 49 (1990): 227–35.
14. For two rather thorough summaries, see R. B. Pollnac and S. J. Littlefield, "Sociocultural Aspects of Fisheries Management," *Ocean Development and Inter-*

national Law Journal 12 (1983): 209–46; P. H. Fricke, "Use of Sociocultural Data in the Allocation of Common Property Resources," *Marine Policy* 9 (1985): 39–52.

15. A Scott, "Development of Economic Theory on Fisheries Regulation," *Journal of the Fisheries Research Board of Canada* 36 (1979): 725–41.

16. J. A. Crutchfield and G. Pontecorvo, *The Pacific Salmon Fisheries: A Study in Irrational Conservation* (Baltimore: Johns Hopkins University Press, 1969); J. A. Gulland, *The Management of Marine Fisheries* (Seattle: University of Washington Press, 1974), 135–45.

17. Scott, "Development of Economic Theory," 732.

18. J. A. Crutchfield, "Economic and Social Implications of the Main Policy Alternatives for Controlling Fishing Effort," *Journal of the Fisheries Research Board of Canada* 36 (1979): 742–52, quotation from p. 744.

19. Ibid., 745.

20. S. J. Langdon, *Transfer Patterns in Alaskan Limited Entry Fisheries,* Final Report for Limited Entry Study Group of the Alaska State Legislature (Juneau: Alaska, 1980); K. Schelle and B. Muse, "Efficiency and Distributional Aspects of Alaska's Limited Entry Program," in *Fishery Access Control Programs Worldwide: Proceedings of the Workshop on Management Options for the North Pacific Longline Fisheries,* ed. N. Mollett (Juneau: Alaska Sea Grant Report 86–4, 1986), 317–52.

21. Crutchfield, "Economic and Social Implications;" Scott, "Development of Economic Theory;" J. E. Wilen, "Fisherman Behavior and the Design of Efficient Fisheries Regulation Programs," *Journal of the Fisheries Research Board of Canada* 36 (1979): 855–58.

22. J. B. Gatewood and B. J. McCay, "The Role of Job Satisfaction Data in Selecting among Alternative Regulatory Policies," in *Marine Resource Utilization: A Conference on Social Science Issues,* ed. J. S. Thomas, L. Maril, and E. P. Durrenberger (Mobile: University of South Alabama Publication Services, 1989), 51–62; Gatewood and McCay, "Comparison of Job Satisfaction."

23. A. Scott, "The Fishery: The Objectives of Sole Ownership," *Journal of Political Economy* 63 (1955): 116–24, quotation from p. 116.

24. Ibid., 121–23.

25. For an extended critique arriving at the same conclusion, see J. R. McGoodwin, *Crisis in the World's Fisheries: People, Problems, and Policies* (Stanford, CA: Stanford University Press, 1990).

26. For a recent assessment of restricted entry systems, generally, see R. E. Townsend, "Entry Restrictions in the Fishery: A Survey of the Evidence," *Land Economics* 66 (1990): 359–78.

27. National Marine Fisheries Service, *Fisheries of the United States,* Annual reports covering the years 1980–1989, respectively, prepared by the Department of Commerce, NOAA, NMFS (Washington, D.C.: Government Printing Office, 1981–1990), quotation from 1990 report, 72–73.

28. Ibid., xv, quotation from 1990 report.

29. P. Drucker, *Indians of the Northwest Coast* (Garden City, NY: The Natural History Press, 1963).

30. S. J. Langdon, *The Native People of Alaska* (Anchorage: Greatland Graphics, 1987), 74.

31. S. J. Langdon, "Technology, Ecology, and Economy: Fishing Systems in Southeast Alaska" (Ph.D. diss., Stanford University, 1977), 215–46.

32. R. J. Browning, *Fisheries of the North Pacific: History, Species, Gear, and Processes* (Anchorage: Alaska Northwest Publishing, 1974), 106.

33. G. W. Rogers, *Alaska in Transition: The Southeast Region* (Baltimore: Johns Hopkins University Press, 1960), 96.

34. Ibid., 103.

35. Ibid., 12.

36. Rogers, *Alaska in Transition;* Langdon, *Technology;* Langdon, *Transfer Patterns;* and for the broader cultural significance of "resident" in Alaska, see J. B. Gatewood, "Competition for Cultural Images: Fisherman versus Logger in Southeast Alaska," *Maritime Anthropological Studies* 2 (1989): 87–104.

37. J. Rearden, ed., "Alaska's Salmon Fisheries," *Alaska Geographic Quarterly* 10, no. 3 (Anchorage: Alaska Geographical Society, 1983).

38. Langdon, *Transfer Patterns.*

39. Rogers, *Alaska in Transition.*

40. E. Dale, J. Owens, and A. Stenseth, "Tilling the Sea: Prospects for Norwegian Aquaculture," *Marine Policy* 11 (1987): 229–39; T. Bjørndal, "The Norwegian Aquaculture Industry," *Marine Policy* 12 (1988): 122–42.

Regulation, Competitiveness, and the Role of Public Participation

CAROLE GORNEY

Early in 1990 the U.S. Senate held a series of hearings on the international competitiveness challenge facing American industry. Testimony identified a complex variety of factors contributing to a decline in U.S. competitiveness, including a financial environment unsupportive of long-term capital investment and research and development,[1] as well as government policies that further exacerbate the problem by increasing financial and legal uncertainty.[2]

Ironically, even as Congress was seeking solutions to the competitiveness challenge, it also was considering the most stringent and costly environmental legislation in history. The 1990 amendments to the Clean Air Act were approved with an estimated nationwide price tag of $22 billion a year,[3] but some estimates are even higher. Analysts predict that these costs could have a crippling economic effect on businesses and industries already facing a precarious competitive environment.

Why the inconsistency in government policy? How do we fare in relation to other, less regulated countries? Are there more efficient, less costly regulatory options that could help us out of the regulatory-competitiveness dilemma? What role could public participation play in fostering those options? Are there specific public participation models that work better than others?

In attempting to answer these questions, I will first discuss the origin and evolution of government regulation, specifically environmental, health, and safety legislation. I focus on these areas for manageability and because historically they have been the object of much of the public activism that has contributed to the current regulatory climate.

Second, I will make correlations between regulation and competitiveness, noting differences in the nature, application, and competitive impact of legislated regulation. I will include a discussion of approaches to regulation in other competitor nations, particularly those with more flexible regulatory systems than the United States.

Next, I will provide an overview of and a rationale for public participation, indicating the use and effectiveness of various forms of public involvement in the regulatory process. Finally, I will offer a model for public participation that promises to work best in the current competitive environment.

REGULATION IN PERSPECTIVE

Current federal regulation has evolved from nearly a century of legislative activity aimed at protecting the economic, health, safety, and environmental well-being of the country. Much of this activity occurred in three distinct periods of social and economic change.[4]

The first two decades of the twentieth century were marked by passage of the Pure Food and Drugs Act, the first minimum wage law, and the Federal Trade Commission Act. These and hundreds of other reforms were a reaction to uncertainties created by expansions in immigration, industrialization, and urbanization.

The next major wave of regulatory controls was generated in the New Deal period of 1933–38. During those years, encompassing much of the Great Depression, many of today's regulatory agencies were created, including the Securities and Exchange Commission, the Federal Communications Commission, the Interstate Commerce Commission, the Federal Aviation Administration, and the National Labor Relations Board.

The 1960s ushered in a third era of regulatory activity, connected with anti-establishment protests and civil rights activism. Lasting nearly twenty years, until the Reagan Administration's flurry of deregulation, this regulatory period gave us the Occupational Safety and Health Administration and the Consumer Product Safety Commission. The following is a list of the most significant health, safety and environmental legislation passed since the 1960s:

1962 Food, Drug, and Cosmetic Act Amendments
1962 Air Pollution Control Act
1965 Cigarette Labeling and Advertising Act
1966 Fair Packaging and Labeling Act
1966 Traffic Safety Act (Includes safety standards for motor vehicles)
1966 Coal Mine Safety Amendments

1967 Flammable Fabrics Act
1969 National Environmental Policy Act
1970 Poison Prevention Packaging Act
1970 Clean Air Act Amendments
1970 Occupational Safety and Health Act
1972 Consumer Product Safety Act
1972 Federal Water Pollution Control Act
1972 Noise Pollution and Control Act
1973 Safe Drinking Water Act
1974 Hazardous Materials Transportation Act
1976 Toxic Substances Control Act
1977 Surface Mining Control and Reclamation Act
1977 Saccharin Study and Labeling Act
1980 Comprehensive Environmental Response, Compensation
       and Liability Act (Superfund)
1986 Superfund Amendments and Reauthorizaation Act
       (SARA)
1986 Emergency Planning and Community Right-to-Know
       Act (SARA Title III)
1986 Safe Drinking Water Act
1987 Clean Water Act
1990 Clean Air Act Amendments

The most intensive period of federal regulation came in the decade between 1970 and 1980, a period marked by an emphasis on so-called social legislation. Up until that time, industries impacted by traditional economic regulation accounted for only about one-tenth of the gross national product.[5] This low rate of impact was due in great part to the fact that most government jurisdictions were limited to very specific industry categories. By contrast, the newer regulatory agencies were given jurisdiction over broad issues that cut across a wide range of industries, both large and small. The current Clean Air legislation is one very good example.

The proliferation in federal regulation during the 1970–80 period can be viewed in several ways: in terms of the number of agencies, total increase in expenditures, or increases in staff. During this period, some twenty new regulatory agencies were created, representing nearly a fifty percent increase over the previous decade. Federal expenditures for social regulation, which includes consumer safety and health, job safety and working conditions, and environment and energy, totaled $4.9 billion, an increase of 944% during the 10-year period. Full-time staff positions exploded from

9,700 to more than 66,000, a 584% jump.[6] This is significant information to consider later in my discussion of costs of regulation.

The first five years of Reagan-era deregulation were marked by a very slight drop in the number of federal regulatory agencies, a 6% decline in staff, and only a 10% increase in expenditures.[7] However, the 1986 Superfund and 1990 Clean Air Act amendments have reversed any downward trend while greatly expanding federal control over the private sector.

The history of regulation has been one of both evolution and accumulation, with many concepts, rationales, and methods being carried over from earlier social and economic contexts. As a result, what prevails today are traditional standard-setting approaches that emphasize centralized control, bans on products, and rules and regulations that detail specific methods of, and equipment for achieving compliance. This emphasis on process, rather than on goals, accounts in part for the criticism, especially from economists, that existing approaches to regulation no longer are appropriate or efficient in today's social and economic environment. Critics argue that regulation has become inflexible and unnecessarily costly because it fails to make use of local knowledge and initiative in developing alternative approaches to meeting desired goals.[8]

I will return to local initiative as a resource in my discussion of public participation. Meanwhile, there are two other factors that have impacted on the nature and effectiveness of regulation: the emergence of single-issue politics, and the accompanying vulnerability of public policy to special interests. The emergence of these legacies of the 1960s and 1970s was a major factor in the accompanying focus on legislated social regulation. The source of this change is summarized in the following statement:

> The acceleration of inflation, the emerging energy crisis, and the continuing breakup of party discipline within Congress created a confusing situation that could be exploited for the benefit of almost any interest group, left or right, pro or anti, reform or reactionary. If a group could mobilize or appear to mobilize public opinion, and if it could construct a powerful, intelligible, and factually supported case for a particular program, then the odds for success might be good, irrespective of the ideology behind a particular lobbying campaign.[9]

This observation offers an illuminating explanation of why Congress could play Janus in the 1980s, deregulating some industries and increasing regulations on others simultaneously, and why today it appears to see no incongruity in giving with one hand and taking away with the other, promoting competitiveness with legislation while legislating anti-competitive environmental regulation.

Another interesting consequence of single-issue manipulation can be found in the acid rain policy developed as part of the 1970 and 1977 amendments to the clean Air Act. The legislation imposed some of the most costly technology, especially on new rather than older plants, while failing to solve some of the most critical acid rain problems. The reason was that environmentalists, aware that they alone could not get pollution-control legislation through Congress, allied themselves with legislators from states with vested interests in discouraging local industries from moving to new plants in the "sunbelt." The environmentalists also got support from legislators from states supplying high-sulphur coal. This resulted in the most costly technology being required on all plants, regardless of the type of coal burned, so as not to put sales of high-sulphur coal in jeopardy.[10]

Murray Weidenbaum summarizes the drawbacks of the U.S. style of special-interest-dominated social regulation:

> ". . . although important benefits may be gained by the newer form of social regulation, limited attention is given by the regulators to the basic mission of the industries they regulate: to provide goods and services to the public. Also ignored or downplayed are crosscutting concerns and matters broader than those dealt with in the specific charter of the regulating agency, such as productivity, economic growth, employment, cost to the consumer, effects on overall living standards, and inflationary impacts.[11]

He adds that not only are regulators and special interests oblivious to economic factors, but they also view any consideration of them in discussions of health, safety, or environmental concerns to be callous, or worse. "In this respect, therefore, the new wave of government regulation is a markedly different phenomenon."[12]

REGULATORY COSTS AND COMPETITIVENESS

The relationship of regulatory costs and international competitiveness may be discussed from a number of different perspectives: the direct operating and capital costs of compliance, the impact on production and pricing, the impact on capital improvements and research and development, the comparative-advantage factor in relation to less regulated countries, and plant siting decisions.

Direct compliance costs have risen dramatically as government regulations since the early seventies have become more pervasive, detailed, and complex. This has been especially true in the areas of consumer protection, health, safety, and environment. The immediate compliance costs to business and industry for anti-pollution controls under the new amendments to the Clean Air Act are estimated to be $22 billion a year or more.[13] Another source estimates that when provisions are fully implemented in ten to fifteen years, the bill could go as high as $120 billion annually.[14]

It is reasonable to accept a higher rather than a more conservative price tag after comparing pre-amendment costs. In 1987, for example, $31 billion was spent on air pollution control alone in the United States. The figure is for both operating and capital costs. It compares with $81 billion spent the same year for pollution abatement of all types.[15] A year later, combined operating and capital costs for air pollution rose to more than $42 billion; expenditures for all pollution jumped to nearly $93 billion.[16]

Imposed technological solutions, called technology forcing, are one contributor to the high price tag. While regulators do not often require specific technologies for solving pollution problems, the regulators often impose specific standards that are only achievable with the most expensive technological systems. Consider, for example, the varying costs of reducing sulfur dioxide emissions from coal-burning electricity-generating plants. Depending on the method, the costs can range from $250 per ton, by converting to low-sulfur coal, to $1,000 a ton, if scrubbers are used. If standards are set that can only be achieved by using scrubbers, the costs are quadrupled[17] over those of conversion.

Related to this point, and another reason why regulatory critics accuse the U.S. system of being cost inefficient, is the policy of requiring uniform emissions reductions from all sources. Continuing with our previous example, suppose that three plants in an area each emit sulfur dioxide, but that it costs each $100, $600, and $1,000 per ton, respectively, to reduce emissions. Let us further suppose that the goal of applicable regulations is to reduce emissions by thirty tons. Cost-wise, it would make more sense to reach the thirty ton goal by requiring more reductions from sources that spend less to achieve those reductions.[18] When we look later at comparisons with other countries, many of whose industries are major marketplace competitors of U. S. industries, we will see that they have developed much more flexible systems that allow for adaptation to specific industry costs and needs on a localized basis.

Another cost of regulation is management overhead. With the

expansion of regulation since 1970 has come confusing overlaps in agency jurisdiction and staggering amounts of written codes and paperwork. Frequently, a company must receive permits from myriad federal, state, and local regulators before beginning, or even continuing specified operations. A graphic example is Dow Chemical Company's facility in Pittsburg, California, which must file 563 separate permit applications each year to cover its direct emissions into the air. The company also must obtain 370 additional permits for the source that generates the materials that escape through the emissions point.[19]

In another example, Dow canceled plans to build a $300 million petrochemical complex in California because of regulatory red tape. After two years, and expenses of more than $4 million to secure environmental approval, the project had obtained only four of the required 65 permits from federal, state, local, and regional regulatory agencies.[20]

Similar costly delays are caused by lawsuits and the intervention of activist groups in regulatory proceedings. Economists Bardach and Pugliaresi dscribe the federally required environmental impact statements (EIS) as a process used for legal and political warfare in which environmentalist critics "exploit the opportunities for harassment and legal delay."[21] Such delays increase the direct cost of doing business, but it can also be argued that there are still greater indirect losses to the economy through unrealized expansion in production and accompanying loss of potential jobs.

How these direct and indirect costs affect the nation's competitiveness depends on the specific industry, its product and location, and the degree and nature of its competition. Industries in highly competitive markets are unable to add environmental control costs on to the price of the product. Instead, they may decrease output to reduce their average total cost (unit cost). Some industries may actually go out of business, thus reducing productivity. Still others, in less competitive markets, may choose to pass through the costs to the consumer. Whatever the case, "if domestic producers face higher pollution control costs than competitive foreign suppliers, they will eventually lose in international competitiveness."[22]

There is some disagreement among economists as to the actual impact that regulation has on business productivity. A study conducted at the Brookings Institution concluded that business productivity was 1.4% lower in 1975 than it would have been had it not been for pollution and job safety regulatory costs. Considering that the total annual gain in productivity is measured on an average of only two to three percent, this was considered to be a significant cost amounting to about $20 billion of the total $1.6 trillion GNP in 1975.[23]

A more recent report, from 1985, also argues that the United States is at a competitive disadvantage because of the depressing effect that regulation has on productivity.[24] A 1989 study by Conrad and Morrison comparing regulatory impacts on Germany, the U.S., and Canada, concluded that even after adjusting for a downward bias in the traditional way productivity measures have been computed, there was still some evidence that regulation-control investment did depress productivity, with the greatest impact affecting the U. S. and Canada.[25]

Nevertheless, other economists argue that composition, rather than level of GNP, is more likely to be affected by regulation.[26] By this is meant that while certain sectors of the economy might decline, there would be spending and price tradeoffs that would keep total GNP fairly constant. Regulatory costs also are believed to be linked to a reduction in available resources needed to modernize facilities and support research and development. At the 1990 competitiveness hearings in Washington, the Office of Technology Assessment reported that investment in machinery and equipment in the United States during the past fifteen years has remained static at about 7 to 8% of GNP, while Japan's comparable investments have continued to rise to a present high in excess of 20% of GNP.[27] Furthermore, nondefense expenditures for research and development have been stagnant at about 1.8% of U.S. GNP, while West Germany and Japan not only have outstripped us for the past twenty years, but also have continued to widen the gap significantly each year.[28]

The president of the Council on Competitiveness summarized the situation for hearing members: "Last year, with an economy that is about sixty percent of ours in terms of size, Japan actually invested (gross) more dollars than the United States. That puts the latest technology to work in Japan's factories and the best tools in the hands of the Japanese worker."[29]

COMPARISONS WITH COMPETITORS

The point was made earlier that if U. S. producers face more stringent regulations than their foreign counterparts, they will lose competitiveness. In fact, the United Kingdom, France, and Germany have very few legally enforceable codes in the areas of health, safety, and the environment. They rely instead on limits or guidelines that can be modified quickly and easily in reponse to current technical and economic constraints. For example, the British Nuclear Installations Inspectorate uses a system of consultative regulation and inspection, with elements of public participation.[30] The British Alkali and Clean Air Inspectorate works according to the following official description:

> The Chief Inspector, with the help of his deputies, lays down the broad national policies and provided they keep within their broad lines, inspectors in the field have plenty of flexibility to take into account local circumstances and make suitable decisions.[31]

Sweden is a highly industrialized country with a percentage of GNP in manufacturing comparable to that in the United States.[32] Furthermore, it supports a wide range of heavy and polluting industries from metals to chemicals. Mills and Graves conclude that, unlike the United States, the Swedish system is based on trust, responsibility, and consultation:

> Many decisions are made by formal and informal cooperation and consultation between government and private representatives of business and labor. It is the envy of those who favor a society based on consultation and cooperation instead of on competition and a careful distinction between the rights and responsibilities of the government and the private sector.[33]

The Swedish Environmental Protection Act provides for broadly defined criteria for attaining limits on pollution emissions, taking into consideration the likelihood of damage, available technology, costs of abatement, and the impact on the country's international competitiveness. Compare this with the U.S. approach described earlier that promulgates narrowly defined standards within an attitudinal climate that condemns as callous the consideration of costs in relation to health, safety, or environmental controls.

Japan, too, is a highly industrialized country facing some of the world's worst environmental problems. Its environmental regulations were developed later than this country's, in large part in response to strong pressure from grassroots citizens groups. The Japanese government has much less control over business activities than in Sweden or the United States, and its pollution control laws are simple and procedural. Japan's Environmental Agency is responsible for setting standards and determining their stringency. While Japanese standards have proven to be more stringent than in this country, they "appear to result from prolonged negotiation between agency officials and managers from private industries."[34] As in Sweden, Japanese standards are set for particular plants with consideration given to the plant's existing technology and economic viability, as well as to the costs of alternative pollution control methods.

South Korea has undergone substantial industrialization since the end of the Korean War, but it still has one foot in the Third World. Thus it faces environmental problems characteristic of both poor nations and industrialized ones. Until recently, observe Mills and Graves, the South Korean government and its people have considered industrialization a much higher priority than the environment. In particular, air pollution has received very little attention.[35] Although South Korea has a broad anti-pollution law, pollution-control costs are seen as a threat to the competitive advantage now held by that nation.

Many other countries, particularly in Asia, have little or no constraints on industry regarding the environment. If they do, infractions may be overlooked or the costs of abatement may be offset by government subsidies. These conditions lead to another potential consequence of overregulation, namely, the siting of more U.S.-owned facilities in foreign countries. Transnational companies already have the option of shifting their production locations, and they may be encouraged to do so more readily if U.S. regulatory costs and red tape become significantly skewed in relation to the rest of the world.

THE ROLE OF PUBLIC PARTICIPATION

Background

Studies of group process at the University of Iowa in the 1930s popularized the notion of interactive participation in decision making by affected publics. But the concept of public participation goes back even further. It is rooted in the principles of democracy, and one of its most common manifestations is voting. Even under American democracy, however, public participation in decision making has been far from perfect or even extensive. Jacobson notes: "Many of America's founders feared the political influence of persons uneducated and untrained in the ways of governance. Participation was therefore deliberately restricted in order to establish government by those thought best able to contribute."[36]

The elitist view is still in vogue today among those technicians, bureaucrats, and corporate decision makers who resist more than token public participation on the grounds that issues are too complex to be understood by the masses. In the same vein, elitists often dismiss public concerns about health and safety issues as irrational fears of the uninformed. The elitists seem to be swimming against the tide, however.

Citizen participation in policy making currently is mandated for most federal agencies and programs. Its influence on the national level emerged with the advent of Watergate and the decline in public confidence in government, together with the rise of consumerism and single-issue politics. Recently, state and local governments have moved to mandate direct citizen participation both in decision making and in policy implementation. Even business and industry on their own are implementing public participation initiatives in response to mounting community hostility over a variety of environmental and safety concerns.

Rationale

Health, safety, and environmental regulation is a predictable result of fear and distrust brought on by years of ignoring public concerns. Yet the resulting centralized, standard-legislated regulation, as it has developed in the United States, has proven itself to be costly and ineffective, placing American business and industry at a comparative competitive disadvantage with the rest of the world. This further exacerbates any decline in international competitiveness, such as that faced in the past ten years by the U.S. steel industry. The steel industry is competing with government subsidized foreign competitors, while at the same time being particularly vulnerable to clean air and clean water legislation. Its decline since the early 1980s is well documented.

Less publicly known is the competitive struggle of the U.S. chemical industry. While this industry is the third largest in the world and a mainstay of America's international competitiveness, there has been some worrisome erosion in its position. Michael T. Kelley, Deputy Assistant Secretary in the Department of Commerce, testified at a 1988 Senate hearing on the Competitiveness of the U.S. Chemical Industry, that in the period 1983–88, chemical imports grew an average of 11% while exports lagged at only 6% annual growth. He concluded that heavy environmental and safety regulation, particularly in the pharmaceutical, biotechnology, pesticides, and organic chemical producing industries, should be recognized as adversely affecting the American chemical industry's position in the world marketplace.[37]

Both the steel and chemical industries are subject to a double whammy when it comes to environmental legislation. Both are heavy users of electricity—electric power production being another industry reeling under environmental and safety regulatory costs. According to Douglas Biden, economist and secretary-treasurer of the Pennsylvania Electric Association, the United States used to have the second lowest electricity costs in the world. "It is now fifth or sixth," he said. "Canada has always had the lowest costs because it has a wealth of hydro (water) resources and it is run by the government and subsidized by it. France has passed us as it is 75% nuclear, and it is also subsidized. Sweden is 40 to 45% nuclear."[38]

Solutions to the inefficiency dilemma can be found in approaches used by countries like Great Britain, France, or Sweden, where regulations are confined to broad guidelines or statements of goals and where the greatest amount of local determination is encouraged. Given the current regulatory structure and the political climate in Washington, however, it is unlikely that great strides will be made by attacking from the top. I contend that the battle needs to begin at the other end of the process, at the local level.

First, a brief explanation of how local concerns wind up as national legislation. Issues management literature in public relations explains that when the actions, policies or behaviors of an organization have a consequence for some group, an issue emerges and a public arises.[39] "Awareness and concern on the part of a public brings about a resolve to 'do something.' Lines become drawn and conflict emerges."[40]

The evolution of the issue to the level of public policy takes place through the mediation and amplification stage, during which more publics arise and individuals and groups with similar concerns and reactions align themselves together. At this point, the mass media may play a role in increasing awareness. With media attention, the public issue has a strong possibility of becoming part of public policy through legislation or litigation.[41]

An organization has the greatest impact on the direction and development of an issue at the very early stage of mediation and amplification.[42]

"Once issues receive the attention of public officials and enter the policy process, either through proposed legislation or through regulation, efforts to resolve the conflict become protracted and potentially costly.

Resolution becomes a goal in and of itself, regardless of the 'merits' of the issue. Parties to the conflict seek legislation or regulation, the passage of which will have impact on all concerned."[43]

Thus, early identification and intervention in issues development is key to containment. This logically must be achieved at the local level, but doing so necessitates a high degree of public participation. As risk communication studies confirm, "Citizens in a democratic society will eventually interfere with decisions in which they do not feel represented."[44]

Other rationales for broad-based public participation are that non-experts often see problems, issues, and solutions that experts miss; also, people are the best judge of their own interests and, in a democracy, have the right to participate in decisions that affect them and their communities. "If we lack mechanisms for lay participation, then the current crisis of confidence afflicting risk institutions can only deepen. In addition, broader participation may contribute to better decision making, incorporate a broader range of values into decisions, and reduce the probability of error."[45]

In a study I made of consumer committees and citizen advisory panels developed by Pennsylvania Power and Light (PP&L) and South Central Bell Telephone (SCB), it was determined that public participation works best as an early intervention, preventative measure. This is accomplished in six specific ways by:

1) acting as an early-warning system to identify public concerns and needs,
2) serving as a sounding board for proposed organizational programs,
3) providing two-way communication among organizations and specific communities and special interest groups,
4) creating a credible channel through which organizations can disseminate accurate information on a timely basis,
5) securing understanding and support for organizational goals, and
6) encouraging appropriate modification of policies and procedures before major opposition develops.[46]

Criticisms arise that projects could be implemented much sooner without the time and effort spent on public participation. It is true that time must be spent up front on public participation, but the cost in time and money to counter opposition may turn out to be far greater, especially when the opposition translates into expanded regulation. PP&L operates on the rationale that no matter how good a proposal or solution may seem technologically or economically, or even legally, if it cannot be implemented because of public opposition it is no good.[47]

As an example underscoring the wisdom of this position, PP&L cites an ill-fated proposal to incinerate PCB-contaminated oils in one of its plants. The proposal had been approved by both the Department of Environmental Resources (DER) and the Environmental Protection Agency (EPA). The company held an open meeting to tell the affected community what it planned to do, but there was so much public concern expressed that PP&L abandoned the project. The company had invested money and time to modify its boiler for the incineration process, only to be prevented from using the boiler after a spate of protests and negative publicity. If public involvement had been sought earlier, the results might have been different, and the company might have achieved its goals; at worst, it would have saved time and money spent in pursuing an unachievable goal, not to mention the animosity and notoriety it earned.[48]

In a report on *Public Involvement in Corporate Technology Decision-Making: The Case of Pennsylvania Power and Light,* the authors wrote:

> A public advisory committee is worthwhile because it creates one more mechanism through which different interest groups can work together to solve problems which have a direct impact on all of us. This is perhaps the greatest value and the one most intangible to assess. No doubt there are other forms of public participation which other corporations and government agencies can use. Presumably no two companies or corporations would proceed in exactly the same manner, but the crucial point is the recognition that public participation is important, even necessary, to the vital well-being of our society. . . .[49]

Definition and Discussion

But what is this thing called public participation? First, a definition of "public." A public is a "loosely structured system whose members detect the same problem or issue, interact either face to face or through mediated channels, and behave as though they were one body."[50] In order for a public to form, there must be some consequence affecting the individuals in the group, and those individuals must recognize or detect that consequence.

The concept of public participation is harder to define because it encompasses so many forms, approaches, and expectations. Generically speaking, however, public participation has been called both a "mechanism and a process for the public to have meaningful input and dialogue with decision makers on issues of mutual concern."[51]

This definition is useful because it underscores the two-way communication aspects of public participation, that is, that the decision makers must listen to what citizens have to say and discuss the issues with them. It fails, however, to specify to what end the input and dialogue is conducted. The term "meaningful" also presents a problem. How do you define meaningful, and from whose perspective?

What is meant by meaningful public participation varies depending on the purpose and method used. From the perspective of regulation and competitiveness as it is discussed here, "meaningful" is defined as two-way symmetric communication[52] in which concerned parties with differing opinions come together under circumstances in which they can mutually pursue solutions to problems that take all relevant factors into consideration.[53] It is on the basis of definition that the major types of public participation will be evaluated later in this section.

Inherent in two-way symmetric communication is a "balance" between involved parties, with no one viewpoint or interest being favored. Using two-way symmetric communication does not imply changing opinions. Rather it takes those opinions into consideration and makes modifications to accommodate them within a framework of negotiation and compromise. What *is* implied is that not only are publics allowed to impact on decisions before they are made, but also they are actively involved in the decision process itself.

Researchers at the University of Michigan in the 1970s were the first to consider public participation in terms of two-way communication. They identified three types of participation: information/ educational (output), review/reaction (input), and interaction/dialogue (two-way).[54]

Buchholz identifies four approaches to issues management—reactive, accommodative, proactive and interactive—and concludes that the interactive method, which fits the two-way symmetric model, works the most effectively.[55]

Unfortunately, many of the forms or mechanisms of public participation do not allow for interactive, symmetric involvement. Fiorino has identified five mechanisms used for citizen participation in the area of environmental risk: public hearings, voter initiatives or referenda, public surveys or opinion polls, negotiated rule making, and citizens panels.[56] To this list I will add advisory committees.

Public hearings are by nature reactive and potentially adversarial. They also can have other flaws as identified in one study:

> . . . weak prehearing procedures, poor and overly technical presentation of information, a bias toward participation by parties having a clear economic stake in the decision, and minimal evidence that hearings affected agency decisions.[57]

Initiatives allow citizens to place issues on the ballot that can impact on public policy. This approach has its benefits, but in terms of broad public participation, it fails to provide for consensus or compromise.[58]

Public opinion polls can help assess the views of a broad base of affected citizens, especially when direct participation is limited, but the method is a poor substitute for active involvement. Furthermore, polls tend to reflect opinions held in isolation rather than those formed after consideration of specific social, economic and community realities.

Negotiated rule making provides for interested parties to negotiate as equals to reach consensus and promulgate rules within statutory authority. The process, however, relies entirely on interest group representation.

Citizens review panels are based on the jury model, and have applications in technical policy areas that might normally be closed to nonexperts. One model used in environmental issues consists of laypersons who hear testimony, question experts, draw conclusions and, if appropriate, prepare written recommendations and/or meet with decision makers.[59] The drawbacks of such citizen panels are that they reach only a small portion of the affected public, require substantial time and money, may raise unrealistic expectations as to impact and results, can cause frustration for participants, and involve potential risk for the regulatory agency.[60]

The last participation form to be considered is the advisory committee. Such committees are mandated under the Federal Advisory Committee Act (FACA) and are used extensively by such agencies as the Food and Drug Administration (FDA). By law the committees must be "fairly balanced in terms of points of view represented and the functions to be performed by the advisory committee.[61] But the law does not specifically mention representation by the public or consumers, and in practice few members of the public appear, let alone participate, in committee hearings.[62] This is due to cost, lack of notification except in the *Federal Register,* and citizens' perceptions of themselves as lacking the expertise to participate and, therefore, lacking potential effectiveness as well.[63]

It is clear from the preceding review of participation mechanisms that only negotiated rule making, citizens review panels, and advisory committees have potential for fulfilling the two-way symmetric criteria for meaningful public participation. Nonetheless, each of these also falls short of the mark.

Rule making provides for symmetric communication before decisions are made, but as it is now used at the national level, it encourages rather than alleviates the problem of special interest pressure. Review panels involve nonexperts before decision making, but the method is not truly symmetric as it does not utilize negotiation with decision makers in a balanced setting, nor does it necessarily guarantee that input will have any impact. Advisory committees have similar shortcomings.

The negotiated rule making process would provide a particularly useful framework if the narrow focus implied in its name could be eliminated and if representation could be broadened.

SUGGESTED MODELS

Public Sector

The State of New Jersey has created an Office of Public Participation within its Department of Environmental Protection (DEP). Working with the Office of Public Participation and Rutgers University, the DEP's Bureau of Water Quality Standards and Analysis developed a two-way communication model for public participation prior to drafting ground water quality regulations in 1987–88. Rather than addressing the public in general, the participation process utilized a concentric circle approach to identifying target publics:

*The inner circle consisted of a **task force** that included representatives of groups directly affected by the standards. The representatives, who were required to commit to day-long monthly meetings, were selected by the specific interest groups. Participating groups included those expected to be hostile.

*The middle circle consisted of affected publics that did not have the time to commit to the process. They participated in informal **round-**

table meetings that provided valuable early warning of potential problems.

*The outer circle included less interested but affected publics.[64]

A model such as this allows for appropriate flexibility, not only in terms of membership and degree of participation, but also in regard to location. The system can be implemented on a statewide level or in a specific community. It can be applied to nearly any issue, and can encompass a variety of affected publics, including industry representatives. Most importantly, the model represents the kind of decentralized public participation that is responsive to local needs and circumstances, and considerate of economic, ecological, and political diversity.

> Life is lived in specific communities. That is where locational and land use decisions are made and tradeoffs between competing strategies occur. That is where citizens learn to appreciate, and agonize over, the coexistence of self-interest and public interest. As Tocqueville first recognized, the American states and municipalities are far more than an administrative convenience. They are the schools of citizenship, and their elected officials have a unique perspective from which to consider the political and ethical, as well as the technical content of policy choices.[65]

Private Sector

The Chemical Manufacturers Association (CMA) has developed a two-level initiative that involves public participation at both the national and the local level. The purpose of the initiative, called "Responsible Care: A Public Commitment," is to improve the chemical industry's response to public concerns. Public participation is achieved through a national Public Advisory Panel and through local Community Advisory Panels.[66]

Citizen participation in the private sector is not new; utilities have been using participation on a company-by-company basis for years. However, the CMA initiative is unique in several respects.

1) It is an industry-wide effort, not an individual company initiative.

2) The initiative is grounded in a written statement of Guiding Principles and Codes of Management Practices.

3) CMA member companies, which represent about 90 percent of so-called basic chemical industry capacity in the United States,

are obligated to participate in Responsible Care and to subscribe to its Guiding Principles in order to retain their membership.

4) Through the national Advisory Panel, concerned and informed citizens with interests and concerns related to the environment, health, and safety are directly involved in the development and evaluation of the initiative. The panel meets four or five times a year to identify and define areas of concern they believe warrant industry response, to critique all proposed Codes of Management Practices, and to assist the industry in identifying and developing responsive programs and actions.

5) Member companies are encouraged to establish Community Advisory Panels, and the CMA provides consultation and support materials to facilitate this effort.

CMA allows for flexibility in panel format based on the size and location of the community, the size and resources of the facility, and the specific needs to be addressed. It has identified four variations on the same theme, but all with the intent of fostering two-way communication:

When company resources are limited, or when a community is in a rural, well-defined area, CMA recommends an **Ad Hoc Community Panel** invited by the company to meet periodically to deal with specific projects or problems. This might be done when a company is considering siting a hazardous waste disposal facility, or expanding, or cleaning up a Superfund site.

When there are long-term projects or goals to be met, or when a company determines that it wants an ongoing relationship with the community, CMA suggests the **Company-Organized Panel.** In this type of panel, the facility invites the participants and remains at the center of its organization, usually providing a preliminary agenda to guide discussion. "Even though the company is providing the structure and support for the group, real progress will come only through an open exchange."[67]

When there are two or more companies in the same community, they may want to organize a **Joint Panel** to pursue mutual problems and goals. The challenge is to serve the collective needs of all the companies before those of any one company.

Finally, **Independent Panels** may be established through third party resources in the community. The CMA states, "These panels provide the most open exchange of information because they are run independent of the facility(ies). Panelists are more likely to convey the true feelings of the community, thus providing the best barometer of attitudes toward the company(ies). Industry may find that this option offers a broader forum for explaining its position and getting accurate feedback."[68]

The CMA model provides flexibility while ensuring two-way communication. The potential benefits are enumerated by the association:

—It helps industry leaders better understand citizens' concerns.

—It helps facility managers identify issues that concern local citizens but are not apparent.

—It offers facility managers a unique opportunity to explain the often complex issues associated with chemical production to lay people in a setting that fosters open and complete discussion.

—It provides an opportunity for dialogue between citizens and facility managers about future projects at the facility, such as a new production unit, landfill, or incinerator.

—Most important, the panel builds trust between companies and the communities in which they operate.[69]

SUMMARY

Current federal regulation has evolved into a centralized, standard-setting approach that specifies detailed methods and equipment for achieving compliance. In turn, such compliance has become an extremely costly and time-consuming procedure for business and industry trying to function competitively against rivals in countries with either little or no regulation, or with regulations that are goal rather than process oriented. Some of the ways that costly overregulation impacts negatively on U.S. competitiveness include increased pricing and decreased production, as well as reduced research, development, and capital investment.

Because regulation is a predictable result of public concerns that develop from local consequences to public issues and to public policy, the solution to the overregulation dilemma rests with early and meaningful intervention at the local level. Meaningful intervention, in turn, necessitates public participation in decision making that utilizes a two-way symmetric approach involving negotiation and compromise.

A review of six current public participation mechanisms indicates that all are flawed in terms of the two-way symmetric model. This points to the need for development of models to meet the suggested criteria similar to ones implemented by the State of New Jersey and the Chemical Manufacturers Association.

NOTES

1. Senate Committee on Banking, Housing, and Urban Affairs, *Making Things Better: Competing in Manufacturing,* Office of Technology Assessment Report, 101st Cong., 2d sess., 1990, 13.

2. Ibid., 53.

3. "House Passes Clean Air Law Overhaul," *The* [Allentown, PA] *Morning Call,* 27 Oct. 1990, sec. A.

4. For a detailed discussion of the evolution of Federal regulation see U. S. Congress, Joint Economic Committee, *Government Regulation: Achieving Social and Economic Balance,* Special Study on Economic Change, 96th Cong., 2d sess., 1980, 1–17.

5. Murray L. Weidenbaum, *Business, Government and the Public* (Englewood Cliffs, NJ: Prentice-Hall, Inc., 1986), 23.

6. Ibid., 15–16.

7. Ibid.

8. Edwin G. Dolan and John C. Goodman, "Acid Rain: The Economics of Opportunity Cost," *Economics of Public Policy* (St. Paul, MN: West Publishing Co., 1989), 15.

9. *Social and Economic Balance,* p. 14.

10. Robert W. Crandall, *Controlling Industrial Pollution* (New York: Norton, 1978), cited by Dolan and Goodman, 19.

11. Weidenbaum, 30.

12. Ibid.

13. Denny Technical Services, "Clean Air Act Legislation: House/Senate Side-By-Side Comparison." Report prepared for the Clean Air Working Group, 30 July 1990, 1.

14. "Congress debates: What Price Clean Air?" *The Morning Call,* 16 Sept. 1990, A3.

15. Kit Farber ad Gary Rutledge, "Pollution Abatement and Control Expenditures, 1984–87," *Survey of Current Business* (June 1989): 19–27.

16. Weidenbaum, 96.

17. Michael R. Edgmand, Ronald L. Moomaw, and Kent W. Olson, *Economics and Contemporary Issues* (Chicago: Dryden Press, 1991), 152–153.

18. Ibid., 152.

19. *1978 Annual Report* (Midland, MI: Dow Chemical Co., 1979), 2.

20. Murray Weidenbaum, *The Future of Business Regulation: Private Action and Public Demand* (New York: AMACOM, 1979), 19.

21. Eugene Bardach and Lucian Pugliaresi, "The Environmental-Impact Statement vs. The Real World," *Public Interest* (Fall 1977): 11.

22. Ingo Walter, "A Survey of International Economic Repercussions of Environmental Policy," in *Economics of Environmental and Natural Resources Policy,* ed. J. A. Butlin (Boulder, CO: Westview Press, 1981), 171.

23. Edward F. Denison, "Effects of Selected Changes in the Institutional and Human Environment upon Output per Unit of Input," *Survey of Current Business* (January 1978): 111.

24. J. P. Kalt, "The Impact of Domestic Environmental Regulatory Policies on U.S. International Competitiveness," John F. Kennedy School of Government

Energy and Environmental Policy Center Discussion Paper No. E-85-02, 1985. Cited in Klaus Conrad and Catherine J. Morrison, "The Impact of Pollution Abatement Investment on Productivity Change: An Empirical Comparison of the U.S., Germany, and Canada," *Southern Economic Journal* (January 1989): 685.

25. Conrad and Morrison, 696.

26. Edgmand, Moomaw and Olson, 154.

27. *Making Things Better,* 31.

28. Ibid., 30.

29. Senate Committee on Commerce, Science, and Transportation, *The Competitiveness Challenge Facing the U. S. Industry,* 101st Cong., 2nd sess., 1990, 22.

30. Giandomenico Majone, "Science and Trans-Science in Standard Setting," *Science, Technology & Human Values* 9, no. 1 (Winter 1984):20.

31. *Annual Report of H. M. Alkali and Clean Air Inspectorate for 1973* (London: Her Majesty's Stationery Office, 1974), cited by Michael Hill, "The Role of the British Alkali and Clean Air Inspectorate in Air Pollution Control," in *International Comparisons in Implementing Pollution Laws,* ed. Paul B. Downing and Kenneth Hanf (Boston and the Hague: Kluwer-Nijhoff Publishing Co., 1983), 90–91.

32. For a detailed comparison of pollution-control programs among the United States, Sweden, Japan and South Korea see Edwin S. Mills and Philip E. Graves, *The Economics of Environmental Quality* (New York: W. W. Norton & Company, 1986).

33. Ibid., 306.

34. Ibid., 312.

35. Ibid., 319.

36. Thomas L. Jacobson, "Old and New Approaches to Participatory Communication for Development" (Paper presented at the Annual Meeting of the International Communication Association, San Francisco, CA, 25–29 May 1989), 5.

37. Senate Committee on Commerce, Science, and Transportation, *Competitiveness of the U.S. Chemical Industry,* 100th Cong., 2nd sess., 1988, 1–5.

38. Douglas Biden, Economist and Secretary-Treasurer, Pennsylvania Electric Association, interview with author, 14 August 1990.

39. James E. Grunig and Todd Hunt, *Managing Public Relations* (New York: CBS College Publishing, 1984), 10.

40. Richard E. Crable and Steven L. Vibbert, "Managing Issues and Influencing Public Policy," *Public Relations Review* 11 (Summer 1985): 6.

41. Brad E. Hainsworth, "The Distribution of Advantages and Disadvantages," *Public Relations Review* 16 (Spring 1990): 35.

42. Earl C. Gottschalk, Jr., "Firms Hiring New Type of Manager to Study Issues, Emerging Troubles," *Wall Street Journal,* 10 June 1982, sec. 2, 38, cited in Hainsworth, ibid.

43. Hainsworth, 36.

44. Baruch Fischoff, et al, *Acceptable Risk* (Cambridge: Cambridge University Press, 1981), 148.

45. Daniel J. Fiorino, "Citizen Participation and Environmental Risk: A Survey of Institutional Mechanisms," *Science, Technology & Human Values* 15:2 (Spring 1990): 228.

46. Carole M. Gorney, "How to Use Public-Participation Groups Successfully," *Public Relations Journal* 43, no. 6 (June 1987): 29.

47. Bernard J. Bujnowski, Supervisor, Community Planning, Marketing & Economic Development, Pennsylvania Power & Light, interview with author, 27 March 1986.

48. Ibid.

49. Eleanor W. Winsor and Stephen H. Cutcliffe, *Public Involvement in Corporate Technology Decision-Making: The Case of Pennsylvania Power and Light,* in *Public Involvement in Energy Facility Planning,* Dennis W. Ducsik ed. (Boulder, CO: Westview Press, 1986), 377–406.

50. Grunig and Hunt, 144.

51. Jean Mroscko, Director Office of Public Participation, Department of Environmental Protection, Trenton, New Jersey, interviews with author, September 1990.

52. Grunig and Hunt, 23.

53. Ibid.

54. Bruce Stiftel, "Dialogue: Does it Increase Participant Knowledgeability and Attitude Congruence?" in *Public Involvement and Social Assessment,* ed. Gregory A. Daneke, Margot W. Garcia, and Jerome Delli Priscoli (Boulder, CO: Westview Press, 1983) 61.

55. Rogene A. Buchholz, *Business Environment and Public Policy* (Englewood Cliffs, NJ: Prentice-Hall, 1982) 464, cited in Grunig and Hunt, 306.

56. For a detailed discussion of public participation mechanisms, their strengths and weaknesses, see Fiorino.

57. B. Checkoway, "The Politics of Public Hearings," *Journal of Applied Behavioral Science* 17 (1981): 566–582, cited in Fiorino, 231.

58. Daniel J. Fiorino, 233.

59. N. Crosby, J. M. Kelly, and P. Schaefer, "Citizens Review Panels: A New Approach to Citizen Participation," *Public Administration Review* 46 (1986):170–178, cited in Fiorino, 235.

60. Fiorino, 233.

61. Federal Advisory Committee Act, 5 U.S.C. app. 2, 5(b)(2).

62. Joseph L. Lakshmanan, "An Empirical Argument for Nontechnical Public Members on Advisory Committees: FDA as a Model," *Risk: Issues in Health and Safety* 1, no. 1 (1990): 62–63.

63. Ibid., 63–64.

64. Caron Chess, "Drafting Ground Water Quality Regulations: A Case Study in Public Participation" (Report to Division of Water Quality, New Jersey Department of Environmental Protection, 25 Oct. 1989), 1–2.

65. Marc K. Landy, Marc J. Roberts and Stephen R. Thomas, *The Environmental Protection Agency: Asking the Wrong Questions* (New York and Oxford: Oxford University Press, 1990) 300.

66. The following information on Responsible Care is contained in a variety of handouts and support material provided by the Chemical Manufacturers Association, 2501 M Street, N.W., Washington, D.C. 20037.

67. *Advisory Panels: Options for Community Outreach* (Washington, D.C.: Chemical Manufacturers Association, n.d.), 8.

68. Ibid., 15–16.

69. Ibid., 3.

Management, Innovation, and Competitiveness: A Vision of a New Era in Manufacturing

STEVEN L. GOLDMAN AND ROGER N. NAGEL

Since the rise of the modern industrial corporation little more than a century ago, technological innovation has been a determinant of successful manufacturing in open, competitive markets. The impact of a firm's innovation policies on its competitiveness is, however, far from straightforward. Decisions to innovate or not to innovate are not a matter of "picking winners." The success of a firm is not guaranteed by committing it to what becomes the next technology success story; nor does deciding not to adopt a successful innovation necessarily imply competitive decline. The timing of innovation decisions is crucial, as are the particular form in which an innovation is introduced and the scale on which it is introduced. Technology pioneers often pay a heavy price for the privilege, while firms can sometimes find niche markets that allow them to bypass an innovation and remain profitable.

In this essay, we explore two underappreciated factors influencing the impact of innovation decisions on a firms's competitiveness. Both of these factors are managerial, not technological. One has to do with management's responsibility for the technical resources available to it, the other with management's responsiveness to the managerial implications of newly introduced technologies.

The impact of innovation commitments by the management of a firm is affected by the coordination between management practices and distinctive organizational requirements of new technologies. The optimal utilization of a technology may require significant changes in a firm's managerial values, in its internal "culture," even in its organizational structure. Conversely, attempting to assimilate

a new technology into existing managerial practices may well viti-
ate, and will certainly limit, the competitive impact of an innovation, as we will illustrate below and in our "vision" of an emerging
new era in manufacturing.

At the same time, innovation commitments by management cannot be derived objectively either from technical knowledge itself
or from an examination of new technologies. The reverse is closer
to the truth, namely, that the technical resources (the knowledge
and the technologies) available to the management of a firm at
a given time are themselves the products of value-laden, hence
subjective, managerial decision-making processes. It is the management of a firm that decides, on managerial grounds, the kinds
of technical expertise and the directions of research and development that will be supported internally, or acquired from other firms
in the form of personnel, patents, licensing agreements, or reverse
engineering. It is, again, management that decides, for each firm,
what technical knowledge and which technologies are to be used,
how they are to be used, what they are to be used for, and on what
scale. Technological innovation is thus driven by extra-technical
value judgments. These value judgments are embedded, in part
explicitly but more often tacitly, in enterprise-specific decisions
that are invariably the prerogative of management. They are the
expression of a firm's managerial agenda together with the management processes organized for the express purpose of executing that
agenda.[1]

Such a view of innovation flies in the face of the popular view that
innovation is a universal and objective process, driven by innate
characteristics of theoretical knowledge, and of artifacts that somehow dictate the terms of their own unfolding. This view was supported by traditional notions of material progress that saw as
inevitable the introduction, application, improvement, and dissemination of steam power, electricity, and internal combustion engines,
for example, in just the forms that those technologies actually
took.[2] Many critics of technology, however, especially in the 1960s
and 1970s, warned of an "imperative" in technical knowledge and
in artifacts that threatened to overwhelm humanity's ability to manage their humane implementation.[3] Both of these groups ignored
the fact that the domain of the technical, in spite of having been
shaped by value judgments, cannot include the terms of its own
application. The application of technical knowledge can only be
determined by the addition of extra-technical value judgments,
such as those mentioned above.

Furthermore, the application of technical knowledge is always a particular and context-specific process. Each instance of it must take place within an organization whose management must decide—in addition to what knowledge to use and how to use it— what the best interests of that organization, its management, and its stakeholders are (three sets of interests that overlap but rarely coincide); what the projected near- and middle-term social, economic, and competitive situation of the organization is likely to be; how the interests of the organization, its management, and its stakeholders would be served by employing technical knowledge innovatively, rather than by pursuing financial, legal, political, or marketing initiatives; and how well innovation opportunities match the organization's culture, the prevailing conceptions of what objectives and procedures are, or are not, "right" for it.[4]

The task that management confronts in formulating innovation policies for a firm (or for a government agency, or a laboratory) is very much like the task that applied scientists and engineers confront in solving a design problem. There is no one correct solution to a design problem, nor can the reductive analytical techniques familiar from mathematics and physics be applied to design problems. Their solution requires assigning values on extra-technical grounds to a set of factors that have been identified, also on extra-technical grounds, as relevant both to the definition of the problem and to what will be considered an acceptable solution to it. Typical factors in industry, for example, would include manufacturability, cost, compatibility with existing products, facilities and inventory, competitive pressures, legal restrictions, marketing projections, aesthetics, corporate image requirements, and managerial experience and prejudices.[5] The very same sorts of considerations apply, as well, to the solution of the managerial problem of designing a role for technological innovation within a corporation's strategic plan.

This characterization of technological innovation is supported by numerous historical studies of technology and business, and by a host of theoretical and case studies by philosophers, sociologists, and policy analysts.[6] David Noble's history of the introduction of numerically controlled machine tools, Tracy Kidder's account of the interaction between management and engineers in the design of a new Data General computer, Margaret Graham's analysis of RCA's Videodisc project, and Peter Temin's discussion of Western Electric's manufacturing objectives before and after the "break-up" of AT&T are representative of many similar studies published in the last twenty years.[7] The interplay among political agenda, parochial corporate interests, and selective utilization of available knowledge in shaping the development of new technologies has been described in detail for electric utility networks, broadcast radio, commercial nuclear power, fusion power research, and America's space and weapons programs, again among many others.[8] The common denominator of all these studies is that technological innovation, indeed the evolution of technical knowledge itself, cannot be explained without reference to the essential influence on innovation and research of social, political, economic, and cultural factors. The impact of innovation decisions on a firm's competitiveness is also dependent on the coordination of new technologies with management practices and values. General Motors' early 1980s attempts to improve productivity by installing billions of dollars worth of robotics and computer-aided manufacturing technologies, but without changing the relationship between management, technical resources and the workforce, proved abortive. By contrast, NUMMI, the joint manufacturing agreement GM entered into with Toyota, employing an existing "low tech" GM plant with little new technology, achieved dramatic productivity increases just by changing the organization and operation of the plant's managerial structure. A study of the use of flexible manufacturing systems by U.S. and Japanese companies revealed a similar influence of management decisions on the impact of new technologies.[9] Japanese companies typically use flexible machining clusters to produce more new products, maintaining volume per product by adding work shifts. American companies typically choose to use the new tools to manufacture more of the same product per shift, settling for unit cost savings instead of greater market penetration.

Technological innovation is not simply synonymous with the introduction of new artifacts. Managerial decisions relating to the scale of new production capabilities can have major consequences for their impact on a firm's competitiveness. The integration of a new production technology with a harmonized product redesign can result in the projection of new families of products, the opening of new markets, and the ability to change, improve, and customize products on new schedules of cost and delivery. Black and Decker management realized dramatic increases in productivity and quality, along with decreases in costs, when its engineering staff was permitted to redesign their electric motors as part of management's investment in improved production facilities. The result was a new, integrated family of power tool products that enjoyed a competitive advantage over even their lowest-price foreign rivals.[10] Harley

Davidson realized similar improvements with the introduction of its redesigned, integrated "Evolution" family of Sportster motorcycles.

Many of the Japanese industrial success stories of the past thirty years have been the result of creative managerial "inventions" introduced collaterally with new technologies. These include the invention of new markets (consumer VCR, Sony Walkman), new marketing strategies keyed to rapid introduction of new models and products (motorcycles, automobiles, consumer electronics), and new directions in which to push borrowed technical knowledge leading to qualitative manufacturing advantages (statistical quality control, CNC machine tools, industrial robotics, photovoltaic and semiconductor device manufacturing, among many others).[11] Allen Bradley Corporation management redefined its self-perception, from the managers of a company manufacturing large volumes of uniform products that its sales staff had to push out the door, to one using the latest technology to manufacture low-cost customized products that customers pulled out the door. The production technologies utilized did not dictate the purpose for which they were installed. That had to come from management which, in turn, had to redefine its relationship to the Allen Bradley workforce. The result was the transformation of a corporation hard pressed to survive into a profitable, aggressive competitor.

The increasing electronic content of automobiles is creating new approaches to vehicle design in order to optimize computer control and monitoring of vehicle functions. In the process, the redesign is also creating new commercial diagnostic, maintenance, and repair services, and thus new competitive opportunities as well, to which management must be responsive. Computer network technologies are making simultaneous engineering practical. Simultaneous engineering ties together design, research, manufacturing, and sales, suppliers and customers, into an integrated product development program. It offers significant competitive advantages to manufacturers of complex products, but requires a commitment on the part of management to adapting organizational structures to the requirements of simultaneous engineering, as well as investment in the hardware, software, and training required to integrate the various divisions of an enterprise. It is the process that has been implemented at Boeing to design, develop, and manufacture the new Boeing 777 aircraft, without drawings or physical models, by dispersed, multi-functional work teams.[12]

Recent technological innovations have highlighted the value of information as a commercial product and as an element of the total manufacturing process. American Airlines SABRE reservation system, for example, has been a major profit generator as a commercial information service offered to competitor airlines and travel agents—in recent years, a greater profit generator than American's flight operations. In the current information-intensive business environment, management cannot blindly suppose that protecting proprietary information protects competitive advantage. Sharing information, even with competitors, can sometimes be profitable, and can even confer competitive advantage.[13] Again, new technologies have created new opportunities for their creative utilization, but only by managements alert to those opportunities. DEC management discovered that managerial processing of information was responsible for well over 90% of the time it took to respond to orders for its VAX mini-computers. By implementing an expert systems-based computerized ordering system linked to purchasing, inventory, production scheduling, and a rationalized managerial monitoring process, the time between order and delivery was reduced by more than half. Information may be immaterial and may move very rapidly, but its flow through a production system must be accounted for and optimized. Indeed, its value is such that the organization of the production system must be adapted to the optimization of information flow through it, rather than the reverse.

Every firm's management manifests in its decision-making some set of stock values, some fixed ways of doing things linked to a particular vision of what the objectives of that firm are and ought to be. Such a repertoire of internalized values makes managing the status quo easier to perform and easier to measure, but they militate against challenging the status quo, let alone changing it. Today the rate of change in business practice, driven by the increased pace of managerial as well as of technological innovation, is too rapid for competitive practices to be derived from past practices. The belief that improving product quality and increasing product variety necessarily entailed increased production cost was shown by the Japanese to no longer be true. The price to American industry of persisting in that belief in the face of new possibilities opened up by new production technologies has been enormous.

These few illustrations highlight the dependence of the competitiveness impact of a firm's innovation commitments on its management's selective utilization of technical knowledge. Optimal utilization requires sufficient familiarity with technical resources on the part of management to be able to perceive new production and marketing possibilities. It also requires sufficient flexibility on the part of management to change prevailing managerial values and organizational structures in order to exploit those possibilities. Optimal utilization also requires that a firm's technical professionals have internalized the managerial agenda. Historically, engineers in industry have not understood the relationship of their technical knowledge to the business goals of their firms. This is largely an expression of prevailing managerial decisions regarding the place of technical resources in corporate organizational structures.[14]

There are signs that this situation is beginning to change in order to bring technical resources into closer coordination with management agendas. The pivotal factor, however, is the willingness of management to adjust organizational structures to the requirements of new technical possibilities. Management needs to reconsider the dogma that only managers understand which decisions are in the firm's best interests, and that only they know how the firm's resources can best be brought to bear on achieving the firm's objectives. Ideally, the entire workforce, embracing managers, professional technical personnel, and production and service employees, needs to understand the relationship of their work to the firm's immediate and long-term objectives.[15] A knowledgeable workforce, possessing such understanding and organized in such a way as to spontaneously exercise it, wielding state-of-the-art manufacturing and management technologies, constitutes a competitive force of potentially awesome power. It is the contemporary analogue of the early modern industrial corporations that created the mass production system by tying a patchquilt of existing production, communication, and transportation technologies to a new management structure: the vertically integrated, centrally administered, hierarchically organized corporation.[16]

The current globalization of industry is creating new opportunities for manufacturing enterprises and forcing new choices on management and on societies. As a matter of fact, U.S. industry today stands at the threshold of a new era in manufacturing. An opportunity beckons to reverse the decade-long decline in American industrial competitiveness. If it is seized, the manufacturing sector of the U.S. economy will expand and a foundation will be laid for broadly distributed improvements in the quality of American life. Other nations, as indicated above, already stand at that threshold, indeed are moving across it. If U.S. industry lingers, its manufacturing capability will soon be outdated, its competitiveness in domestic markets will continue to decline, and it will effectively be locked out of many world markets. A decline in the American standard of living is almost certain.

The implications for American society of the transformation of manufacturing that is underway are profound. Consider the following capsule scenarios. *The year is 2006. The automotive Big Three are the No-Longer-So-Big Two, and their partnerships with Japanese and Korean automakers account for the bulk of their domestic sales. Japanese and German robotics devices and numerically-controlled machine tools dominate American manufacturing operations. Flat-panel TV screens, a Japanese monopoly, have displaced the color picture tube. The booming market for bioengineering products is controlled by a joint Swiss-German-Japanese corporation with exclusive rights to the basic research they fund in hundreds of small U.S. commercial and academic laboratories. A Franco-German consortium has created a universal access, global information network through which it has achieved dominance in computer networking, and in telecommunications, software, and equipment. The U.S. economy continues to weaken from the chronic trade deficit and from the burden of a defense budget swollen by the need to maintain dedicated manufacturing facilities and large stockpiles of weapons designed for every projected mission requirement.*

All too believable, given current trends?

The year is 2006 and the United States enjoys world leadership in manufacturing. Domestically, overall employment in manufacturing at both large and small companies has increased and industry profits are at record high levels. In the European Community, in developing countries around the world, and at home, U.S. companies compete aggressively for market share and are respected producers of quality goods and services. They have an especially strong position in leading-edge computer hardware and software, biotechnology, telecommunications, industrial process control equipment, and state-of-the-art consumer electronics products. The level of education of the U.S. workforce is among the highest in the world. Management has long since integrated social concerns—environment, energy, workforce structure, community impact—into the setting of company agenda, alongside technical and economic concerns. Maintaining U.S. military superiority requires a smaller fraction of the federal budget as DoD weapons requirements can quickly be met by commercial manufacturing facilities.

Unbelievable?

The very developments that today are driving the transformation of the mass production system of manufacturing can serve as a springboard for the United States to regain manufacturing competitiveness by the year 2006. The technologies required by the new system are well defined and will become available, at a price, to whoever has the ability to use them. This ability, however, will depend upon innovations in the organization of the management of manufacturing enterprises. American industry must acquire the necessary technologies in a timely manner, but the technologies alone are not enough. The technologies will have to be integrated into organizational frameworks that fully utilize the knowledge, creativity, and, above all, the initiative of the human resources available to industry. Even this is not enough. Industrial enterprises must have access to generic social resources—an appropriately educated workforce, adequate communication and information networks, a supportive political, legal, and economic climate. Together, technologies, their organization within enterprises, and the linkages of these enterprises to their social contexts, constitute a system. New technologies and new organizational structures are today converging in a new manufacturing system, embodied in a new kind of industrial enterprise: agile manufacturing enterprises.

Increasingly powerful information and communication technologies are being incorporated into the tools of manufacturing. Networks of computer-controlled production machinery are creating new kinds of industrial goods and services. In the process, a competitive environment is emerging in which the existing mass production system of manufacturing is at a disadvantage. Where the mass production system achieved low unit costs by producing large quantities of uniform products, the new system achieves agility. It is capable of low unit costs while producing far smaller quantities of high quality, highly customized products. In an agile enterprise, manufacturing machinery can be reprogrammed quickly to produce new products in many variations. Products with a high information content and related commercial services are being created that will increasingly come to define the competitiveness of a nation's industrial apparatus.

In the mass production system, even with the enhancements of just-in-time and "lean" production, corporations attempted to do everything themselves. Competition favored large-scale comprehensive operations. The agile manufacturing system favors smaller scale, modular production facilities, and cooperation between enterprises, each of which contributes a part to a new capability. Agile manufacturing alters the meaning of industrial competition as competitor, supplier, and customer firms occupy changing roles in relation to one another. Competition and cooperation become mutually compatible. In such a system, competitive advantage is determined by speed to market, by the ability to satisfy individual

customer preferences (whether consumer or commercial customers), and by responsiveness to intensifying public concern
about manufacturing's social and environmental impacts.

In the United States, Japan, and western Europe, a recognition
is spreading that this new manufacturing system has already begun
to take shape. A host of reports by government agencies and by
private and public institutions address the, as yet dimly perceived,
outlines of that new system.[17] Congress has become increasingly
involved in what is now a decade-long public debate on the U.S.
industrial competitiveness "crisis." It has passed legislation that
enables the formation of certain kinds of consortia among competitors, funds the consortial development of "pre-competitive" generic technologies and—in the case of Sematech—of competitive
technologies, encourages the commercialization of innovations developed with public funds, and accelerates the transfer of new technologies from the 700+ federal laboratories to private industry.

Many corporations and industrial organizations also have recognized that a transition to a new mode of manufacturing has begun.
The rate of formation of consortia and of joint ventures has accelerated sharply in the past decade. They reflect an awareness that
only a cooperative effort can manage this transition successfully.
Such highly publicized recent joint ventures as those of GM, Ford,
and Chrysler, of IBM, Motorola, and Apple, and of IBM and Sie-
mens are symptomatic of initial responses to a recognition that
innovative measures are called for to remain competitive in the
new industrial environment.

In western Europe, concern over competitiveness in a new global
manufacturing environment has precipitated an unprecedented
subordination of national prerogatives to regional unification. The
Single Market Act of the European Community rests on the conviction that, divided, the national markets of the EC member states
could not withstand the competitive pressure that Japanese and
U.S. manufacturing, employing new production technologies,
would soon be bringing bear on them. United, however, they had
a chance to achieve at least competitive equality by jointly recon-
structing a common manufacturing system employing those same
technologies.[18] The political price these countries have indicated
they are willing to pay to avoid industrial obsolescence is a sign of
how seriously those communities take the imminence of a new era
in manufacturing. To date, their paper commitments are reinforced
by their funding of trans-national consortia to develop jointly a
common competence in a wide range of manufacturing technologies.[19]

The Japanese have since 1986 been engaged in an exercise whose objective is articulating the next mode of competitive manufacturing, the one that comes after mass production.[20] They have identified the strengths and the weaknesses of the manufacturing system that has been the vehicle for their rise to a prosperity and international economic power unparalleled in their history. But, for them, the limits of this system have been reached. Quality control and just-in-time inventory management have done as much as they can do. More importantly, they are doing the same things for other manufacturing nations, not just for a resurgent United States and newly dynamic western Europe, but for east Asian rivals as well. In fact, the mass production system has reached such a degree of sophistication, its managerial and technological structures are now so robust, that it can be installed virtually anywhere in the world. Wherever some natural, social, or political factor creates a competitive advantage, a factory can be located. Quality alone cannot make enough of a difference to keep the manufacture of standard products, using mature technologies of production, an attractive investment in developed societies for much longer.

Already the Japanese see signs of decline in the functionality of the current system of manufacturing. The number of young Japanese engineers going into industry is dropping. Of those who go into industry, the number going into manufacturing is also dropping. Young Japanese, having grown up in a prosperous and peaceful society, are not displaying the devotion to work or the company loyalty that characterized their parents' generation. Increasingly, the Japanese public is taking up the concerns about the environmental and social impacts of industry that have been prominent in the United States, Canada, and western Europe since the late 1960s.

At the same time, a consensus has taken shape among Japanese industrialists about a new manufacturing system, one that will complement mass production, not replace it, and be profitable even in Japan.[21] This system poses problems, too, the least of which are technological. The new system will depend on spontaneous workforce initiative and on innovative creativity at the operatoinal level of an enterprise. It will depend on globally distributed authority as well as globally decentralized manufacturing facilities. Both at home and abroad, Japanese managers will have to deal with women who will merit, and expect, promotion to positions of authority. Finally, the successful implementation of the new technologies will be critically dependent on the software linking human workers at all levels with a national information network capable of controlling manufacturing operations.

All of these requirements pose special challenges to entrenched

values of Japanese management, society, and culture. Japanese corporations nevertheless have already begun to explore the potential
of the latest manufacturing technologies for rapid product development, for offering multiple models of basic designs with many cus-
tomization options, and for profitable production of relatively small
product lot sizes.

In its global operations, U.S. industry has an established record
for respecting and rewarding the abilities of professional national
personnel, including promotion to the highest managerial positions
in U.S.-owned foreign operations. American society has moved
steadily, over the past twenty years, towards eliminating the disparity between workplace treatment of men and women. The promotion of women to positions of authority in industry has become a
familiar, though not yet a routine, phenomenon for U.S. companies.
Entrepreneurial initiative and technical creativity have been hall-
marks of American industry for over 150 years. Software development is one of the technologies in which America holds a
commanding world leadership position. More generally, the United
States is a world leader in information science. It also possesses a
diverse supplier base that constitutes a major resource for cooperative ventures in an agile manufacturing environment. Linking these
two could create a significant competitive advantage for U.S. industry.

Attracting a larger number of intelligent, creative young people
into manufacturing than now choose such careers is a problem that
U.S. and Japanese industry share. The "pipeline" into science and
engineering careers has received considerable attention in recent
years. It remains poorly understood and, after reaching the highest
levels in U.S. history in the early 1980s, undergraduate engineering
enrollment has been declining since 1986. The number of women
entering the engineering profession had increased ten-fold between
1970 and 1986, but it has since levelled off at about 12% of first
degree recipients. Minority engineering enrollment over the same
period doubled and it, too, has levelled off. Apart from quantity
and diversity issues, American science and engineering educators
need to identify the distinctive requirements of agile manufacturing
for technical professionals and to reform undergraduate and graduate curricula to satisfy those requirements.[22]

A growing number of American companies (among them Apple,
Becton Dickinson, Cypress Semiconductor, and Xerox) have already begun to experiment with inverting the pyramid of managerial authority to permit the formation, and to allow the execution,
of new project initiatives "from below." It will be necessary to

exploit the flexibility and the rapid response capabilities of the new production technologies. To excel at multi-disciplinary teamwork, Americans will have to overcome the national prejudice for "going it alone," for valuing individual achievement above team achievement. On balance, however, the transition to a system of manufacturing with these infrastructure requirements appears to give U.S. industry an opportunity to build on a number of strengths in effecting the transition from mass production to agile manufacturing.

The agile manufacturing enterprise confers decisive competitive advantage in an open market because it is able to bring out totally new products quickly. It assimilates field experience and technological innovations easily, continually modifying its product offerings to incorporate them. Its products are designed to evolve. As the needs of users change, as improvements are introduced, users can readily reconfigure or upgrade what they have bought instead of replacing it. Reprogrammable, reconfigurable, continuously changeable production systems, integrated into a new, information intensive, manufacturing system, make the lot size of an order irrelevant. The cost of production is the same for 10,000 units of one model, as for one unit each of 10,000 different configurations of all the models of a single product. Agile manufacturing thus produces to order, where mass production manufacturing produced to stock and sell, basing its production schedule on marketing projections. Similarly, quality in agile manufacturing advances from being measured in defects per part when sold to customer gratification over the full life of the product.

Because of the longevity of its evolutionary product lines, the agile manufacturing enterprise develops strategic relationships with its consumer as well as with its commercial customers. In place of the sale-and-limited-warranty relationship, it offers customers a continuously variable mix of products, services, and value-adding information. To facilitate this relationship, it communicates with its products while they are in their users' possession. Information is exchanged, software upgraded, diagnostic servicing performed, and individual product histories maintained. Customer confidence is maintained over long product lifetimes by continuous investment in the skill base of the agile enterprise's workforce, which is valued as the enterprise's central long-term asset. The workforce is responsible for innovative product evolution and for manufacturing process improvements that allow cost increases to be recovered internally rather than through price increases.

Mass production enterprises are operationally focused and emphasize short-term financial performance. Because of the limited flexibility of their production technologies, they extend the status quo as long as possible in order to amortize sunk costs. Agile enterprises are strategically focused, and emphasize long-term financial performance. They see opportunities for growth and profit in constant change that their production technologies and managerial organization, both highly flexible, are able to exploit. Authority is diffused in the agile enterprise, not concentrated in a chain of command. Instead of a static corporate structure based on fixed, specialized departments, agile corporations have a dynamic structure keyed to the evolving needs of cross-functional project teams. Where technology under the mass production system is perceived as the key to solving manufacturing and marketing problems, under agile manufacturing people optimally utilizing technology are the problem solvers.

The agile enterprise is the natural next development of industry. The modern industrial corporation created in the 1880s integrated relatively inflexible production machinery, a largely illiterate workforce, and an international network of technological innovations in communication and transportation into a centrally administered, hierarchically ordered, managerial structure of great competitive power. Local manufacturers in industry after industry succumbed to the competitive advantages of centralized mass production and national distribution. Except for high-quality, customized niche markets, companies that did not emulate the modern corporation could not compete with it for long. It has prospered through 100 years of revolutionary social, political, and technological change, but it is being challenged today.

Agile manufacturing is accomplished by integrating three resources—technology, management, workforce—into a coordinated interdependent system. Highly flexible production machinery is a necessary condition for the emergence of agile manufacturing enterprises, but it is not sufficient by itself to bring them about. The required production technologies are either already here, in embryonic form, or are foreseeable: flexible, programmable machine tools grouped in reconfigurable, modular, and scalable manufacturing cells; "intelligent" manufacturing process controllers; closed-loop monitoring of manufacturing processes employing sensors, samplers, and analyzers coupled to intelligent diagnostic software; the computer power and the manufacturing process knowledge base to design complex products digitally, to simulate their properties and behaviors reliably, and to model the processes of their manufacture accurately. Short product cycle times—the rapid creation, development, and manufacture of new products—

requires linking these technologies to organizational structures that can fully exploit their power.

Agile enterprises are totally integrated organizations. Information flows seamlessly among manufacturing, engineering, marketing, purchasing, finance, inventory, sales, and research departments. Work proceeds concurrently rather than sequentially. The development of new products and the development of the process for manufacturing and marketing them take place concurrently. Design is not the province of engineering, not even of engineering and manufacturing jointly. Instead, representatives of every stage in a product's life cycle, from materials employed in its manufacture to its ultimate disposal, participate in setting its design specification. Information thus flows seamlessly between agile manufacturers and their suppliers, as well as between manufacturers and their customers, who play an active role in product design and development under agile manufacturing. Every product can be dealt with on a highly interactive network, allowing physically dispersed and organizationally segregated personnel from the same company to work collaboratively with one another and with personnel from other companies.

Distributed enterprise integration and distributed operational concurrency are made possible by strict universal data exchange standards, by robust "groupware"—software allowing many people to work on the same project at the same time, constructively— and by broadband communication channels capable of carrying the amount of information involved in these exchanges. The synthesis of these into off-the-shelf enterprise integration software and hardware—analogous to the emergence of off-the-shelf computer network technologies in the late 1980s—will signal the onset of the agile manufacturing era. With reliable integration technologies, safe large-scale changes that do not disrupt system operations will become routine.

Enterprise integration is also made possible by an atmosphere of mutual responsibility for success, within enterprises and between cooperating enterprises. The ethics of agile manufacturing will be mutual trust based on the need to make cooperation a first-choice approach to problem solving, and sharing relevant information with all project collaborators. Trust and mutual responsibility together bear on the capacity for localized decision-making that is a major determinant of agility. Agile enterprises can make and implement many decisions at the point of information. They do not have to wait for requests to act to move up and then back down the organizational hierarchy. The issues locally resolvable include production scheduling changes, error detection and response, and cooperation with other units of the enterprise in setting and pursuing shared goals and in changing pathways to those goals when problems arise.

The ultimate expression of trust, given the proprietary attitudes towards information that prevail today, is the routine formation of "virtual" companies by groups of agile manufacturing enterprises. Speed to market with complex new products is a major competitive advantage. Often the quickest route to the introduction of a new product is by selecting resources from different companies and synthesizing them into a single electronic business entity: a virtual company. If the various distributed resources, human and physical, are "plug compatible" with one another, that is, if they can perform their respective functions jointly, then the virtual company can behave as if it were a single company dedicated to one particular project. For as long as the market opportunity lasts, the virtual company continues in existence; when the opportunity passes, the company dissolves and its personnel turns to other projects.

The "Safari" notebook computer introduced by AT&T in the spring of 1991 captures the spirit of such an inter-firm alliance. AT&T marketing personnel identified a corporate market niche not being served well by the many available notebook computers. Together with AT&T engineers, they defined a set of specifications for the size, weight, and performance characteristics a notebook computer would need in order to compete in that market. Most important, at the same time a series of upgrade paths were specified that established for buyers the product's longevity and its development in parallel with the likely growth of their own computer needs. The market opportunity would long since have vanished if AT&T had had to create the facilities necessary to fully design and produce such a computer. Instead, they created a Safari Computer Division linking the necessary internal managerial, sales, and technical support resources. The Safari Division, in turn, contracted with Marubeni Trading Company to organize the machine's manufacture, utilizing Marubeni's extensive network of manufacturing sources in Japan and the Far East. Concurrently, AT&T contracted with industrial designers Henry Dreyfus Associates to create a distinctive look for the machine. Marubeni arranged for Matsushita to actually produce the machine, which is assembled in the United States out of components, almost all of which are manufactured abroad by various companies. (Interestingly, Marubeni and Matsushita belong to different keiretsu.)

The upshot of all this activity was that four months after AT&T

management decided to proceed with the product, a functional prototype was displayed at the fall 1990 Comdex Consumer Electronics Show and shipping began in the spring. The immediate success of the computer with the corporate buyers it targeted was AT&T's first unqualified triumph in the personal computer market.

In addition to accelerating speed to market, inter-firm alliances can bridge fragmented markets and use generic technologies to satisfy specific customer preferences. The recent agreement among IBM, Apple, and Motorola to jointly develop an operating system and a new series of computers is an illustration of this tactic. Currently the two largest fragments, by far, of the personal computer market are those served by the IBM PC "family" of computers and those served by Apple's Macintosh line. Under the new agreement, Apple and IBM will each introduce a line of computers, using a common processor chip to be manufactured by Motorola, that will be software-compatible with one another. The differences between Macintoshes and PCs will have been bridged regardless of how the computers "look and feel" to users.

The ability to form virtual companies routinely is a powerful competitive weapon. It exploits a number of distinctive American strengths, notably, world leadership in information science, and a vast diversified supplier base. Having achieved distributed enterprise integration, agile manufacturing enterprises routinely form virtual companies. The medium they use is a national industrial network, a Factory America Network (FAN). FAN combines a comprehensive industrial data base with services that allow groups of companies to create and operate proprietary virtual entities. Its operation assumes the removal of legal barriers to multi-enterprise collaboration and the creation of standard consortium formation models that make forming a virtual company as straightforward as making a will or forming a corporation. Intellectual property rights issues generated by collaborative ventures need to be resolved. Techniques need to be developed for managing companies that promote workforce initiative at the operational level, as well as performance measures for self-directed inter-enterprise project teams. These are formidable tasks. The alternative, however, is repeatedly showing up in the marketplace with too little, too late.

More broadly, change is required in the prevailing attitude in American society toward antitrust legislation as well as in the legislation itself. The historical foundation of antitrust legislation in the United States has been superceded by events. The driving concern in the late nineteenth and early twentieth centuries, when this legislation was framed, was to protect the American public from anti-competitive practices by then-new corporate manufacturing giants. Until the 1960s, these corporations did dominate the domestic market and this domination was the foundation for the public's fears of collusion and price manipulation. Today the American market is a global competitive battleground in which American manufacturers have few protected positions, if any. Furthermore, the very definition of "competition" is changing. Competitors are no longer self-sufficient enterprises as U.S. Steel and Standard Oil of New Jersey were, producing standardized products for markets where cost was the primary fact about a product. Cooperation among competitors to create products and services that satisfy individual customer preferences is today the distinctive feature of advanced manufacturing and retailing. Antitrust legislation based on a conception of competition that is no longer operative loses its functionality. By inhibiting cooperation, it neither achieves the dynamic marketplace it sought to create nor protects consumers from potential price manipulation by foreign manufacturers who control whole market segments.

Cooperative initiatives between firms and cooperation among functionally-divided branches of the same firm are central to agile manufacturing. The premium placed on the rapid creation, development, and marketing of new products makes cooperation inevitable. There are many more advantages to cooperation. Cooperation allows the sharing of costs and of risks in an environment of intense competitive pressure. It permits sharing unique technological and human resources, as well, and managing variable rather than fixed costs. In the course of cooperating on the solution of a common problem, a whole new body of knowledge is created out of what had been individual parts proprietary to the cooperating firms. Concurrently, by integrating their respective contributions to the whole project, a new resource is created with capabilities that had not been possessed before by the separate parts. At the same time, interactions among highly qualified individuals with complementary expertise, focusing on a narrow well-defined problem, are themselves stimulating. The probability is high that they will provoke innovative solutions to familiar as well as to new problems.

Agility is becoming a condition of survival. An intensely competitive environment for advanced industrial goods and services has already begun to take shape. Markets are fragmenting and changing rapidly as a steady flow of new products appear in a wide range of continually changing models. Stimulated by the variety of models available, commercial customers and consumers alike are becoming more demanding. They want to buy high quality, low cost, high performance products configured with only the features they feel they need. Performance and cost remain objective measures, but the meaning of "quality" is changing. Quality as reliability, which is an objective attribute of a product, no longer confers competitive advantage. Consumers are learning to take reliability for granted. "Quality" is coming to mean "satisfaction," the subjective response of a customer to owning and using a product.

At the same time, more and more products are being designed to compete in highly diversified global markets. Their design, manufacture, distribution, and servicing are being managed by transnational corporations using globally distributed assets and resources. Increasingly, manufacturing companies are being required to satisfy locally imposed constraints reflecting environmental, safety, and energy efficiency concerns as well as social, political, and economic values; in such an environment, classical forms of vertical integration, attempting to do everything "in house," is a recipe for failure.

An agile enterprise has the organizational flexibility to adopt for each project the managerial vehicle that will yield the greatest competitive advantage. Sometimes this will take the form of an internal cross-functional project team with participation by suppliers and customers. Sometimes it will take the form of a virtual company. The guiding principle of agile enterprise management is not automatic recourse to self-directed work teams or to virtual companies, but full utilization of corporate assets. In a dynamic competitive environment, the key to utilizing assets fully is the workforce. Flexible production technologies and flexible management enable the workforce of agile manufacturing enterprises to implement the innovations they generate. There can be no algorithm for the conduct of such an enterprise; the only competitively viable long-term managerial agenda is providing physical and organizational resources in support of the creativity and initiative of the workforce.

It is a cliché that technological innovation is unpredictable. In the agile manufacturing era, constant innovation in the creation and evolution of products and services, and in the improvement of manufacturing processes, is synonymous with competitive advantage. Agile manufacturing enterprises are able to manage unpredictability by maximizing the scope for human initiative. A knowledgeable workforce, expected to display initiative and provided with the means to exercise it, is the single greatest asset of such an enterprise. Continuous workforce education and continuous growth in the quality of the workforce are therefore long-term investments aggressively pursued by management. The better able every employee is to assimilate information and to respond creatively to new possibilities suggested by it, the more successful the enterprise. This is as true of managers and production line workers as of technical professionals. The involvement of scientists and engineers in strategic planning, as well as in operational activities, is crucial to the agile enterprise. Scientific knowledge of the manufacturing process and coordination of engineering expertise with all phases of product creation and development are central resources.

Everyone in an agile enterprise needs to understand that flexibility transforms the enterprise into a general purpose tool, one whose applications are determined only (and are limited only) by the imaginations of those working with it. Mass production enterprises, with their dedicated manufacturing facilities, are special purpose tools. The limiting factor in mass production is the fixed nature of the manufacturing systems. The agile enterprise, by contrast, has continuously evolving manufacturing systems. Thus the capabilities of the agile manufacturing system are limited by the imagination, creativity, and skills of the workforce, not by equipment.

These characteristics of the agile manufacturing enterprise dictate attitudes toward managing the workforce very different from those prevailing in mass production enterprises. Adversarial relationships between management and employees are insupportable, as are policies of limited access to information about the enterprise and its operations. Information must be open to an unprecedented degree, entailing an atmosphere of trust and of mutual stakeholder relationships. The workplace must not only be safe, but positively attractive to intelligent creative people at every level of the enterprise. Expectations of high levels of employee involvement must be created, sustained, and rewarded, again, at every level, from production line workers to executives. Routine creation of cross-functional project teams and virtual companies poses additional managerial challenges. Elitist organizational values are incompatible with the egalitarian character of project teams. Parochial managerial attitudes, privileging the accomplishments of one's "own" participants in an inter-enterprise collaboration, are incompatible with "best effort" commitments to such collaborations. A new kind of "social contract" between employer and employee is called for. The employee must be tied to the company through mutually perceived long-term benefits that anchor their loyalty in the face of routine participation in projects outside the boundaries of the company as traditionally conceived.

The evolving relationship of U.S. industry to the U.S. economy is similar to the relationship of U.S. agriculture to the economy. Over the past century, agricultural employment has fallen from 60% of the total workforce to 3%, with the bulk of production coming from only a small fraction of that 3%. At the same time, American agriculture's extraordinary productivity is a major contributor to the standard of living Americans enjoy through low food prices and through plentiful and highly varied food supplies. Furthermore, while direct farm labor has shrunk almost to insignificance as a factor in employment, employment in the total food production and supply system—extending over farm machinery, chemicals and services, food processing, new product development, research, distribution, packaging, advertising, marketing, and sales—continues to increase.

Similar to agricultural labor trends, production line labor, even with a resurgent U.S. manufacturing capability, will continue its slow, long-term decline from its peak in the late 1940s. Today, manufacturing employment accounts for approximately 17% of the U.S. workforce. Even as that figure declines further, total empoyment in the agile manufacturing system will grow as personnel are added to the manufacturing enterprise apparatus within which agile production operations are embedded. In addition, the quality of all agile manufacturing jobs, including those in production, will be enhanced by the premium placed on initiative, knowledge, and active involvement by all levels of the manufacturing organization in setting and executing production agenda. Furthermore, as with agriculture, the productivity of agile manufacturing will be central to the quality of American life through the kinds of customer-focused products it will provide and through the value of goods and services that it will contribute to the American economy. A competitive manufacturing system will make a balanced trade account possible; and an agile manufacturing system, developed in coordination with DoD needs, will permit significant savings in the defense procurement budget while retaining military leadership.

It is the overall system, not its individual elements, that generates wealth for society, that creates resources and opportunities, and that affects social institutions, practices, and values. It is a serious mistake, therefore, to infer from declining blue-collar employment the decreasing significance of manufacturing to America's future prosperity. Such an inference ignores the fact that production operations are always embedded in a manufacturing system with a wide range of social ramifications. That was true of mass production, as it was true of earlier craft-based production, and it is true of agile manufacturing as well. The requirement of a more knowledgeable workforce under agile manufacturing than satisfied the needs of mass production has important implications for education. Mass-production factory workers tended relatively inflexible machines. The work was commonly routine, repetitive, and required little initiative or understanding either of the particular job being done or of the wider production scheme into which each job fit. Agile manufacturing, on the other hand, requires that all workers understand the production scheme into which their jobs fit, and that each displays initiative and is routinely capable of changing what he or she does and the way it is done.

If competitive pressures are "pulling" a transformation of manufacturing into existence, it is also the case that social pressures are driving manufacturing in the same direction. Environmental concerns are the most obvious source of pressure, ranging from anxiety over the global impact of manufacturing to local pollution issues. Energy concerns, natural resource depletion, manufacturing workplace safety, and the social impact of manufacturing are drivers second in visibility only to environmental ones. The posture of industrial management toward these manufacturing-related social issues has, until recently, been reactive, treating them as negative externalities to be coped with as they arose. The implementation of a new manufacturing system, more explicitly coupled to a broad range of social institutions and values than mass production manufacturing was, offers an opportunity to adopt a new proactive posture.

In an agile manufacturing environment, it is natural for management to assimilate into the managerial decision-making process the total impact of manufacturing. The concept of manufacturing expands from a narrow focus on production of consumable/disposable goods to the comprehensive process of creating, developing, selling, and maintaining products over their entire life cycles, which for many products will be highly extended by reconfiguration and upgrade capabilities. With this expansion comes a complex set of interdependencies among manufacturers, suppliers, customers, and public institutions that make it advantageous for manufacturers to internalize social drivers rather than have them constrain manufacturing from the outside—for example, from political responses to special interest activism.

The rise to dominance of the mass production system threatened the extinction of small producers who could not, or would not, adopt the production technologies or the managerial structure of the new corporations. The emergence of agile manufacturing, by contrast, enhances opportunities for small businesses through the wider access to their services that a national manufacturing network would allow. The routine formation of virtual companies, as well as of smaller scale electronic alliances, diminishes the attractiveness of single enterprise vertical alliances. The complex of small suppliers, machine shops, and specialty manufacturers that is an internationally acknowledged strength of American industry can in this way be knit into a new national resource. Doing so will require equal access to comprehensive-coverage broad-band communication channels, and the creation of a national industrial data base with uniform data exchange standards for sharing digital engineering drawings and 3-dimensional parts descriptions.

If an agile manufacturing system is to be implemented, many currently held management "truths" need to be unlearned—among them, that cooperation is less desirable than succeeding on one's own; that labor management relations must be adversarial; that information is power and can be shared only to one's detriment; that trust makes one vulnerable; that there are single technological solutions to complex problems; that breakthroughs are the only targets worth aiming at; that markets will appear by themselves once better mousetraps are invented; that infrastructure requirements will take care of themselves once pioneers have thrown up superstructures; that standards are constraining and their formulation dull work; that only parts can be invented, not whole systems.

The task of effecting the transition to a new era in manufacturing is a social task, though one that must be led by industry if it is to be accomplished at all. The transition must be led by industry because only through experience in the new competitive arenas can the requirements of the agile manufacturing system be identified and the effectiveness of mechanisms for meeting them evaluated. Nevertheless, society is a mutual stakeholder in effecting the transition along with industry, and society, too, must anticipate changes in social institutions and in social and personal values. The rise of mass production manufacturing profoundly affected all of the societies adopting that mode of industrialization. The imposition of compulsory public education, the urbanization of populations, the ways people lived, worked, and played, the financial, commercial, legal, and political structures of industrial life, all were influenced to a greater or lesser degree by the implementation of mass production manufacturing as conducted by modern corporations.

The rise of agile manufacturing will exert an analogous social influence. Some of the changes that will take place can be foreseen, at least in part, because they will be deliberate. Some of the changes, perhaps the most profound, cannot be foreseen. With the experience of the Industrial Revolution and of Western societies' responses to it before us as a sobering lesson, the course of wisdom is to move into the industrial future open to learning lessons as far in advance of their social or environmental impact as possible.

Managerial agenda setting, decision-making, and judgments of the scope and relevance of projected innovation activities are social processes. They reflect the reciprocal action of social institutions and values on corporate interests, as well as the influence of corporate interests on social institutions and values. The legal, political, and economic climate, public opinion on a spectrum of issues, and a wide range of conscious and unconscious values all enter into what the management of a particular firm identifies as in the best interests of that firm. Given the competitive challenge that American industry confronts today, together with the opportunity presented by the emergence of agile manufacturing, an understanding of the nature of managerial decision-making is more important than ever before. What we have attempted to suggest here is that innovation policies are crucially dependent on management in two ways: management's judgment of the competitive possibilities latent in available or new technical knowledge, and management's willingness to adapt managerial values and organization to the optimal realization of those possibilities. The notion that new technologies confer competitive advantage through some intrinsic properties they possess is a fundamental misconception. Competitive advantage is created by managerial initiatives that selectively utilize technology in ways that are consistent with the social context of their enterprise and interact synergistically with the enterprise's organizational structure and procedures.

NOTES

This essay incorporates material from the (1991) report *21st Century Manufacturing Enterprise Strategy: An Industry Led View* edited by Steven L. Goldman. The report was partially funded by the Office of the Secretary of Defense Manufacturing Technology Program (U.S. Navy contract #N00014–91–C–0151) through the Iacocca Institute at Lehigh University. The co-principal investigators were Roger N. Nagel and Rick Dove. Copies of the full report can be obtained from the Iacocca Institute, Lehigh University, Bethlehem, PA 18015.

1. This view is developed in detail in Steven L. Goldman, "The Social Captivity of Engineering," in Paul T. Durbin, ed., *Critical Perspectives on Non-Academic Science and Engineering* (Bethlehem, Pa.: Lehigh University Press, 1991), pp. 121–45.

2. The essays in Steven L. Goldman, ed., *Science Technology and Social Progress* (Bethlehem, Pa.: Lehigh University Press, 1991), discuss the relationship between improvement of the human condition and scientific and technological advances. The essays by Hill, Noble, and Staudenmaier are particularly relevant.

3. Jacques Ellul's *The Technological Society* (New York: Knopf, 1964), trans. John Wilkinson, is an important vehicle for the dissemination of this view. So is Langdon Winner's development of Ellul's ideas in *Autonomous Technology* (Cambridge, Mass.: MIT Press, 1977) and Lewis Mumford's *The Myth of the Machine* in two volumes (New York: Harcourt, 1968, 1970).

4. While the discussion in this article focuses on industrial firms, the same characterization of innovation applies equally well to public or private agencies charged with setting an agenda that includes support for scientific research or technological development, for example, the over 700 federal laboratories, as well as such agencies as the National Science Foundation, the Department of Energy, the National Institutes of Health, and the Advanced Technology Program at the National Institute of Standards and Technology.

5. The distinctiveness of engineering problem-solving in relation to physics and mathematics and the nature of engineering design is discussed in Steven L. Goldman, "Philosophy, Engineering and Western Culture," in Paul T. Durbin, ed., *Broad and Narrow Interpretations of Philosophy of Technology* (Dordrecht, Netherlands: Kluwer, 1990), especially pp. 127–32 and notes 8 and 16. The very same sort of considerations apply as well to the solution of the managerial problem of designing a role for technological innovation within a corporation's strategic plan.

6. Ibid., notes 7 and 22.

7. David Noble, *Forces of Production* (New York: Knopf, 1984); Tracy Kidder, *The Soul of a New Machine* (New York: Avon, 1981); Margaret B. W. Graham, *RCA and the Videodisc: The Business of Research* (Cambridge, Mass.: Cambridge University Press, 1986); Peter Temin (with Louis Galambos), *The Fall of the Bell System* (Cambridge: Cambridge University Press, 1987).

8. Thomas Hughes, *Networks of Power* (Baltimore: Johns Hopkins University Press, 1986); Hugh G. Aitken, *The Continuous Wave: Technology and American Radio 1900–1932* (Princeton: Princeton University Press, 1985); I. C. Bupp and J. C. Derian, *Light Water Reactors: How the Nuclear Dream Dissolved* (New York: Basic Books, 1978); Stephen L. Del Sesto, *Science, Politics and Controversy: Civilian Nuclear Power in the United States 1946–1974* (Boulder, Co.: Westview Press, 1979); Joan Lisa Bromberg, *Fusion: Science, Politics and the Invention of a New Energy Source* (Cambridge, Mass.: MIT Press, 1983); Walter McDougall, . . . *the heavens and the Earth: A Political History of the Space Age* (New York: Basic Books, 1985); John Logsdon, *The Decision to Go to the Moon* (Chicago: University of Chicago Press, 1970); 417–24; Sylvia D. Fries, "2001–1994: Political Environment and the Design of NASA's Space Station System," *Technology and Culture* 29 (July 1988): 568–93; Nick Kotz, *Wild Blue Yonder:*

Money, Politics and the B-1 Bomber (New York: Pantheon, 1988); and Patrick Tyler, *Running Critical: The Silent War, Rickover and General Dynamics* (New York: Harper and Row, 1986).

9. Ramchandran Jaikumar, "Post Industrial Manufacturing," *Harvard Business Review* (November/December 1986): 69–76.

10. Alvin Lehnerd, "Revitalizing the Manufacture and Design of Mature Global Products," in Bruce R. Guile and Harvey Brooks, eds., *Technology and Global Industry: Companies and Nations in the World Economy* (Washington, D.C.: National Academy of Engineering Press, 1987), pp. 49–64.

11. Ezra Vogel, *Comeback: Building the Resurgence of American Business* (New York: Simon & Schuster, 1985).

12. *New York Times,* Sunday, 10 November 1991, sec. 3, p. 1; also, Richard G. O'Lone, "777 Revolutionizes Boeing Aircraft Development Process," Michael A. Dornheim, "Computerized Design System Allows Boeing to Skip Building 777 Mockup (CATIA System)," and Philip J. Klass, "New Avionic Concepts Make Debut on Boeing 777," *Aviation Week and Space Technology* 134 (June 1991): 34–35, 50–51, 60–61.

13. Achieving competitive advantage through sharing information that would today be considered proprietary is discussed in the report *21st Century Manufacturing Enterprise Strategy* (see prefatory note above), especially the scenarios "USASICS," pp. 27–32, and the chapter "Cooperation Mechanisms," pp. 43–45.

14. For historical background on the relationship of engineers and their corporate employers, see Edwin T. Layton, Jr., *The Revolt of the Engineers: Social Responsibility and the American Engineering Profession* (Baltimore: Johns Hopkins University Press, 1986). For the subordinate role assigned to engineering and manufacturing in U.S. industry in the 1960s, see "Technology in the Modern Corporation: A Strategic Perspective," a special issue of *Technology in Society* 7, nos. 2 and 3, 1985, Mel Horwitch guest editor.

15. G. Hamel and J. K. Prahalad, "Strategic Intent," *Harvard Business Review* 67, no. 3 (May/June 1989): 63–76.

16. Alfred B. Chandler, Jr., *The Visible Hand: The Managerial Revolution in American Business* (Cambridge, Mass.: Belknap Press, 1977).

17. Among them, *Gaining New Ground: Technology Priorities for America's Future,* (Washington, D.C.: Council on Competitiveness, 1991); *Report of the National Critical Technologies Panel* (Washington, D.C.: Office of Science and Technology Policy, 1991); and *The Department of Defense Critical Technologies Plan* (Washington, D.C.: Department of Defense, 1991).

18. See Michael Hodges' essay in this volume, "Stacking the Deck: The 1992 Single Market Initiative and the Promotion of European Industrial Competitiveness."

19. The major consortia include BRITE (Basic Reserach in Industrial Technologies for Europe), ESPRIT (European Strategic Program for Research and Development in Information Technologies), EUREKA (European Research Coordination Agency), JESSI (Joint European Semiconductor Silicon Initiative), and RACE (Research and Development in Advanced Communication Technologies in Europe).

20. Robert Hall, *Manufacturing 21 Report—The Future of Japanese Manufacturing* (Wheeling, Ill.: Association for Manufacturing Excellence, 1991).

21. Japanese management science is occupied with holonics, a theory of the relationships among parts and wholes in systems composed of distributed autonomous modules. See, for example, Hall, above and I. Suda "Future Factory System

Formulated in Japan (2)," *Techn. Japan* 22 (October 1989). The term "holonics," and an original theory of wholes composed of quasi-independent parts, was presented by Arthur Koestler in *The Ghost in the Machine* (London: Hutchinson, 1967).

22. For a recent review of science and engineering education issues, see the Office of Technology Assessment Report entitled *Educating Scientists and Engineers: Grade School to Grad School* (Washington, D.C.: Government Printing Office, June 1988), 128 pp. For a bibliography of reports on U.S. engineering education from 1919 to 1987, see Steven L. Goldman, "The History of Engineering Education: Perennial Issues in the Supply and Training of Talent," a report prepared for the Office of Technology Assessment (Washington, D.C.: GPO NTIS #PB 88–177 951/AS, 1988).

Technological Leadership and International Competitiveness: A Comparative Approach

GAIL COOPER

Technological leadership is a key element in American competitiveness. Technology has been called "the lever of riches" for its promise of wealth for the individual, the company, or the country that successfully controls it.[1] However, a comparison with Japan suggests that Americans may have put an undue emphasis on invention and technological leadership both at the company level and at the national level. Notable examples suggest that despite continued American technological creativity, U.S. firms have often failed to capitalize economically upon their technological leadership. Despite a strong patent position, they have lost the advantages of technological pioneering when others have been more successful at bringing the product into the market place. In contrast, a great deal of Japan's economic success has come from a fresh approach to manufacturing and production values rather than from patent primacy. These successes are not due to the competitive advantages of a low wage economy but from technological innovation in production. I will take a historical look at the issue of technological leadership in the United States and Japan in the postwar era to discover how the balance between invention and production has developed at the national and the firm level.

It is striking that each country has utilized technology to achieve different national goals. The United States has pursued international political goals and has hoped that domestic economic prosperity and civilian technological leadership will be the by-product. Thus the postwar emphasis on the international containment of communism has led the U.S. government to budget countless dollars for military research and development and for the production of technically sophisticated defense systems in the hope that technological "spin-offs" would also fuel economic growth and new consumer products. In a mirror-image strategy, Japan has pursued economic goals in the belief that they will be the mechanism to implement international political ends. Japan's international vision was discredited by her wartime defeat and a purely defensive military posture written into the Constitution of 1946. As a result, Japan has concentrated on domestic economic growth and foreign exports with the hope that through economic primacy she could forge new ties with her Asian neighbors. Given this great disparity between the guiding force behind each country's technological growth, it can be said that at the national level these two countries have, in one sense, not been competing with one another at all. Clearly, a look at technology policy at the national level in both countries can provide useful insights for the American competitiveness issue.

The management of technology, however, also takes place at the level of the individual firm. Here, too, are intriguing contrasts in the culture of creativity and technological innovation. In the continuum of invention and innovation, Americans have been fascinated by invention and the break-through technology that establishes entirely new industries, while the Japanese have put their efforts into adaptive research and innovation. While this is a generalization with numerous exceptions, it has been through process innovations that Japan has made the most striking contributions. Indeed, through continuous improvements in this area, Japanese companies have developed a new system of production that differs significantly from Henry Ford's mass production. While competing for the same markets, Japan's just-in-time production has changed the paradigm for industrial competition. On the firm level Japanese and American companies are competing intensely for the American consumer market, but a disproportionate reliance on technological leadership has meant that American companies have not always developed the capacity to manufacture sophisticated products. Thus, in certain areas of electronics, for example, Americans no longer try to compete with Japanese firms despite their early lead. This is another way in which the two countries are not competing at all.

Against this historical overview of national policy and culture, I will examine the postwar transfer by American experts and government authorities of the techniques of statistical quality control that have played such an important role in reforming Japanese postwar production methods. This example can perhaps serve as an illustration of the differences between the two countries in their attitudes toward creativity in production technology.

TECHNOLOGY, NATIONAL CULTURE AND INDUSTRIAL POLICY

In the now bulky literature that seeks to explain Japan's postwar "economic miracle," two broad explanations have emerged. One is that Japan's success is due to cultural values that make the Japanese particularly hardworking and mold each individual into a strong and loyal supporter of his company and colleagues. This cultural base at the heart of Japan's economic system has recently been dubbed "Confucian capitalism," and, as an explanatory model, has gained in popularity as it seems relevant for all Asian industrialization. A second group maintains that cultural explanations prevent us from seeing that specific modern policies rather than a centuries-old culture nurtured Japan's economic growth. In their eyes it is the government rather than the individual that is the key actor in Japan's postwar drama. For example, Chalmers Johnson emphasizes the importance of the Ministry of International Trade and Industry (MITI), whose augmentation in power and prestige following the American Occupation allowed the agency to exert a powerful impact on the structure as well as the methods of Japanese industry. Behind the stress on the formulative impact of governmental policies is the idea that concrete policies are much more easily duplicated in a different country.[2]

At the risk of diluting such important insights, one can see clearly that these two views are only different positions on a continuum. Few would deny that governmental policies reflect cultural as well as political values. Both cultural values and governmental policies have shaped the industrial system we now have. Technology is an integral part of that system, equally responsive to politics and culture, and technological leadership is a matter of both attitudes and policies.[3]

Historically, Japanese cultural attitudes toward technology have been mixed. Rather than being a technological leader, Japan has often seen herself as a technological borrower. The Meiji Restoration of 1868 placed in power a group of young leaders who were willing to use western technology as a means of strengthening the country from foreign encroachment. But the ambivalence of the country toward imported technology is captured in a popular slogan of the 1850s which urged the adoption of "Western science and Eastern ethics." Despite this reluctance to accept western technology wholeheartedly, Japan from 1868 to the 1930s was an avid borrower of foreign technology as the basis for both a modern military and a modern industrial sector, shopping selectively to acquire the best of each nation including British engineering.[4]

Generally Japan saw herself as a nation handicapped by a late start in industrialization and playing catch-up against her western rivals. Often this view was self-serving, as when Japanese manufacturers in the interwar period resisted labor reforms on the basis that Japan could not afford the social niceties common to western industrial leaders with whom they had to compete.[5] And sometimes the view was modified by the achievements of Japanese inventors such as Sakichi Toyoda, who perfected a narrow-gauge loom in the 1920s that was subsequently licensed abroad. But against the background of a nation that made tremendous strides in technical sophistication and national strength, Japan's self-identity often continued to encompass elements of the late industrializer who borrowed the necessary tools from abroad and adapted them to Japan's special culture.[6]

Japan's postwar era saw a variation on this theme. After 1945 this nation struggled to overcome the handicap of their humiliating and disastrous military defeat. The country faced the problems of a hungry population swelled by nationals repatriated from an overseas empire, an industry squeezed by the demands of military production and wartime destruction, and a greatly narrowed resource base. Once again, the Japanese felt they had to catch up with the West. One clear solution was a national effort to import modern technology and to export manufactured products to pay for the imports of food and raw resources. Technology thus became an important part of the larger national goal of rebuilding, and the govenrment supervised the importation of new technology.

In contrast, technological inventiveness has long had an important place in American culture. In the early days of the United States' political independence from England, technical creativity was deemed the high art of a practical society, and Americans who liked to contrast the vigor and freedom of the New World to the stultification and stratification of Europe found their artists and scholars in mechanical inventors.[7]

This conviction of a special tie between freedom and creativity that captured the uniqueness of American society appeared in a new form in the postwar era when the United States pitted their technology against that of the Soviet Union—one more venue in which Americans could prove the merits of their political system. The use of American technology to counter the spread of communist political systems had a practical aspect to it. President Harry Truman proposed in his inaugural address in 1949 that American technical assistance overseas could help provide a strong material base on which to build stable democratic governments. Democracy was not likely to flourish among poverty, disease, and isolation. As a consequence, the Point Four Program was established that same year to send American technical experts abroad. In addition, however, technology often took on symbolic importance in the Cold War confrontation. When the Soviets launched the Sputnik satellite in 1957, the response of the United States was not simply to Sputnik's military potential but also to its challenge to the prestige of American science and technology. The space race became an analogous, but not identical, effort to the arms race in which American technology would help establish the primacy of the United States.[8] Thus technological leadership in the national culture, from the national period through the post-World War II era, has been seen as the proof of the vigor and wisdom of our social and political system.

In these two countries, the nations have a very different historical relationship to technology. In the United States, technology is the blossom of the native democratic culture; in Japan, it is the pathway to participation in a larger international culture. However, it would be a mistake to characterize all American technology as native and all Japanese technology as imported. The United States borrowed or stole the technology for her own industrial revolution from Europe, particularly from England. Despite sweeping British laws that forbade the export of advanced machinery or the emigration of skilled craftsmen, the United States smuggled machine parts on successive packets and seduced workmen with jobs and bonuses to begin her own textile and machine industries in the late 1700s.[9] Similarly, in contrast to the nation's tradition as a borrower, Japan has enjoyed the creative achievements of talented men like Sakichi Toyoda, Soichiro Honda, and Masaru Ibuka.[10]

Each country's strengths should not be taken as its limits. Michael Adas has shown that nineteenth- and early twentieth-century thinkers enshrined technology as the distinguishing characteristic of a higher western culture, which many endowed with a racial basis as well. The railroad symbolized that superiority, and its evident power as it passed among colonial peoples seemed convincing proof of the argument. But the remarkable success of Japan's industrialization, as symbolized by the defeat of China in 1894 and

Russia in 1905, challenged that belief. Gustave Le Bon, a late nineteenth-century theorist of colonialism, fell back upon the assertion that though the Europeans might be outproduced or undersold, they retained a unique capacity for invention and scientific discovery. The colonialist and racist history of the belief that technological creativity distinguishes eastern and western cultures should alert us to the probability that, while modern Japan has shown a particular talent for adaptive research and production innovations, Americans would be mistaken to suppose that adaptation is the limit of Japan's capabilities.[11]

Just as technology has different meanings in different cultures, technology has also been handled very differently by each government. In the postwar era, Japan's bureaucracy inherited the power that had been concentrated in the hands of Occupation authorities, and powerful ministries like MITI became influential policy makers. Johnson has distinguished between the United States' "regulatory" industrial policy, which is essentially prohibitive, and Japan's "developmental" industrial policy, which characteristically consists of positive incentives. Industrial policy in Japan is marked not simply by the encouragement of all industry but by the Ministry's willingness to target new industries that they perceive to be important for Japan's future growth. The first effort to shape Japan's industrial structure came in the 1950s when MITI decided to build Japan's economic basis not on labor intensive industries, which might have been the most obvious choice, but on heavy chemical industrialization.[12]

Ministry officials have worked not only to shape the structure of Japanese industry but also to blunt the destructive effects of excessive competition. They often felt that a weakened Japan could ill afford the degree of domestic competition that Occupation officials promoted when they sponsored the passage of the Anti-Monoploy Act and established the Fair Trade Commission to enforce it. Soon after Japan achieved its postwar independence, MITI sponsored the first rationalization cartels among struggling textile firms who could not find markets to support their increased capacity at the end of U.S. government contracts for Korean war supplies. Through the fifties, sixties, and seventies, MITI promoted mergers in several industries—successfully in steel, less successfully in automobiles, where several companies stubbornly resisted MITI policy—to increase economies of scale and decrease excessive domestic competition.

Competition in Japan since the war has often taken on the characteristics of insider versus outsider. Clearly, until international

pressure forced Japan to sponsor a series of economic liberalization measures in the early 1960s, which loosened restrictive capital
and trade regulations, Japan erected a number of protective barriers around domestic firms, at the same time placing heavy emphasis on foreign exports and international competition.[13] This is one
aspect of the insider versus outsider competitive stance.

In addition, the effect of Japan's developmental industrial policy
has led to similar domestic distinctions by reinforcing the *keiretsu*
structure of postwar industry. *Keiretsu* are business groupings, coordinated at the top by a bank, that have in some cases informally
reunited the interfirm ties of the old *zaibatsu*. Firms within the
keiretsu are tied to together through the sharing of lucrative contracts and management expertise, and through joint stockholding.
A large percentage of business is kept within the group. Thus Japanese firms take a cooperative approach to business within the *keiretsu,* but a more highly competitive stance to companies in other
groups. The inter-*keiretsu* competition intensifies when the government offers rapid depreciation, cheap financing, and new construction subsidies to firms entering new technological areas, because
each group feels it must have an entrant in the competition for
these government incentives. Thus, new high-tech firms are
spawned within the *keiretsu* with easy access to the capital and
management expertise of established firms as part of the domestic
insider/outsider competitive structure.[14]

The postwar importation of foreign technology was shaped by
these attitudes and institutions. Through their power to approve
foreign currency exchanges, all applications for the importation of
new technology was controlled by MITI. The ministry's handling
of licenses for foreign technology showed a similar concern with
limiting competition in terms of technology. Foreign exchange was
not used to pay for the same technology twice; that is, for a second
company also to acquire similar rights within the introductory period. MITI's typical pattern was to select a strong company as the
sole importer of a new technology in its introductory stages. That
domestic monopoly assured the favored company easy access to
the loans necessary to implement their rights. Increasingly, the
technologies that Japanese companies licensed required substantial
capital outlays to implement, and their temporary domestic monop-
ogy assured them of favorable decisions on bank loans. MITI allowed duplicate technologies to be licensed, after a few years, to
competing firms.[15]

Japan's domestic policies identifying the rebuilding of industry
as a primary national goal profoundly influenced international rela-

tions. Japan was a loyal supporter of United States anticommunist policies in the Far East throughout the Cold War era despite their disagreements over the policy of economic isolation of the People's Republic of China. Yet as Japan developed independent international goals, resource diplomacy increasingly began to dominate Japan's foreign relations. With few of the natural resources necessary to pursue industrial growth, international diplomacy was important in securing access to both markets and resources. Rather than forge a special relationship with a few Asian neighbors, Japan followed the strategy of spreading her resource dependence over a number of foreign sources. Sometimes war reparations and foreign aid were tied to domestic credits to facilitate Japan's goals. She pursued the domestic goal of industrial growth with the hope that her economic strength would facilitate favorable relations with foreign countries.[16]

Despite the continued importance of technological creativity to our national identity, the United States has not had a coherent technology policy or industrial policy that promotes technological research and development for the consumer economy in the post-World War II era. That is not to say that the development of technology is independent of governmental policy. Instead, the development of technology has been greatly influenced by government policies that have been formulated to achieve disparate goals. The result is the existence of an ad hoc technology policy consisting of the combined effects of patent policies, tax measures, national security export restrictions, health and safety legislation, and environmental regulations, on the one hand, and national defense spending on the other. While the former shape the regulatory climate for new technologies, the latter has all the positive power of massive government spending. In the sense that it provides incentives rather than disincentives, national defense spending most nearly equates to Japanese developmental policy. In the postwar period, then, the United States' ad hoc technology policy has been dominated by strategic concerns and the drive to contain communism.

Without a self-conscious industrial policy, American technology has been shaped willy-nilly, influenced by larger government programs of which technology has played an important part. The nation's foreign policy—defense, international prestige, and third-world development, all aimed at the defeat of communism—became technology policy in the absence of an independent industrial viewpoint. The influence upon the technical community of government defense contracts was magnified not only by the absence of

similar civilian incentives but also by the vastly increased scale of
government spending. Research and development expenditures by
the federal government rose from $74 million in 1940 to $15.9 billion in 1966.[17] Critics charge that after 1945 the United States entered a permanent wartime economy.[18]

The United States' massive defense spending has often been justified in terms of the creation of "spin-off" technologies suitable
for commercial development. Yet defense-financed projects have
produced patents at a very low rate. From 1951 to 1956 defense-
financed R&D represented more than half of all corporate R&D
activity, but military R&D accounted for only 4% of all patent
applications in the United States in the same period.[19] The efficacy
of spin-offs from military research and development as engines of
economic growth came under public questioning as early as 1962.
After critical articles appeared in such public forums as the *Harvard Business Review* and the *New York Times Magazine,* the
United States National Commission on Technology, Automation
and Economic Progress took up the issue in 1965. The transfer
of technology from federally-funded programs to the commercial
sector became an explicit goal of the U. S. Congress, written into
the enabling legislation of some agencies and strengthened by annual Congressional hearings on appropriations. The four principal
technology transfer programs were found in the Atomic Energy
Commission, the National Aeronautics and Space Administration,
the Department of Commerce, and the Department of Agriculture.
Of these programs, the Department of Agriculture was the oldest
and most successful. Their Cooperative Extension Program, established by the Smith-Lever Act of 1914, created a network of county
agricultural agents whose responsibilities included bringing scientific research to the individual farmer. The youngest of the technology transfer programs was NASA's Technology Utilization
Program (TUP), established in 1963, which was only marginally
successful. Studies showed that reporting of new patents from contracting firms was low, and TUP continued to be primarily a response to political pressure as "a device for partial justification of
NASA R&D funding, rather than as a technical program in its own
right."[20]

One characteristic of government spending has been its high concentration both in the number of industries receiving federal funds
and in the number of companies within those industries that gain
federal contracts. For example, in 1969, 82% of all industrial research and development expenditures took place in five industries:
aerospace, electrical equipment and communications, chemicals,

machinery, and motor vehicles.[21] That concentration profoundly influenced the kinds of commercial technologies that emerged, leading logically to large computers, supersonic aircraft, and nuclear reactors. In 1966 the President's Commission on Technology, Automation and Economic Progress complained that too little was being spent by the government for research and development in urban transportation, housing, and pollution control.[22] Defense spending as an engine for economic growth, then, has proven to be inefficient and as an agent of social change it has been unresponsive.

PRODUCTION VERSUS INVENTION

While commercial firms may maintain their competitiveness through patent control, price advantage or monopolistic power in the area of military technology, technological innovation is the only effective key to leadership. That perception underlay the escalation of the arms race between the United States and the Soviet Union that characterized the Cold War period.[23] In fact, it may be that technological leadership is more a strategic imperative than a commercial one. The defense-tinted lenses through which the United States has viewed technology since World War II may have made it easier to conflate the needs of the military and the business community. While invention provides an enormous potential for the prosperity of individual companies, the disproportionate emphasis on new products rather than new production methods that has characterized postwar American industry may have limited the ability of U.S. companies to garner the benefits of their technological creativity.

Once a dominant design for a new product emerges, the originator is vulnerable to competition from follower firms whose own production efficiencies enable them to compete on the basis of price.[24] This concept describes the relationship between many U.S. and Japanese firms in the postwar period. U.S. firms were willing sellers of technology and the Japanese were eager buyers. From 1951 to 1961, payments by Japanese companies for patent licenses and know-how increased over 30% each year.[25] Foreign firms were willing to license their patents to Japanese companies for a number of reasons: the ready availability of alternate suppliers in international industry, the barriers put up by the Japanese government against effective exploitation of patents by foreign companies, the lack of skills to exploit their patents in an unfamiliar market, the perception that real competition came from domestic rivals, and that foreign licensing represented windfall profits. American firms sometimes added to this list their conviction that the rate of technological innovation was so rapid that any licensee would be competing with old technology within a short period.[26] Receipts for the sale of technology by U.S. firms increased from $711 million in 1961 to $2,465 million in 1971.[27] American firms put their faith in continual invention rather than efficient production.

American companies have been prone to place a greater emphasis on new products rather than new production methods. A survey in the early 1960s found that 47% of firms reported the purpose of their research and development was to develop new products, 40% to improve existing products, and only 13% to develop new processes.[28] Among companies conducting both private and government-funded R&D, the emphasis on product versus process was marked; indeed, most cited new product opportunities as the primary motivation for taking on government-funded research and development.[29]

In contrast, Japan has been notably successful with adaptive research and production innovations. The most famous of these is the pull-system or the "just-in-time" system of production.[30] The pull-system of manufacturing was given only a brief trial in U.S. aircraft manufacture during World War II before it was picked up and brought to fruition by Toyota engineer Ono Taiichi from 1947 to 1975. Sometimes called the *kanban* system of production for the re-order cards that regulate the flow of materials through the assembly or production process, it represents a virtual reinvention of Ford's assembly line. While Ford's original line regulated the pace of the work by pushing automobiles through the factory as they became available (a push-system of production), Ono's variation pulled parts through the system as workers needed them (a pull system, also called a market basket approach). Workers ordered parts or materials as they finished one batch by returning the *kanban* attached to the completed batch. Management regulated the pace of work by determining the number of *kanban* in circulation.

Ono instituted this new system to reduce the costs and delays associated with supply. A push-system left excess supplies to clog the factory or a missing part to bring production to a halt. In dealing with outside suppliers, Toyota's experience was that a delay in the arrival of a large shipment of parts could idle the factory for half the month while the timely delivery of large batches cost the company in warehousing fees. The logical solution was an extension of the pull-system to subcontractors as well. Toyota's suppliers began to make frequent small deliveries of parts as needed, giving the *kanban* system the alternative name "just-in-time" production.

Toyota's talented engineer also pioneered alternative strategies to American-style mass production. The century-old feeling among Japanese industrialists, that western approaches to industry that had been conceived from a position of strength were not always applicable to a small late developer like Japan, led Ono to devise methods for economies that were less dependent on scale. Specifically, he wanted to achieve variety in the styles of automobiles produced without relying on long runs to keep the costs down. He achieved his goal by handling machine tools differently. He greatly reduced the downtime associated with changes in dies and increased the number and variety of machine tools per worker. This flexible production allowed Toyota to extend their demand-driven production approach to the arena of customer relations. By coordinating automobile orders with factory output, a coordination made possible by frequent retooling of the production line, few completed cars were left to clog dealers' small lots. Cars were produced as needed.

This innovation suggests that it is not simply what the Japanese produce but how they produce it that has led to their success. Japan's success has come less from path-breaking inventions than from innovative engineering design and efficient production technologies. In postwar Japan cultural creativity and economic success centered on innovation rather than invention. Japan's success with engineering innovations and production technologies offers us a new pattern of industrial production. "Flexible production" or "lean production," as Japanese manufacturing is sometimes called, seems better suited to modern demands. The success of Japanese manufacturing allows historians to recognize better historical examples of flexible production that provide alternatives to mass production. The Japanese example is not unique but simply calls our attention to a different style of production.

THE CASE OF QUALITY CONTROL

The transfer of technology to Japan in the cold war era was shaped by the United States' concern with an anticommunist international policy. The Occupation Army, in fact, changed its policy toward the recovery and modernization of Japanese industry with the outbreak of tensions in Korea. Initially, Occupation policy aimed at keeping the Japanese standard of living at a level not to exceed that of the Asian victims of Japanese aggression. In the same vein, the Pauley Commission in 1946 recommended dismantling Japanese industrial plants and shipping them abroad as reparations.

As the United States built a political and economic bloc to oppose communism, governmental help in rebuilding Japanese industry increased substantially. No longer was the rebuilding of Japanese industry aimed at democratization or demilitarization. With the outbreak of war in Korea Japan served as a convenient supplier of war material. Numerous military contracts were given to Japanese industry at a time when outdated plants made their products expensive and uncompetitive internationally.[31] In addition, the Japan Productivity Center sent numerous small groups of academics, business executives, managers, and engineers on tours of American plants to foster the ready transfer of American know-how and technology—with the U.S. government providing foreign exchange credits. America's decision to build Japan into the keystone of American anticommunist policy in the Far East greatly affected technology policy. Just as at home, the United States harnessed industry and technology in Japan to the service of its international political goals.

This famous "reverse course" in United States policy in Japan, which traded sweeping democratic reforms for political stability on the one hand, and demilitarization and decentralization for industrial efficiency on the other, provided an encouraging climate for the transfer of American production technology to Japanese industry. Statistical quality control was one such important production technique. The history of Japanese attempts to apply statistical quality control was short and unpromising. Experiments in statistical quality control were first tried by Japanese manufacturers of light bulbs independent of American influence, followed by some less-than-successful applications in the manufacture of dry batteries, bearings, and aircraft during World War II. The greatest success came about following the promotional efforts of the Occupation government.

Statistical quality control encompasses a wide array of statistical techniques, including control charts, Pareto diagrams, histograms, sampling, and so on, with a variety of uses. The greatest benefit derived from statistical quality control is not in the final inspection, when defective products are rejected, but rather in its application to process control and analysis of data. Statistical process control is based on the premise that random variations in the manufacture of any part are inevitable and little can be done to prevent them. The key to quality manufacture is to pinpoint when, where, and why defective parts are being systematically produced due to identifiable causes. A misaligned machine, bad materials, or a poorly trained workman might be responsible for the production of systematic errors. Successive applications of statistical tests can help the company identify when, where, and why defects creep into their products, and that information forms a basis for corrective action.

Because it pushes the concern with quality back into the manufacturing stage, process control can save a company the material and labor wasted in assembling a product with a defective part. Statistical quality control, therefore, benefits the company by eliminating sloppy manufacturing, while final inspection simply shields the consumer from its effects. It is easy to see how statistical quality control was used to produce a cheaper product invariably consistent with its design. Japanese manufacturers have utilized that consistency to produce both inexpensive transistor radios and expensive luxury automobiles.

Statistical quality control is American in origin but was never widely adopted in postwar United States industry. It was the product of AT&T's Bell Laboratories' Walter Shewhart, who in May 1924 first articulated his ideas about the control chart. Shewhart and his colleagues in the inspection engineering department developed a number of statistical techniques that included both acceptance sampling methods and production control. Statistical quality control found a congenial atmosphere within AT&T. The special relationship between AT&T and Western Electric, their manufacturing arm, meant that imposing new standards for acceptance procedures was relatively easy, and the expertise for training inspectors in the new techniques was readily available. Indicative of that close working relationship was the formation of a Special Committee on Inspection Statistics composed jointly of Bell Lab and Western Electric staff to establish the new inspection techniques at Western Electric's Hawthorne plant in 1926.[32]

Shewhart promoted the spread of statistical quality control throughout American industry. In 1929, under the auspices of the National Academy of Sciences, he organized a joint committee of the American Society of Testing Materials, the American Society of Mechanical Engineers, the American Mathematical Society, and the American Statistical Association for the development of statistical applications in engineering and manufacturing. Despite his enthusiasm, however, statistical quality control did not spread widely in U.S. industry. Curious visitors who came to the plant did not believe that the new techniques were applicable to production outside the telephone industry.

Perhaps the most notable exception to this neglect was the adoption of Shewhart's concepts by U.S. Army Ordnance. Beginning in 1936, Shewhart worked as a consultant on ammunition specifications for the War Department and, through the advocacy and enthusiasm of Lt. Col. Leslie E. Simon, statistical methods were adopted first at Picatinney Arsenal and then at Aberdeen Proving Ground. With the outbreak of World War II, the inevitable conflict between quality and quantity loomed very large. No one wanted to contemplate the effect of substandard equipment upon American soldiers on the front lines, yet the percentage of defects ran up to 80% in factories that manufactured unfamiliar parts with an inexperienced labor force. Statistical quality control enjoyed a brief popularity in American industry during the war because the use of the process control chart in manufacturing insured goods of a consistent quality and boosted production by eliminating scrap and rework. Its effectiveness was recognized by a small but influential group of academics, military officers, and AT&T personnel who used the persuasive device of government contracts to insist on new ways for American industry to measure quality. Government purchasers of war material practiced acceptance sampling of goods, and through that mechanism promoted process control charts. They then attempted to use their power of acceptance to reform production processes.

Despite the army's influence, industry resisted applied statistics as impractical. It required the practical example of a successful West Coast training program to convince the Office of Production Research and Development in 1943 to establish industrial training programs. Two aircraft manufacturers chalked up substantial savings and provided persuasive evidence that statistical quality control could be effective. Lockheed Corporation estimated that they saved $10 million annually on one operation alone, and Vega Corporation reduced its inspection force on several operations by 80%.[33] Industrial engineering instructors Profs. Holbrook Working, Eugene Grant, and W. Edwards Deming were successful by selling the benefits of statistical methods to the participants at the same time that they taught the technical skills. The wartime training courses produced quality control inspectors who provided the nucleus for a postwar professional organization. These middle-level experts struggled against great apathy to secure an important place in American industrial production.

After the war, however, most American industry dropped their quality control programs along with their government contracts. Deming came to believe that the failure of statistical quality control was due to the isolated position of middle-level statistical experts caught between the apathy of senior executives and the resistance of factory workers. Most managers were mainly interested in special causes of variation, that is, those instances in which the blame for defective products could be placed specifically at the door of labor. Common causes of variation, those variables outside the control of workers and for which only management bore the responsibility, were not given the attention they deserved. Shewhart's methods had been introduced into an American system of adversarial relationships between management and labor and they suffered accordingly.

If the missionary efforts of this small influential elite of statistical quality control experts failed to convert American industry, they had a second chance in the postwar period in occupied Japan. The initial statements of Occupation policy reflected the American hard line. "Members of the Manufacturing Branch are under no circumstances to assist management by advising as to, or imparting information on improved production techniques or processes," an early memo declared.[34] The quality of Japanese manufactured goods soon became a major concern of the Occupation government. In June of 1947 Frank Jewett, director of Bell Laboratories and president of the National Academy of Sciences, appointed a Scientific Advisory Group that included William Coolidge, former director of research for General Electric, to evaluate Japanese science and technology and to advise the Supreme Commander of the Allied Powers (SCAP). Not surprisingly, given its origins and personnel, the report of the committee in the spring of 1948 heavily emphasized the importance of science to technology and the industrial research laboratory to industrial production. After pointing out that Japan was attempting to feed a greatly increased repatriated population without access to former overseas resources through imported food, the Advisory Group wondered how those imports were to be paid for given Japan's reputation for poor quality manufactured goods.

Soon the Occupation Army became the conduit for introducing statistical quality control technique into Japanese industry. Occupation experts were often AT&T personnel on loan, and as the ban on improving Japanese production techniques was gradually set aside their suggestions often reflected Western Electric practices. Had Japanese industry modelled itself on general American practice it is uncertain if statistical quality control would have been among Japan's borrowings, but the Occupation government drew heavily upon American ideals for inspiration and upon American experts for techniques. W. S. Magil of Western Electric and Homer M. Sarasohn introduced quality control at Nihon Denki Kaisha in the manufacture of vacuum tubes in 1948.[35]

In 1950, at SCAP's urging, the Union of Japanese Scientists and Engineers (JUSE) invited Deming to Japan to lecture on statistical quality control to a broader segment of Japanese industry. After the first lecture to middle managers, however, he had a sinking feeling that his efforts would not succeed, that he was talking to the wrong group of people. Anxious to avoid the twin pitfalls of apathy by senior executives and misuse of the techniques against workers, Deming presented his next lecture to members of the *Keidanren,* Japan's most powerful manufacturers' association. When Deming donated his honorarium to establish two prizes for the best new theory and the best application in Japanese industry, he effectively launched statistical quality control as an independent Japanese concern. By October 1957 nearly 38,000 people had received at least ten hours of training outside of their company.[36] Deming's plea for the support of top executives paved the way for the success of management consultant and former Western Electric manager Joseph Juran in 1954. Juran advocated company-wide statistical quality control, a concern with quality throughout the company. These American experts found a much more receptive audience for industrial reform in Japan than they did in the United States.

Statistical quality control was important to Japanese firms because it recast the company's relationships with its customers, it suppliers, and its workers. By improving the quality of Japanese manufactures, it allowed Japan to succeed in new markets. As important as export credits were to the nation in the 1950s, foreign markets became increasingly important to Japanese manufacturers in the early 1960s when trade liberalization threatened their international competitiveness. Many manufacturers explicitly chose quality as one issue on which to base their international exports. Second, statistical quality control facilitated the cooperative relationship between contractors and subcontractors, which is at the heart of "just-in-time" production, by setting agreements on standards and methods. Only such explicit technical linkage between firms could cope with the increasingly complex technology. Just as the U.S. military had used acceptance sampling as a lever to improve production processes, large Japanese firms who were pioneers in statistical quality control used the dependency of small subcontractors to insist not only on standard levels of quality but also on consistent production methods. Third, statistical quality control led to each Japanese worker's becoming a "factory expert" by giving him the analytical tools with which to improve his own performance. While the general direction of American industrial management such as Taylorism has contributed to the deskilling of factory workers, statistical quality control as it is practiced in Japanese quality control circles enriches the skills of workers. Japan has tried to maintain a healthy manufacturing sector in a mature industrial economy by capitalizing on a highly skilled work force. The adoption of statistical quality control in postwar Japan illustrates the Japanese emphasis on improving production over invention and the benefits to be gained from that approach.

CONCLUSION

The United States is now emerging from an era in which Cold War concerns dominated many aspects of our culture and politics. Americans' concern with "international competitiveness" since 1945 has consisted, more often than not, of worrying about the struggle for the hearts and minds of third world developing countries. That political struggle has reemphasized Americans' long-standing cultural attachment to invention, for technological leadership has become the mainstay of military strategy. The American pride in technological inventiveness is not misplaced, but a look at Japan's success with adaptive research and production excellence suggests that a reliance on that historical legacy for economic competitive advantage may be. Clearly, a balance between inventive creativity and manufacturing innovation provides the strongest base for international competitiveness. Technology has caught the attention of government decision makers only in its relationship to U.S. international policy and national defense. In the absence of a national industrial policy for economic competitiveness, American technology policy has responded to the positive incentives of national defense spending. A look at the history of technology transfer between the United States and Japan in the postwar years clearly shows how technology responded to the push of American concern with foreign policy and the pull of Japanese concern with production innovation.

NOTES

1. Joel Mokyr, *The Lever of Riches: Technological Creativity and Economic Progress* (New York: Oxford University Press, 1990).
2. Chalmers Johnson, *MITI and the Japanese Miracle: The Growth of Industrial Policy, 1925–1975* (Stanford: Stanford University Press, 1982), and *The Industrial Policy Debate* (San Francisco: ICS Press, 1984).
3. The essential connection between values and policy has been made in Ezra Vogel and George C. Lodge, eds., *Ideology and National Competitiveness: An Analysis of Nine Countries* (Boston: Harvard Business School Press, 1987).
4. For the role of foreign experts in Japan's modernization, see Hazel J. Jones, *Live Machines: Hired Foreigners and Meiji Japan* (Vancouver: 1980); Ardath W. Burks and Clark Beck, Jr., eds., *Aspects of Meiji Modernization: The Japan Helpers and the Helped* (New Brunswick, N.J.: Rutgers University Press, 1983); Ardath W. Burks, ed., *The Modernizers: Overseas Students, Foreign Employees and Meiji Japan* (Boulder, Colo.: Westview Press, 1985); and Akira Iriye and Edward Beauchamp, eds., *Foreign Employees in Nineteenth Century Japan* (Boulder, Colo.: Westview Press, 1990).
5. For business ideology see Byron K. Marshall, *Capitalism and Nationalism in Prewar Japan: The Ideology of the Business Elite, 1868–1941* (Stanford: Stanford University Press, 1967).
6. For a brief discussion of adaptation of western technology to Japanese condition, see Ryoshin Minami, *Powerful Revolution in the Industrialization of Japan, 1885–1940* (New York: Kinokuniya, 1987).
7. For American values toward technology, see John Kasson, *Civilizing the Machine: Technology and Republican Values in America, 1776–1900* (New York: Grossman, 1976).
8. For a discussion of the relationship between international prestige and the United States space program, see Walter A. McDougall, . . . *The Heavens and the Earth: A Political History of the Space Age* (New York: Basic Books, 1985); J. M. Logsdon, *The Decision to Go to the Moon: Project Apollo and the National Interest* (Cambridge, Mass.: MIT Press, 1970); and V. Van Dyke, *Pride and Power: The Rationale of the Space Program* (Urbana: University of Illinois Press, 1964).
9. For the smuggling of machinery out of England, see David J. Jeremy, "Damning the Flood: British Government Efforts to Check the Outflow of Technicians and Machinery, 1780–1843," *Business History Review* 51 (Spring 1977): 1–34.
10. For the contributions of Japan's own inventors, see Michael A. Cusumano, *The Japanese Automobile Industry: Technology and Management at Nissan and Toyota* (Cambridge, Mass.: Harvard University Press, 1985); Tetsuo Sakiya, *Honda Motor: The Men, the Management, the Machines* (Tokyo: Kodansha International, 1982); and Akio Morita, *Made in Japan: Akio Morita and Sony* (London: Fontana Paperbacks, 1987).
11. For a fascinating discussion of Japan's first challenge to Western industrial supremacy, see Michael Adas, *Machines ad the Measure of Men: Science, Technology and Ideologies of Western Dominance* (Ithaca: Cornell University Press, 1989).
12. Chalmers, *MITI.*

13. Merton Peck, "Technology," in Hugh Patrick and Henry Rosovsky, eds., *Asia's New Giant: How the Japanese Economy Works* (Washington,D.C.: Brookings Institution, 1976); Terutomo Ozawa, *Japan's Technological Challenge to the West, 1950–1974: Motivation and Accomplishment* (Cambridge, Mass.: MIT Press, 1974); and Johnson, *MITI.*

14. Peck, "Technology," and Johnson, *MITI.*

15. For the policies governing postwar importation of technology, see Terutomo Ozawa, *Japan's Technological Challenge to the West: Motivation and Accomplishment* (Cambridge, Mass.: MIT Press, 1974).

16. For Japan's use of foreign aid and technical assistance to bolster her international economic position, see Sukehiro Hasegawa, *Japanese Foreign Aid: Policy and Practice* (New York: Praeger, 1975).

17. Samuel I. Doctors, *The Role of Federal Agencies in Technology Transfer* (Cambridge, Mass.: MIT Press, 1969), 10.

18. For the effect of the continuance of high levels of defense spending, see Seymour Melman, *The Permanent War Economy: American Capitalism in Decline* (New York: Simon & Schuster, 1974).

19. Merton Peck and Frederic M Scherer, *The Weapons Aquisition Process: An Economic Analysis* (Cambridge, Mass.: Harvard University Graduate School of Business Administration, Division of Research, 1962), 215–16 as quoted in Peck, "Technology."

20. Samuel I. Doctors, *The Role of Federal Agencies in Technology Transfer* (Cambridge, Mass.: MIT Press, 1969), 161. See also Doctors, *The NASA Technology Transfer Program: An Evaluation of the Dissemination System* (New York: Praeger, 1971).

21. Edwin Mansfield, "The Contribution of R&D to Economic Growth in the United States," *Science* 175 (4 February 1972): 480.

22. Mansfield, "Contributions of R&D."

23. For a discussion of the impact of changing technology and strategic advantage, see Henry M. Sapolsky, "Science, Technology and Military Policy," in Ina Spiegel-Rosing and Derek de Solla Price, eds., *Science, Technology and Society: A Cross Disciplinary Perspective* (Beverly Hills, Calif.: Sage Publications, 1977), 443–72.

24. See David Teece, "Capturing Value from Technological Innovation: Integration, Strategic Partnering, and Licensing Decision," in Bruce R. Guile and Harvey Brooks, eds., *Technology and Global Industry: Companies and Nations in the World Economy* (Washington, D.C.: National Academy Press, 1987), 65–95.

25. Peck, "Technology," 525–85.

26. Terutomo Ozawa, *Japan's Technological Challenge to the West, 1950–1974: Motivation and Accomplishment* (Cambridge, Mass.: MIT Press, 1974).

27. Peck, "Technology."

28. Mansfield, "Contributions of R&D."

29. Guy Black, "The Effect of Government Funding on Commercial R and D," in William H. Gruber and Donald G. Marquis, eds., *Factors in the Transfer of Technology* (Cambridge, Mass.: MIT Press, 1969), 202–18.

30. For the new production methods associated wtih Toyota, see James P. Womack, *The Machine That Changed the World* (New York: Rawson Association, 1990); Japan Management Association, ed., *Kanban: Just-in-time at Toyota* (Stanford, Conn.: Productivity Press, 1986); Michael A. Cusumano, *The Japanese Automobile Industry: Technology and Management at Nissan and Toyota*

(Cambridge, Mass.: Harvard University Press, 1985); and Taiichi Ono, *Toyota Production System: Beyond Large-Scale Production* (Cambridge: Productivity Press, 1978).

31. Johnson, *MITI*. See also Peck, "Technology."

32. H. F. Dodge to R. L. Jones, 14 November 1927, Inspection Methods-Case 18015-2, AT&T Archives 32.

33. W. E. Deming to Stuart A. Rice, 18 September 1943, National Archives, RG 12, E219, box 9.

34. J. S. Bail, 20 February 1946, National Archives, RG 331, box 3190b.

35. "Quality Control in Japan," *Report on Statistical Applications Research, JUSE,* 6 (Special Issue 1959): 1–54.

36. "Quality Control in Japan," 6.

Part III
Competitiveness and
Social Values

Competitiveness as Propaganda

EDWARD P. MORGAN
and
ROBERT E. ROSENWEIN

> In capitalist democracies, there is a certain tension with regard
> to the locus of power. In a democracy the people rule, in prin-
> ciple. But decision-making power over central areas of life re-
> sides in private hands, with large-scale effects throughout the
> social order. One way to resolve the tension would be to extend
> the democratic system to investment, the organization of work,
> and so on. That would constitute a major social revolution,
> which, in my view at least, would consummate the political
> revolutions of an earlier era and realize some of the libertarian
> principles on which they were partly based. Or the tension
> could be resolved, and sometimes is, by forcefully eliminating
> public interference with state and private power. In the ad-
> vanced industrial societies the problem is typically approached
> by a variety of measures to deprive democratic political struc-
> tures of substantive content, while leaving them formally intact.
> A large part of this task is assumed by ideological institutions
> that channel thought and attitudes within acceptable bounds,
> deflecting any potential challenge to established privilege and
> authority before it can take form and gather strength.
> —Noam Chomsky, *Necessary Illusions:*
> *Thought Control in Democratic Societies*
> (1989, vii)

United States competitiveness is an entirely valid and important
concern in the twilight years of the Pax Americana. In the past
twenty years, the United States' share of world markets has declined, its status has changed from a creditor to a debtor nation,
and arenas of production once dominated by American-owned
companies (for example, microelectronics, automobiles) are no
longer so. In response to what has become known as the "competitiveness issue," a variety of positions and solutions as to the best

course of action have been proposed, and many of these will be explored in other papers in this volume.

Our focus in this paper is different. It is our contention that the arguments made about competitiveness act as propaganda—that is, as means of advancing the interests and goals of organizations with which the propagandist identifies. In propaganda, interests are advanced in two ways. First, implications of the argument that might alienate certain publics are obscured. Second, the propagandist seeks to mobilize action or win passive support while inhibiting the critical capacity to form independent thought and judgement. In the first instance, propaganda differs from simple persuasion in that intent is hidden. In the second, propaganda is anti-educational (and by implication, anti-democratic) because its function is to suppress rather than stimulate critical capacity. The term "propaganda" carries with it a connotation of conscious intent to manipulate an audience. However, we make no claim that individuals taking part in the competitiveness debate understand or are conscious of the extent to which their comments are propaganda. What we are concerned about is the potential *effects* of propaganda in a democracy, whether those employing propaganda understand these effects or not.

After examining propaganda analysis in more detail, we will consider four approaches to the "American competitiveness problem" and show how each of these acts as propaganda. The four are: (1) a "micro-competitive" perspective in which certain business leaders, firms, or declining sectors advocate greater productivity, innovation, or managerial competence; (2) a "macro-competitive" perspective in which declining sectors of the U.S. economy, or their political representatives, call for governmental intervention to preserve or strengthen these sectors; (3) a "macro-competitive" perspective in which transnational corporations address ways that public policy should meet the stresses of the new global economy; (4) an "American national economy" perspective that advocates public policies focusing on the U.S. workforce and infrastructure assets in the global economy.

In the last section of this paper, we consider what our analysis means for the practice of democracy in America. What are the implications of propaganda for democracy that is grounded in assumptions of an informed, engaged, and critical citizenry? What role does propaganda play in determining which voices affected by the competitiveness "problem" will have access to the decision-making arena?

PROPAGANDA

The study of propaganda can be traced back to the Greek city-states of about 500 B.C. and to the codification of "rhetoric" promoted by Plato and Aristotle. The modern study of propaganda can arguably be traced to Niccolo Machiavelli and his instructions to "The Prince" to use information for practical and manipulative purposes. In democratic societies, the emergence of a "science" of propaganda is associated with the awareness of "publics" that can have "opinions." According to Speier, both the French Revolution and the Industrial Revolution resulted in the spreading of discussion about competing beliefs, ideas, opinions, and the proper role of the "common person" in political life.[1] In the late nineteenth and early twentieth centuries, elites studied public opinion to assess ways in which it might be shaped to serve their economic and political interests. In the twentieth century, of course, we associate propaganda with totalitarian political systems such as Nazi Germany, Stalin's Soviet Union, or George Orwell's *1984.*

In the United States, interest in manipulating public opinion was associated with the growth of mass marketing in the early part of this century as well as with Woodrow Wilson's use of new media to mobilize support for American participation in the First World War.[2] Recently, a number of American analysts have turned their attention to the characteristics of propaganda in the U.S. mass media, corporate public relations, government, and politics.[3] Techniques of "engineering of consent," to use Edward Bernays' term,[4] are widely employed by a multitude of organizations seeking to persuade large publics to see the wisdom of positions they advocate in public discourse.

The most exhaustive theoretical treatment of propaganda to date is Jacques Ellul's analysis of propaganda in totalitarian and Western democratic systems. Ellul makes an important distinction between "direct" propaganda and "sociological" propaganda. Direct propaganda involves the deliberate and calculated attempt to mobilize people for action through the mass media or other public forums. In contrast, sociological propaganda acts as a kind of "pre-propaganda," laying the foundation for active, direct propaganda that will be used in time of crisis. Working through the medium of economic and political structures, sociological propaganda "aims at an entire style of life"; in the United States, this might be popularly called the "American way of life."[5] Sociological propaganda presumably is learned as part of the socialization process in the family and schools; it is reinforced by the media in both its news and entertainment functions.

The language and rhetoric of direct propaganda is often related to times of real or putative crisis. Direct propaganda is used classically to mobilize people for war; however, this kind of propaganda is more diverse and complex. Propaganda is a form of communication. In a communication analysis, messages are formulated by a source and transmitted through one or more channels (media) to one or more audiences. It is a given of the analysis of rhetoric (and propaganda as a form of rhetoric) that the structure and form of the message depends on the nature of the audience to which it is directed. The scholarly form of this paper, for example, is shaped by the characteristics of the audience likely to read it.

In a propaganda analysis, we substitute the word "constituency" for "audience" to capture the idea that propaganda is about groups with tangible interests to protect. In the polity, these groups seek to mobilize various publics in order to influence those in the decision-making arena. We distinguish first between constituencies and counterconstituencies. That is, every propaganda message (diagnosis of a problem or formulation of a solution) has as its goal the mobilization of groups (constituencies) who would or might be sympathetic to one's messages, as well as checking the actions of groups (counterconstituencies) whose interests might be negatively affected by the recommendations.

Second, we distinguish between visible and invisible constituencies and counterconstituencies. Those engaging in propaganda seek to maximize their constituencies and minimize counterconstituencies. To do this, they often seek to universalize the beneficiaries of policies they recommend. That is, the visible constituencies of propaganda are claimed to be "all of us." Left invisible in this process are the constituencies of the policy—the owners or directors of a company or business sector or a class of policy beneficiaries.

A propagandist also seeks to marginalize any counterconstituency of the recommend policies. An important technique for doing this is to render counterconstituencies invisible by ignoring them and implying that "everyone" benefits from a given policy. When counterconstituencies clearly exist, they are often dismissed in derogatory terms that imply or state directly that these counterconstituencies either don't recognize their real interests or selfishly pursue their "special" interests.

Sociological propaganda provides the foundation for this direct propaganda. "Sociological" propaganda refers to assumptions, principles, and "tacit understandings" that provide a set of cultural resources on which elites can draw in using direct propaganda. We see four interrelated elements of sociological propaganda in American life:

1. Abstracted or atomistic individualism: The United States is at one extreme in a long tradition in Western societies that abstracts the individual from community and social contexts, that sees the individual as a free-floating entity who develops relationships with others as suits individual goals or purposes. Society is understood as an aggregate of separate individuals, the sum total of its individual parts. The individual is thus given a privileged ontological status, one markedly different from the individual's status in other cultures. Geertz describes this "bourgeois" individual in terms of a conception of the person as "unique, a more or less integrated motivational and cognitive universe, a dynamic center of awareness, emotion, judgment and action organized into a distinctive whole and set contrastively" against others and the world.[6]

If the individual is the prime mover from which social dynamics flow, it follows that blame for social ills must therefore fall on the individual; if systems are faulty, the explanation and remedy also lie with individuals. It can be difficult for persons who acquire this sensibility to see alternative formulations of selfhood, for example, that the individual takes his or her self definition from within a system of organized social relations.

2. The classless society: It follows from the conception of the person as an autonomous, abstracted entity that "class" is not a *sociological* but a *psychological* concept. While Americans perceive that there are class differences (for example, people readily identify the "poor", the "middle-class," and the "rich"), they also feel that the boundaries between these classes are relatively porous. Thus, it might be expected that Americans would tend to endorse propositions of the following sort: If a person is motivated (and has some talent and perhaps some luck), there is no limit to that person's upward mobility. Class is therefore a psychological phenomoena because it exists only as a result of the internal dynamics of individuals.

3. Economic opportunities versus rights: The perception of America as a "land of opportunity" translates into a sociological formulation such that the economic system is a structure of opportunity ladders waiting to be climbed by those with the motivation and talent to do so. The concept of an economic "right" has been

seen as profoundly antithetical to the ideal of economic opportunity. An economic right implies that, by virtue of one's membership in the group, by one's being an American citizen, one is entitled to certain economic protections over and above the minimalist protections of unemployment insurance and the like: the right to a job, the right to a certain level of income, the right to a certain standard of living. The concept of an economic right has also been taken to imply a more active role for government in the economy. The struggle between "opportunities" and "rights" runs like a thread through American history, surfacing most notably in the Populist struggles of the late 1800s, in elements of FDR's "New Deal" (1933–1938) and in some element of Lyndon Johnson's "Great Society" programs (1965–1967).

4. Competition, cooperation, and the legitimacy of resource control: Our culture values competition both as a motivator of action and as a way of allocating resources. Competition provides a rationale for the unequal distribution of resources. Darwin's theory of evolution has frequently been distorted to "prove" that those with greater accumulations of resources and greater control over resource distribution have arrived at these positions by virtue of their superior qualities. This position therefore legitimates one's "right" to exercise control. The struggle to resist worker demands for greater workplace control was a salient part of the development of industrial capitalism in the late nineteenth and early twentieth centuries. It can be argued that, during the 1950s and 1960s, management and labor cooperated in a kind of social compact in which labor peace was traded for decent wages and benefits.

These four elements converge and support the value of a capitalist "free market." Atomistic or abstracted individuals will flourish best in an economic system grounded on the freedom to optimize motivation, talent, and effort. Differences in power and control will result from these characteristics as well. "Government functions best which functions least" because any intervention within the market moves or distorts, giving economic opportunities to some and taking it from others. If government does intervene, it should do so to restore the "level playing field." Thus, as is clear in the competitiveness debate, many sectors of capital call for government intervention precisely because it is felt that doing so will protect the "freedom" of the market to "work its will." Of course, throughout American history, and certainly in recent times, the state has intervened frequently to secure advantage for some at the necessary disadvantage of others—for example, through taxing policies. As we shall indicate, it is this reality that propaganda obscures.

The point of direct propaganda is to maintain the structure and operation of American capitalism by mobilizing support and repressing, derogating, or marginalizing dissent. To do so, interested parties can draw on sociological propaganda, deeply inculcated, well-rehearsed sets of assumptions, or cultural "resources" that are shared, either in whole or in part, by members of American society. For example, to sing the praises of the "free" market is not difficult because assumptions about the nature of the individual, economic opportunities, the "psychologizing" of class, and the value of competition make it "obvious" that a "free" market provides the only legitimate basis for organizing an economy. Again, arguments can be made for and against this proposition, but *evoking* the value of a free market becomes propaganda when it is used to ignore negative side effects of such a market, to obscure the ways the market system works to the advantage of capital over labor, and so on. It should be noted that our strategy is *not* to give an exhaustive content analysis of all possible statements made in each perspective on competitiveness to "prove" that such statements are "really" propaganda. Rather, we want to show how statements about competitiveness *can* function as propaganda, and, in the last section of this paper, to discuss the importance of this fact for democratic decision-making in America.

PROPAGANDA ANALYSIS OF COMPETITIVENESS PERSPECTIVES

That there are four competitiveness perspectives, each with a somewhat different general formulation of the competitiveness problem, is to some extent a reflection of recent national and world economic changes. The postwar United States economy flourished with the help of a tripartite support system consisting of global military interventionism (the "Pax Americana"), the resolution of severe capital-labor strife through consumption-stimulating higher wages (in exchange for managerial control of the workplace), and a governing ideology that often rendered invisible the social costs of business' quest for profits. All three supports for this system began to erode during the 1960s and early 1970s, and U.S. economic productivity and profitability began to decline.[7] To some degree the declining share of world markets held by U.S. corpora-

tions reflects the inevitable "catching up" of competitor economies—catching up that was itself the express aim of postwar U.S.
policy.

With the election of Ronald Reagan, so-called "Reaganomics"
became the prevailing policy model. It aimed at improving the
profitability of American corporations through deregulation, free-
trade, "supply-side" tax policies designed to enhance productive
investment without exacerbating inflation, a federal spending shift
from social welfare to military spheres, tight money policies designed to curb runaway inflation, and an effort to roll back the
gains of organized American labor. As the federal budget deficit
ballooned and the United States experienced the deep recession of
1982–83, and as a dramatic trade deficit grew, economic priorities
shifted. Pressure mounted for greater trade protection for the least
competitive sectors of American industry: automobiles, steel, and
textiles. Also, pressure grew for devaluation of the strong dollar to
improve trade balance (perspective 2).

In more recent years, as the trade deficit has declined, there has
been a discernible shift from the early to mid-1980s "rust-belt"
focus to concern for the new rules of the "global economy": an
emphasis on free trade (perspective 3), on a stable currency to
maintain national income, and on government support for education and training of the U.S. workforce, infrastructure improvement, and civilian research and development (perspective 4).
Throughout this period, some company executives have been taking a hard look at their internal management policies and external
marketing practices (perspective 1). Arguably, competitiveness
takes on new meaning in a world of contending economic spheres:
North America, Japan, the Pacific Rim, and Europe.

Over time, then, efforts to shape public policy have reflected
shifts in economic priorities, changing economic conditions, and
the rise and fall of different influential political constituencies.

1. The Microeconomic Perspective: Toward the More
Competitive Firm

Microeconomic competitiveness is, of course, the concern of a
rich field of traditional economic theory and practice. Innumerable
business leaders, advocating improved U.S. competitiveness, have
acknowledged the central importance of improving business innovation, efficiency, and productivity, the very watchwords of the
capitalist ethos. Indeed, their commitment to the free market metaphor demands such a position. Certainly, proponents of each "mac-

rocompetitive" position acknowledge that microeconomic changes in U.S. companies are a necessary part of improving American competitiveness, however that is defined. By the same token, virtually all proponents of microeconomic change acknowledge that government can and should play an important role in improving competitiveness. Our review of the competitiveness-advocacy literature yields four distinct microcompetitive emphases: (1) intelligent, long-range management practices; (2) reduction of labor costs and improved cooperation on the part of workers; (3) reduction in management payroll; and (4) intelligent buy-out strategies to improve firm competitiveness.

Each of these positions reflects the economic experience of the advocate's constituency. Thus, a number of executives from so-called growth firms criticize the management and investment practices of traditional U.S. industries. For example, in speaking to business executives in Japan, Jim Manzi, the CEO of Lotus Development Corporation and an advocate of open markets, laments the short-sightedness of many American firms' research and development outlays—the "result of a misguided attempt by many U.S. companies to become more competitive."[8] Manzi maintained that, unlike Japanese firms, American companies have focused on market-driven "applied technology" rather than research and development for "high value technology" designed to meet the needs and demands of customers. He sees this as a symptom of our "10-minute focus", that is, the inability to plan for the long-term. He suggests that, rather than complaining about our loss of market to the Japanese, "we should be doing something about it—out of pure economic self-interest." John Young of Hewlett-Packard advocates productive investment in manufacturing and process technology rather than product technology in order to counter the Japanese advantage in the latter. As he puts it, "the private sector must improve the quality and cost competitiveness of its products through productive investments and innovations in technology and human resource management. Government can't legislate success in world markets; the responsibility lies with us."[9]

Robert Yohe of the Olin Corporation argues that smokestack America can improve its competitive position through its own initiative by "market differentiation" and "niche positioning" geared to customers' needs and one's own manufacturing strengths. As he puts it, "Drifting doesn't work. If business management worries about microeconomics (the things it can affect) and, with detailed competitive analysis and strategies, truly aims to differentiate, then it can make fundamental changes in its company's destiny. . . .

'Smokestack America' must by it own initiative take action to survive."[10] Stephen A. Barre of Servo Corporation of America, urges
"U.S. businesspeople to wake up. . . . If we [the government
through incentives] do not encourage and achieve a more aggressive posture for U.S. business in international markets, our trade
balance will continue to decline along with our economic health."[11]

Finally, Arthur Levitt, Jr. and William Lilley, III, chairmen of the
American Business Conference (ABC), argue that American firms
need to seize the initiative in finding and capitalizing on prospects
in international markets. If we do not "capitalize on prospects in
marketing," there will be an "across-the-board cheapening of our
goods and services through the devaluation of the dollar" that "will
ensure the decline in our standard of living."[12] Addressing other
members of the ABC group, he reports results of a survey of these
ABC executives and concludes that they have "relentless optimism," a "product of self-confidence" that allows them to "take
. . . risks, grants them patience to sustain early losses" and "gives
them and their companies a sense of purpose." He also denies that
moving offshore has to do primarily with finding a cheaper labor
force. Instead, it reflects a concern with controlling total costs,
whose "main components are costs of market access, capital,
taxes, customer support, labor, and manufacturing." He further
suggests that a major problem for American manufacturers is the
"barrier [of] cultural preferences—the unwillingness of foreign
consumers, both individually and companies, to buy American
products and services. Only managerial will and skill can conquer
this trade barrier, through more investment in quality, service, innovation, and strategic marketing."[13]

Reduced labor costs sometimes figure in the microeconomic recommendations of spokespersons for this perspective. They become
central in the rhetoric of more labor-intensive industries. For example, John A. Simourian of Lily Truck Leasing Corporation singles
out high labor costs "due to historically strong unions, a period of
extraordinary inflation . . . and a mature and civilized industrial
society that demands costly fringe benefits and social programs"
as reasons for America's "chronic competitiveness problem." He
advocates "educating our managers to focus on the needs and demands of the customer rather than on short-term profits and instant
bonuses."[14] Not surprisingly, Owen Bieber of the United Auto
Workers offers a counter to this argument: "I am convinced that
excessive executive compensation, authoritarian management,
short-term time horizons, preoccupation with unproductive mergers and acquisitions, and corporate strategies like outsourcing and

exporting capital, technology, and jobs, cause serious harm to the U.S. economy."[15] Still another view is offered by William B. Johnson of IC Industries, who argues that strategic acquisition is crucial for improving a company's competitive capability and value to its shareholders. Johnson recommends honing the competitive edge by "continually redeploying assets" to buy and sell subsidiaries.[16]

The role of U.S. workers in many of these microeconomic strategies emerges clearly in the recommendations of business professor C. K. E. Prahalad, who maintains that underlying the array of microeconomic improvements lies a need for "an obsession with winning that permeates the total organization and is nurtured and sustained for a long period of time. . . . It is something that goes all the way down from the chairman of the board to the lowest level employee. And each employee believes in and shares the same fundamental competitive agenda. . . . [A]ll must recognize that the enemy is outside."[17] Or, as Ralph Z. Sorensen of Barry Wright Corporation puts it, to bolster U.S. exports and replace merchandise imports, "manufacturing executives must imbue their organizations with the missionary zeal to produce tangible products of ever-higher quality at ever-lower cost."[18]

Many of these statements make good economic sense from the microperspective of business management, shareholders, or even employees. Yet all statements contain elements of direct propaganda by seeking to maximize their constituencies and minimize (denigrate or make invisible) their counterconstituencies and, as well, draw on the resources of sociological propaganda. For example, Manzi ("we should be doing something about it"), Young ("the responsibility lies with us"), Yohe ("Smokestack America must by its own initiative take action"), and Levitt and Lilley ("we" must capitalize on prospects in marketing to guard against a decline in "our standard of living"), all universalize their solutions. While the audience—particularly in the *Harvard Business Review,* from which many of these quotations are taken—are presumably other businessmen, the *effect* of the rhetorical "we" is to fuse owners and workers and everyone else in society as if they were all the same constituency, thus obscuring the potential reality of divergent interests between management and workers (see Bieber's remarks).

Further, by attempting to mobilize the workers to identify with the interests of the firm (Prahalad's "obsession with winning" and Sorenson's "missionary zeal"), these spokespersons obscure the fact that the primary responsibility of management is to shareholders, not to employees. Simourian's attack on the demands for "costly fringe benefits and social programs" in a mature industrial society is a good example of derogating a visible counterconstituency. That is, as Simourian can't ignore his union's demands, he attempts to derogate worker interests in having a "safety net" of benefits and programs. The important elements obscured by this attack are a consideration of inequalities between executive and worker pay, and the possibility of substantial executive pay cuts as an alternative solution to the problem of costs (although, to his credit, Simourian does attack management's tendency to go for "instant bonuses").

These statements also draw on the cultural resources constituting sociological propaganda. Thus, there are repeated references to individual responsibility, to ingroup solidarity and outgroup hostility (Prahalad: "the enemy is outside"), to the value of competition itself (again Prahalad: "each employee believes in and shares the same fundamental competitive agenda"), and to the legitimacy of owner control of the workplace. Simourian's denigration of costly fringe benefits and social programs surely draws on the cultural assumption of economic opportunities versus rights.

Finally, all of these voices embrace the value of a "free" market and at the same time call for government support. In brief, microeconomic solutions to the competitiveness "crisis" reinforce the mythology of the free market, yet are not generalizable without the government's providing incentives for those who may not have the wisdom or the capital to make productive long-term microeconomic decisions. In virtually all cases, business leaders voice the refrain "It's up to us" to improve competitiveness, while using this refrain as a means to obscure their interest in guaranteeing business success through government help.

2. Macrocompetitiveness: The Protectionist Response

A competitiveness perspective expressed most commonly during the early to mid-1980s, was that the U.S. manufacturing sector, particularly traditional heavy industries like steel and automobiles (like textiles in earlier years) were in crisis (as textiles were in earlier years). In fact, for a number of years this perspective virtually defined the growing perception of an urgent national crisis. It was so widespread that President Reagan appointed a Presidential Commission on Industrial Competitiveness, and Congress tried on several occasions to pass legislation creating a National Council on Industrial Competitiveness (vetoed by Reagan).

This approach was most commonly expressed by "rust-belt"

companies, by their political representatives, or by dependent constituencies like steel and auto workers' unions. In their boom years,
sustained through the most of the 1960s, many of these companies
monopolized the American market. However, all lost substantial
world market shares through the 1970s and 1980s and have been
frustrated by their inability to penetrate foreign markets or compete with foreign-owned producers. Throughout the early 1980s,
one encounters traditional forms of economic protectionism such
as trade agreements and import quotas, in addition to calls for
concessions by U.S. labor, public investment for research and development, or macroeconomic policies aimed at reducing public
spending and consumption.

The note of urgency is sounded by Armco, Inc.'s Kemptom B.
Jenkins, Corporate Vice President for International and Government Affairs. He asserts that "In the American marketplace, we
are engaged in a street fight for our very existence." He decries
the fact that "passively we sit by and watch the lights go out in the
industrial communities, which we now dismiss as the 'Rust Belt'
of the United States. . . ." Jenkins blames a number of targets for
the current state of affairs: "While the rest of the world nationalizes
its steel industries, the United States, inhibited by antitrust regulations, contradictory trade policies, and a long tradition of high
wage structures, is rapidly losing its own steel industry." He won-
ders how we are to "survive the mercantilist attacks of our NATO
allies in the world grain markets." He is particularly incensed by
"imaginative subsidy techniques that can skew economic values."
Jenkins offers as a solution the creation of a "national trade policy"
which "all members of Congress must be persuaded to share. . . ."
He advocates a single strong U.S. Trade Czar and the establishment
of a high quality blue-ribbon commercial service to promote U.S.
trade around the world."[19]

A common theme of the protectionist perspective is an unresponsive (or even hostile) government. Thus Merle H. Banta of AM
International cites as principal reasons for "our competitiveness
problem" offshore "savings-oriented" societies with "government-
sponsored market-takeover strategies," and "our own government
with its foolish taxation policies and antibusiness bias." He goes
on to say that "unfortunately, our elected representatives lack the
political will to deal with the problem (biennial elections are their
quarterly earning reports)." Banta fears that "we will continue to
hide behind platitudes such as free trade, refuse to use our market
leverage, and pander to the lower common denominator." He calls
for "convincing, coherent political leadership covering fiscal and

monetary policy, education, antitrust and taxation," without which
we will "dissipate our economic power and leave a less acceptable
living standard for our children."[20] Other voices echo the concern
for misguided macroeconomic policies. The same Ralph Sorensen
of Barry Wright Corporation who urged companies to imbue their
organizations with "missionary zeal" urges the reduction of U.S.
military and social welfare spending coupled with a new value-
added tax to raise needed revenues, encourage savings, and discourage consumption.[21] John E. Swearingen of Continental Illinois
Corporation hones in on the trade deficit that threatens to make
competitiveness a "chronic" problem and urges fiscal policies that
will discourage public and private consumption, even at the cost
of a lower standard of living.[22] Even a free-trade advocate like ex-
Congressman Jack Kemp urges the United States to "use the leverage of our large domestic economy to encourage broad trading
agreements" beyond the product-by-product approach.[23] And, finally, Richard E. Heckert of E.I. DuPont de Nemours asserts that
government must face "the fact that our [domestic] market operates like a sponge, soaking up products from abroad." It should
"compensate" for this disadvantage by government intervention to
maintain "workable currency relationships" and "replacing free-
trade ideology with a practical approach to trade issues . . . [O]ther
nations take steps to enhance their competitive position. It is not
protectionism or a *source of embarrassment* if we do the same."[24]
(emphasis added)

Not surprisingly, many protectionist advocates also focus their
ire on U.S. multinational companies. John P. Cregan of the U.S.
Business and Industrial Council (USBIC) observes that ". . . our
primary antagonists are not lobbyists for South Korean or Japanese
firms . . . [but] rather a powerful coalition of American multinationals which are either dependent on dumped components, or
fearful of retaliation in export markets because of our dumping
statute, or are dumping themselves into America from offshore
production facilities."[25] USBIC president Anthony Harrigan indig-
nantly decries the "American domiciled transnational company—
distinct from the American company with foreign subsidiaries"
that operates "as if it has no responsibility to the national interest."[26] Cregan, however, also directs his ire against "liberal democrats" who "back protectionism solely because of labor union
support" and who therefore view "economic nationalism as good
politics—as a way to drape themselves in the American flag." He
also targets those "high-level trade negotiators or mid-level and
high-ranking Commerce, Treasury and State Department officials"

who think about how to "translate their public posts into private-sector gain." It is these people and others who make "foreign influence" on our economic life so powerful.[27]

Given the fact that these multinational companies have declined, and given their past centrality in the U.S. economy, competitiveness is obviously a legitimate concern. However, advocates of the macrocompetitiveness perspective engage in direct propaganda and exploit the resources of sociological propaganda in a number of ways. First, the specific interests of specific companies or sectors are universalized by equating them with the national or public interest under conditions of threat (the need to return to our position as number one.) In this perspective, in other words, one is most likely to find policy statements that draw on the tendency toward ingroup solidarity under conditions of threat (Jenkins; "engaged in a street fight for our very existence", "watching the lights go out in industrial communities"; Cregan: "transnationals," cynical "liberal democrats," "opportunistic careerists," and "foreign influence"). Banta's focus on "our competitiveness problem" is a particularly good example of using direct propaganda to make invisible the particular interests of the business community and to equate the economic health of these industries with everyone's interest. This universalizing makes invisible the potential difference between owner and worker interests so that the advocate can then express the fear of leaving a "less acceptable standard of living for *our* children" without indicating exactly *whose* children are going to be suffering this fate.

From a propaganda perspective, the treatment of government policies in these writings seems to have two foci. Government is adjured to "get its act together" in ways that will support American business in the new global environment. But what must government do? Besides more actively intervening in the service of business interests, government must (as in the first perspective) reduce onerous regulation of *internal* business practices, change tax policies to favor business, and cut into social programs. Thus, government is urged to identify with the interests of business but at the same time to join business in ignoring or marginalizing the interests of workers in health and safety on the job, a decent standard of living, and the like. However, in the case of transnationals failing to act with "responsibility to the national interest", government is asked to exercise greater oversight.

Of particular interest is the way these statements draw upon the cultural belief in economic opportunity. That is, government must intervene *precisely* because businesses (and, through universalizing, "all of us") are having our opportunities for economic growth restricted. Thus, government is intervening not to violate the free market, but instead to make it even more free. Here we see a subtle difference with advocates in the first perspective. The refrain "it's up to us" so characteristic of that perspective is modified here so that the guarantee of business success is less obscured; it is more overt that government should intervene on a more ongoing basis to set policy and to monitor it (the notion of a trade "czar"). This is rationalized, however, in terms of a more explicit external threat to "all of us." Thus, propaganda takes a somewhat different form depending on the circumstances and experiences of a particular sector. The legitimate role for government is to support business generally. Within that framework, it's "up to us."

3. Macrocompetitiveness: Multinationals, Free Trade, and the Global Economy

In recent years, the protectionist emphasis in the competitiveness debate has given way to a variety of voices advocating free trade, opposing "mercantilism" or "trade barriers" such as tariffs, import quotas, and trade agreements. Typically, these voices characterize themselves as "forward looking" leaders in touch with the "globalized economy." As Anthony Harrigan claims, these business leaders, as often as not, represent successful, U.S.-domiciled (and largely U.S.-owned), transnational companies that make large portions of their revenues from overseas markets, employ large numbers of foreign nationals, and have "outsourced" much of their production.[28] They strongly oppose "archaic mercantilism" because it gets in the way of the beneficial free market and it may encourage trade wars or profitability-reducing responses by foreign nations such as Japan. The U.S. Council for an Open World Economy makes explicit this orientation, characterizing itself as an organization "engaged in research and public education on the merits and problems of developing an open international economic system in the overall national interest," not "on behalf of any 'special interests.'"[29]

Addresing Japanese business leaders, Jim Manzi of Lotus Development Corporation asserted that "competitiveness" has become a "current national obsession," serving as a "code word for protection." Observing that the "genie of globalization is out of the bottle," Manzi looks backward through rose-colored lenses, "We've long since passed the time when industries exist only to support the power of the nation-state or the sovereign."[30] In other words, whereas in the 1950s it could be said that "What's good for General Motors is good for the country," in today's globalized economy, it might be, "what's good for Lotus is good for the world." Manzi generalizes from Lotus' success to assert that any company wanting to succeed in the global marketplace ". . . is now required to invest in, and make the best possible use of information technology," a primary example of which is Lotus 1-2-3.[31]

John P. Cregan, of the U.S. Business and Industrial Council, counters Manzi by distinguishing himself from globalist "romantics" who assert that national borders are disappearing, and from "economic libertarians" in the Reagan administration who embrace the "religion" of "laissez faire free trade." Cregan's recommendations include a reduction of the federal deficit to bring down the cost of capital, tax policies that will spur savings instead of consumption, for example, by reducing the "double taxation" of business, relaxation of some antitrust provisions, and federal aid for private research and development.[32]

In a case study of government policy and international competitiveness in the steel industry, Barnette, Patterson, and Hoppe look disapprovingly on foreign governments who became "deeply involved in the operation, financing and control of their steel and other industries." In their version of history, this involvement led to greater and greater government control and a whole host of ills associated with this, primarily "inefficiencies" in the form of closed markets, production quotas, price controls, export incentives, overcapacity, and overmanning. They extol the virtues of bilateral trade agreements as a remedy for protectionism and look to the GATT talks in 1992 as a place where talks will get "all governments out of the steel business and . . . 'level the playing field' once and for all."[33]

In polling the members of the growth-oriented American Business Conference, Arthur Levitt and William Lilley discovered that most believed "the main problem is not unfair competition but competition pure and simple. A combination of misguided macroeconomic policies, exacerbated by deficiencies in American management, prevents companies from penetrating foreign markets at a time when their economic future depends on such penetration." The primary macroeconomic advice of these leaders is for the federal government to "find the backbone to take remedial action" to reduce the deficit. For their part, business leaders "must find and capitalize on prospects in markets they never had reason to tap before."[34] Presumably all business people of consequence fall into this category.

In a report presented to the House Committee on Banking, Finance, and Urban Affairs, Pat Choate of TRW summarized the analysis of 17 separate studies on long-term U.S. competitiveness. Not surprisingly, all studies agreed that "increasing U.S. competitiveness" was "essential to meeting our nation's many objectives." Recognizing that much of the responsibility for long-term competitiveness was up to business itself, government intervention was inevitable. "Therefore, the issue is not whether the activities of business and government are interrelated, but to what extent and how can they be better harmonized." Among the consensus recommendations of these reports were: (a) extending the R&D tax credit, (b) providing incentives that stimulate greater business investment in worker training and retraining, (c) reducing antitrust barriers to cooperative research, and (d) assuming a more assertive role in trade negotiations to eliminate barriers to U.S. exports and foreign investment.[35]

Perhaps in no other perspective is the connection to the cultural resources constituting sociological propaganda so freely drawn on to make the case for a globalized free market. Thus, Barnette, Patterson, and Hoppe can say about the immediate postwar period that the "magic of the market" worked within America's economic system" and that "laissez-faire was the proven and approved public policy."[36] The accuracy of this statement is not the issue. Americans reading this statement, however, are unlikely to be critical because it fits so well with valuing the "free" unfettered individual engaged in open competition, which of course brings out the best in people, thereby raising them to positions of control to which they are entitled by virtue of their hard work and effort. Why not, then, extend this philosophy to the world at large? What is hidden by these arguments are the impacts on workers of capital mobility, of "outsourcing" to cheaper labor markets, and as a means of avoiding worker protection and environmental regulation within the confines of America's borders. And as in other perspectives, one finds the universalizing tendency at work to identify the worker's interests with those of capital.

4. The U.S. National Economy in a Global Economy

Unlike the two prior positions, this perspective is relatively unconcerned about the economic viability of U.S.-owned corporations, especially those that base much of their operations overseas. Instead, these voices focus on the nonmobile economic assets of the United States: the workforce and its skill level, and the social base and infrastructure that supports economic activity. As Robert Reich puts it, ". . . if we hope to revitalize the competitive performance of the United States economy, we must invest in people, not in nationally defined corporations. We must open our borders to investors from around the world rather than favoring companies that may simply fly the U.S. flag. . . . The American corporation is simply no longer 'us'."[37] In fact, by implication, U.S.-based foreign-owned businesses contribute to American competitiveness, especially if they locate fully-integrated business operations in the United States.

The bottom-line concerns of competitiveness are national income and the national standard of living, occasionally refered to as the "quality of life" in the United States. And the key to national income is the competitiveness of the national work force. As Reich argues, "It is all fungible: capital, technology, raw materials, information—all, except for one thing, the most critical part, the one element that is unique about a nation: its work force."[38]

In trumpeting the benefits of open trade in the new global economy, national economy advocates shade toward the free trade rather than the protectionist position. However, as Reich's comments suggest, they are highly critical of offshore capital flight and outsourcing by U.S.-owned companies. Competitiveness is defined as "the capacity of Americans to add value to the world economy and thereby gain a higher standard of living in the future without going into ever deeper debt. American competitiveness is not the profitability or market share of American-owned corporations."[39] As Matthew Burns and Fidel Ramos of Automated Assemblies Corporation argue, U.S.-owned firms that shift production and design overseas to take advantage of tax incentives, relaxed workplace regulations, the absence of unions, and lower wage structures help to stimulate other national economies.[40] By contrast, as former Massachusetts Governor Michael Dukakis put it, "We need to invest in ourselves."[41]

The specific policies recommended under the national economy rubric include: reducing the federal budget deficit to reduce the cost of capital, improved trade policies coordinated with macroeconomic policy, increased government support for civilian research and development, government incentives for plant and equipment investment, and above all, improvement of American education and job training. Wilkinson, for example, argues that "the competitive edge that advanced technology can provide to a national economy is quickly lost if workers capable of being productive users of the technology are not available." He suggests that "the economic competitive edge will belong to those nations that succeed in developing a cost-effective system for educating and training its population to be productive workers in a technology and information driven economy." The task, he suggests, is to build a "human infrastructure" for the economy. Not surprisingly, the market becomes the desired model for educational reform. Wilkinson argues, along with Reich, for much greater financial investment by both the federal government and the states.[42]

There are different shadings to advocates in this perspective, particularly in terms of their regard for the "problems" of the work force. Reich feels that a majority of Americans are becoming shut out from the nature of work in the global economy (symbolic, information transfer), and he expresses considerable concern about the degree to which Americans will feel concerned enough to support government programs through tax dollars to bring American workers into the modern work world.[43] On the other hand, John F. Copper argues that the United States should follow the example of Japan and the four Pacific Rim newly-industrialized countries (NICs) not only for their economies but their politics. As Copper maintains, "most Asian countries" . . . felt that basic freedoms had become license in the U.S., that they were excessive. They did not think it is good for people to criticize their leaders in vulgar terms. . . . They believe the judiciary in the U.S. has become bureaucratic and dictatorial. . . . Asians do not want laws to break up the family and they think that has happened in America. . . . They do not want a welfare system to create a permanent class of unemployed. They want to keep the crime rate down by not giving too many rights to the accused and by punishing criminals quickly and severely. They don't want a drug culture to develop and destroy many of their young people."[44] A more conventional argument is presented by Norway's Ove Hoegh who urges Washington to provide subsidies for technological advance "through the defense contracting mechanism."[45]

This perspective can be distinguished from the others by what appears to be a shift in the visible constituency from the executive/managerial class to that of the worker. For some, there is militancy in their advocacy of this position. Thus, for example, William Winpisinger, former president of the International Association of Machinists contends, "The [competitiveness] problem is not economic nationalism but multinational corporations, which . . . fly a flag of convenience in quest of market penetration or domination and bottom-line cost minimization and profit maximization. Their balance sheets and income statements compete against our national income accounts and balance of payments as well as the bottom-line standard of living for most working Americans. . . . We should license MNC [multinational corporation] behavior in the national interest. . . . In all trade deals, agreements, and treaties, we should insist on uniform standards to raise environmental, labor, and human right conditions to the highest, rather than the lowest common denominator."[46]

The national economy position of labor leaders like Winpisinger, or liberal economists like Robert Reich, raises the interesting possibility of shifting the primary constituency of government policy from corporate shareholders (with their concern for profitability) to the workforce. Reich, Winspinger, and Wilkinson are bringing formerly invisible counterconstituencies into the light and advocating for them. On one level it is hard to fault these individuals for their obvious care and concern for the welfare of increasingly marginalized workers. But there is a subtle issue of definition here. Certainly for Reich and Wilkinson the "worker" is that individual whose training and education is vital in order for American business and industry to remain in economic good health. Thus, the concern is ultimately for the system as it is constituted. There is no need for workers, in order to achieve a sense of dignity, a decent standard of living, and good working conditions, to be involved in control of their situation. The *real* job of the worker is to get fit for the high-tech, information-based demands of the workplace of tomorrow. Thus, the persistent issue of who is in control is made invisible, along with many of the same interests that are made invisible by direct propaganda in other perspectives: health and safety on the job, environmental protection, and so on. In short, although many advocates for this position weigh in on the side of the worker, the real concern is with improving capitalism as an economic system. And while there are many who would applaud this goal, it is still important to understand how these statements also reflect direct propaganda.

The cultural resources from which these authors draw center on economic opportunity and its associated assumptions. Why would we be concerned with an uneducated workforce? Because lack of training and education does not allow people to place their feet on the bottom rung of those opportunity ladders and from there to climb to the rung that optimizes ability, motivation, and training. Indeed, it is taken for granted that once trained (and socialized), people will understand that motivation and hard work will then pay off. Again, we are not dealing with the *validity* of this proposition, but with its power as part of a generally shared belief system in the culture.

DEMOCRATIC VALUES, PROPAGANDA AND THE COMPETITIVENESS "PROBLEM"

We now turn our attention to the implications of our propaganda analysis for democratic values, particularly for public awareness and access to decision-making. To develop our case, we set our analysis of the competitive debate in its historical context. As pointed out earlier, during the postwar period the American capitalist system was driven by mass production and mass consumption, underwritten by the willingness of the United States to intervene militarily to protect overseas markets and investments, stimulated by a heavily military Keynesianism, secured by a labor-capital accord, and protected by the invisibility of conflict between the private quest for profit and public or social concerns. The very foundations of this system have now become the targets of many competitiveness advocates. Ironically, we appear to be reaping the bitter harvest of our earlier economic "boom."

How have we reaped such a "harvest?" First, the stress on mass consumption, built up through mass communications and mass marketing during the late 1940s and 1950s, laid the groundwork for an advertisement-based economy. This consumption-driven economy is now blamed by many for the trade imbalance that endangers American competitiveness. The very propaganda that spread the American "Way of Life" in the postwar years must be reversed. We must save, not consume; we must do without, so in the long run we can "all" prosper. Maintenance of the American capitalist system requires propaganda that modifies American lifestyles in order to maintain the American "Way of Life."

Second, the consumption-driven economy was the economic vehicle that facilitated management-labor peace during the 1950s, that is, higher wages for labor, increased consumption, and control of the workplace for producers. Now management's "concession," higher wages, is cited as a reason for the competitiveness problems of heavy industry as well as for the outmigration of U.S.-owned multinationals. One objective of Reaganomics was the reduction of these "high labor costs" realized through layoffs, give-backs, and union-busting tactics. In fact, these tactics have been so successful that some analysts now feel it impolitic to advocate further reduction of labor costs.

Third, the ideal fit between mass marketing and the medium of television has led some to argue that the medium has contributed to the much-lamented decline of educational effectiveness, thereby, in the view of some competitiveness analysts, reducing the "competitiveness" of the U.S. workforce. Television has been accused by its critics of having a pervasive if subtle impact on such qualities as student attentiveness, a passive demand to be entertained, a disinclination to read, and growing ignorance of fundamental historical and cultural data.[47] Perhaps more directly related to our concerns here are numerous studies of media acting as gatekeepers against voices in political/economic debates (including competitiveness) that are not sympathetic to consensus elite positions, particularly if these counterconstituencies advocate major structural change.[48]

Fourth, the Reagan administration's acceleration of "military Keynesianism" was a throwback remedy for economic decline that fully conformed to (while aggrandizing) the postwar system. In the eyes of competitiveness analysts, the huge defense budget has diverted public resources from civilian research and development (thereby damaging U.S. competitiveness vis-a-vis Japan and Germany) and has contributed substantially to the mushrooming budget deficit, in the process undermining the U.S. economy by increasing the "cost of capital" investment. In terms of the deficit, however, military and social spending are lumped together as equally "bad" (that is, deficit-increasing) for the economy.

In sum, many of the "remedies" advocated by business sectors today are aimed at "problems" that evolved from previous economic "remedies" advocated earlier by business sectors. Hence, we would argue that an implicit aim of current competitiveness propaganda is to make invisible the extent to which American capitalism has been "hoist by its own petard."

What other counterconstituencies does competitiveness propaganda render invisible? There are, in fact, common invisible counterconstituencies of all four competitiveness perspectives. Almost universally applauded by these competitiveness critics is the reduction of government regulation of the economy. (Indeed, as we have seen, government is urged to reduce regulation even further.) What is made invisible by this are the needs and concerns of those who are affected by the across-the-board regulation we have experienced in the 80s. Thus, worker standard of living, the concept that they have "rights" to health and safety on the job and to a decent standard of living are not addressed. To the extent that they are addressed at all (see perspective 4 above), it is in the context of plans to make a "superior", more efficient and productive worker. The notion that worker interests have *intrinsic value as issues of human concern* seems oddly lacking. Of course, we do not mean to imply some image of the cold-hearted capitalist sitting in his castle while the workers go hungry. Rather, we are suggesting that our system is structured so that the competitiveness debate is biased toward the bottom-line concerns of corporate executives and shareholders rather than toward the needs and concerns of the majority who must struggle to make a living.

Another invisible counterconstituency of all four competitiveness perspectives is linked to the decline of local communities and cultures, the spread of mass consumerism, and the environmental degredation and destruction associated with the spread of global capitalist competition. It is ironic, though revealing, in an age when the President touts himself as the "environmental president," that the competitiveness debate proceeds as if competitiveness solutions should not take these problems into central consideration. The propaganda issue here is that by attacking government regulation as the villian in "decreasing competitive advantage," other values of great importance to people in general may be sacrificed.

A final counterconstituency consists of the working people rendered invisible by the lack of discussion about control of the workplace. As we have seen, the universalizing tendency is a way of making invisible both the interests of those in control and, at the same time, getting employees to identify with that system of control.

From the perspective of democracy, these propaganda tendencies raise grave normative concerns. It appears that business and, for the most part, political leaders have a shared sense of the counterconstituencies to be marginalized, repressed, or otherwise made invisible. Think of these counterconstituencies as voices not invited to the debating table because they would articulate, when taken together, a vision of economic and environmental justice that would force the debate onto subjects other than "competitive advantage": power-sharing or shifts in the structure of control, the empowerment of hitherto powerless groups, and the placing of consumer and environmental concerns before those of profit. Thus, the unfortunate effect of the competitiveness debate as propaganda is a corruption of democratic discourse disguised by propaganda strategies that ultimately equate the interests of powerful groups with the greater good.

There is a subtler way in which the propaganda aspects of the competitiveness debate also undercut meaningful democratic discourse. By defining the concern with competitiveness as a *relative* advantage in a contest of "us vs. them," the debate is cast in relative terms. Thus, if some of "us" gain back market share or achieve enhanced market penetration, we will all gain relative to others. But what needs to be done to improve "relatively" renders invisible distributive questions of who is gaining at whose expense, and normative questions of what values are being sacrificed so that other values may prevail. Yet genuine democratic discourse revolves around precisely how best to realize those values of justice, equality, and fair play so central (at least rhetorically) to our political system. Instead, the fact that the competitiveness debate we have reviewed comes far closer to Chomsky's depiction of propaganda in advanced industrial societies underscores how dramatically the discussion of competitiveness departs from democratic principles. Indeed, if the bottom-line issue for a democracy is not just "discourse," but "control over decision-making," then (at the risk of universalizing) we might do well, as Winner suggests, to see economic competitiveness as "a byproduct of ends, practices, and human relationships that we affirm for their own intrinsic worth— that is, for the contributions they make to a more just and democratic society."[49]

NOTES

1. H. Speier, "The Historical Development of Public Opinion," *American Journal of Sociology* 55: 376–88.

2. See D. L. Altheide and J. M. Johnson, *Bureaucratic Propaganda* (Boston: Allyn and Bacon, 1980).

3. See, for example, Lance Bennett, III, *News: The Politics of an Illusion* (New York: Longman, 1989); Noam Chomsky, *Necessary Illusions: Thought Control in Democratic Societies* (Boston: South End, 1989); Edward S. Herman and Noam Chomsky, *Manufacturing Consent: The Political Economy of the Mass Media* (New York: Pantheon, 1988); Mark Miller, *Boxed In: The Culture of TV* (Evanston, Illinois: Northwestern University Press, 1989); Michael Parenti, *Inventing Reality: The Politics of the Mass Media* (New York: St. Martin's, 1986); and Neil Postman, *Amusing Ourselves to Death: Public Discourse in the Age of Show Business* (New York: Penguin, 1985).

4. Edward Bernays, *Public Relations* (Norman, Oklahoma: University of Oklahoma Press, 1952).

5. Jacques Ellul, *Propaganda: The Formation of Men's Attitudes* (New York: Knopf, 1965).

6. C. Geertz, "From the Native's Point of View: On the Nature of Anthropological Understanding," in P. Rabinow and W. M. Sullivan, eds., *Interpretive*

Social Science (Berkeley: University of California Press, 1979), 229. More generally, see R. N. Bellah, et al, *Habits of the Heart: Individualism and Commitment in American Life* (Berkeley: University of California Press, 1985); E. Sampson, *Justice and the Critique of Pure Psychology* (New York: Plenum, 1982); and A. Wilden, *System and Structure,* 2nd ed. (London: Tavistock, 1980).

7. See Samuel Bowles, David M. Gordon, and Thomas E. Weisskopf, *Beyond the Waste Land: A Democratic Alternative to Economic Decline* (Garden City, New York: Anchor, 1984).

8. Jim Manzi, "Globalization and Competition: A Long Term View is a Necessity," *Vital Speeches of the Day* (1990): 559–62.

9. John A. Young, "Competitiveness: 23 Leaders Speak Out," *Harvard Business Review* 65 (1987): 112.

10. Yohe, 115.

11. Barre, 116.

12. Levitt, Jr., and Lilley, 119.

13. Ibid., 118–20.

14. Simourian, 118.

15. Bieber, 117.

16. Johnson, 120–21.

17. C. K. Prahalad, "The Changing Nature of Worldwide Competition: Reversing the United State's [sic] Decline," *Vital Speeches of the Day* 56 (1990): 355.

18. Ralph Z. Sorensen, in Young, "23 Leaders," 112.

19. Kempton B. Jenkins, in ibid., 110–11.

20. Merle H. Banta, in ibid., 111–12.

21. Sorensen, in ibid., 112–13.

22. John E. Swearingen, in ibid., 121–22.

23. Jack Kemp, in ibid., 115.

24. Richard E. Heckert, in ibid., 110.

25. John P. Cregan, "Building an American Consensus: A National Interest Trade Policy," *Vital Speeches of the Day* 56 (1990): 510.

26. Quoted in ibid., 512.

27. Cregan, "American Consensus, 511–12.

28. Quoted in ibid., 512.

29. U.S. Council for an Open World Economy, statement submitted to the U.S. Senate Committee on Finance, Hearing, 29 March 1985 (Washington, D.C.: U. S. Government Printing Office, 1985), 113.

30. Manzi, "Globalization and Competition," 559.

31. Manzi's comments reveal the difference between what might be considered propaganda and democratic models of economic policy when he states, "There is a fine balance that all companies must deliver between *leading our customers' thinking* with new technology and responding to their needs." *ibid.* 560, (emphasis added).

32. Cregan, "American Consensus," 509–11.

33. C. H. Barnette, L. D. Patterson, and W. L. Hoppe, "Government Policy and International Competitiveness, Steel: A Case Study," *Lehigh Business and Economic Review* (1991): 45, 50.

34. Levitt and Lilley, in Young, "23 Leaders," 118.

35. Pat Choate, statement before the Subcommittee on Economic Stabilization of the Committee on Banking, Finance, and Urban Affairs, U.S. House of Representatives, 5 March 1985 (Washington, D.C.: U.S. Government Printing Office, 1985), 30–31.

36. Barnette, et al, "Government Policy," p. 45.
37. Robert Reich, "Who is Us?" *Harvard Business Review,* 68 (1990): 54.
38. Ibid., 59.
39. Ibid., 58.
40. Matthew Burns and Fidel Ramos, in Young, "23 Leaders," 114.
41. Michael S. Dukakis, in ibid., 113.
42. W. G. Wilkinson, "Education Reform and Economic Competition: Critical Issues before the Oxford International Roundtable on Educational Reform," *Vital Speeches of the Day* 56 (1990): 40–41.
43. See Robert Reich, *The Work of Nations: Preparing for 21st Century Capitalism* (New York: Knopf, 1991).
44. John F. Copper, "U.S. Perspectives on the Pacific Rim," *Vital Speeches of the Day* 56 (1990): 485.
45. Ove Hoegh, in Young, "23 Leaders," 114.
46. William W. Winpisinger, in ibid., 120.
47. See Postman, *Amusing Ourselves,* and Miller, *Boxed In.* For a rebuttal, see W. J. McGuire, "The Myth of Massive Media Impact: Savagings and Salvagings," *Public Communication and Behavior* 1: 173–258.
48. See, for example, Bennett, *News,* Herman and Chomsky, *Manufacturing Consent,* R. M. Entman, *Democracy without Citizens: Media and the Decay of American Politics* (Oxford: Oxford University Press, 1989).
49. Langdon Winner, "Let them Eat Competitiveness," *Technology Review* 91 (1988): 70.

America vs. Japan: Competition, Cooperation, and Competitiveness

JOHN KENLY SMITH, JR.

The most visible symbols of the decline of American industrial competitiveness are the Japanese cars and consumer electronics that are central to modern American life. Although we also buy goods made in other countries, Americans seem obsessed with the competition that domestic products face from Japanese ones. We seem to worry about Japan much more than about any other country. When the Swedish firm Ikea opened its newest furniture store at the northern end of the New Jersey Turnpike, 15,000 enthusiastic shoppers jammed the surrounding highways.[1] Ikea has introduced new concepts into the stodgy American furniture business; yet, the sight of Volvos on our roads and Ikea furniture in our homes has not led to a massive investigation of Swedish life and industry. Perhaps the best example of this phenomenon is the difference in public reaction to the acquisition of American firms by European or Japanese interests. It can be argued that America's obsession with Japan is tinged with racism; we do not worry about competition from our distant cousins in Europe, but we fear the influence of a truly foreign culture on our own. That there is some of this is undeniable. However, from my reading of the literature on Japan and in my own growing fascination with that country, I believe that there is another, more important, motive. For intellectuals, especially, Japanese society is a distant mirror. The economic rise of Japan is presented as a fable with lessons in it for all of us. We highlight particular aspects of the Japanese experience to support various agendas for change in American social and economic life. It is not surprising then that Japanese society has been intensely scrutinized under sociological, economic, and historical "microscopes." Both America and Japan are highly industrialized and wealthy countries, but the respective cultures are very different.

So, we apparently have two paths to the same result and, thus, an experimental control of a sort for sociological speculation.

It is not only fascination that we have for the Japanese; we also fear that Japanese, and to some extent European, success has been gained at the expense of the American standard of living. The competitiveness problem has been defined as the key to understanding American economic and social problems. The symptoms are real. Many American industrial firms have lost domestic market share to foreign producers. In order to maintain middle class status, families now need two incomes instead of one. The poor and working class are actually losing ground economically. This collection of problems, some of which are only partly economic, has been lumped together as *the* problem of competitiveness. Japan has come to be seen as both the cause and the solution to this problem. On the one hand, we lament the draining of wealth out of America, but, at the same time, we admire the accomplishments of the Japanese.

What does the Japanese experience mean for Americans? The current debate about the meaning of the Japanese example is nothing more than the latest incarnation of a nearly two-hundred-year-old discussion going back at least to Thomas Jefferson and Alexander Hamilton. The heart of the debate is what makes a society most healthy and productive: individual initiative versus cooperative endeavor.[2] Of course, any society needs both; it is the dynamic relationship between them that is central to social and economic issues. In fact, the recognition that the key to success is the balancing of both individual freedom and group responsibility does much to explain the success of industrial giants. This recognition does not have to be made in the halls of government, or even consciously recognized by citizens. It can and is, perhaps, best expressed in prevailing cultural beliefs and myths that educate us about what is socially useful or socially destructive behavior. As for the role of the individual, both Japan and America have shared a common work ethic, a belief that the process of work is inherently worthwhile almost independent of the particular rewards that might accrue from work.[3] Both cultures emphasize the importance of individual effort for the accomplishment of larger goals. At the other end of the spectrum, the Japanese have well articulated ideas about the importance of collective endeavor whereas, for Americans, teamwork is highly regarded primarily on the athletic field.

For both Americans and Japanese, an important metaphor for the proper relationship between the individual and the group has been baseball. In each baseball play the action moves sequentially from one player to another. The pitcher throws the ball; the batter hits it; the fielder catches it. On a baseball team the fan knows every player because, at some time or another in every game, the spotlight will shine on him. Unlike football, baseball has no interior linemen who battle anonymously in the trenches. Yet, success in baseball does depend on cooperative actions by the players; it is a team game. Differences between American and Japanese society as revealed through their respective approaches to baseball have recently been explored in Robert Whiting's *You Gotta Have Wa.*[4] This book focuses on the difficulties that American players have had adjusting to the Japanese game. The major point Whiting makes is not surprising—in Japan, there is a great emphasis on *wa,* or team spirit. The addition of a talented American player to a team is generally regarded as endangering the all important *wa.* Japanese players generally show respect for their managers and coaches and are modest about their accomplishments. Their dedication to the game is complete: long practice sessions precede each game, players play while hurt, and they never miss a game for personal reasons such as a birth or death in the family. In Japan, dedication to the team and intensity of effort rather than great individual achievements are rewarded. At the level of cultural myth, Americans place more emphasis on individual striving than on group accomplishment. In America, "You Gotta Have Heart," not *wa.*

Americans lack an equivalent to *wa,* a fact that has made it very difficult to interpret our own history.[5] Pertinent examples of this phenomenon are the entrepreneurs of the late nineteenth and early twentieth centuries who built some of America's great industrial corporations. We admire men such as John D. Rockefeller and Andrew Carnegie for the ambition, drive, and competitive spirit that led them to create giant business organizations and amass great personal fortunes. But we are much less comfortable with their creations, Standard Oil and Carnegie Steel, respectively, which put many of their competitors out of business.[6] The Sherman Antitrust Act of 1890 codified cultural beliefs about the inherent goodness of competition. Of course, late nineteenth-century Americans were imbued with the world views of Adam Smith and Charles Darwin, who argued that competition was the regulator of the "machines" of industry and nature. Given our cultural predilection for individual competitive achievement, competition has become an end in itself in America, not only for individuals but also for institutions. With the absence of other models to explain social processes, the competitive one has been dominant, if only because it is so satisfying to the American psyche.

The American myth of heroic individualism has been exploited by some historical figures. Thomas Edison, for example, created a Horatio Alger persona for himself that incorporated nineteenth-century ideas about individual achievement: poor boy makes good, the unlettered tinkerer, invention is 99% perspiration and 1% inspiration. For a long time historians took Edison at his word. Only recently have we begun to see how Edison used American beliefs to sell his products. There is no question that Edison was an outstanding inventor, but as Andre Millard argues, he was not unchallenged by his contemporaries.[7] Edison's real advantage was his *organized* development laboratories that could get his product into the marketplace faster than his competitors could. Customers bought his products because of their faith in Edison—a faith, as in the case of the infamous Edison talking doll which broke easily, that was sometimes unjustified.[8] By looking at Edison and at the methods that he employed, in comparison with contemporaries, historians are beginning to separate the man from the myth.

Although individualism has long been heralded in America, the recent industrial competitiveness crisis derives its vocabulary and rhetoric from the Cold War rivalry between the United States and the Soviet Union. The Cold War prompted Americans to attempt to define what it was that made their society more productive and attractive than others. To heighten the contrast with the collectivist ethic of the Soviet Union, Americans chose to emphasize individualism and competition as the key factors that had made the country rich and dynamic. In the popular culture of the 1950s, Superman fought for truth, justice, and the American way in the cities, while lone cowboys fought evil gunslingers on the frontier.[9] These values promoted on television and in the movies had important policy implications as well. The 1950s witnessed a continued vigorous antitrust policy that had evolved in the late New Deal. The health of American business enterprise was believed to depend on vigorous competition between a significant number of competitors in each business. For many companies, acquisitions and mergers were out of the question because they would have been viewed by the Justice Department as inherent violations of the antitrust laws.[10]

With the launching of Sputnik in 1957, the Russians succeeded in channeling Cold War competition into the narrow arena of high technology symbolized by rockets and satellites: the Space Race. Many Americans, especially scientists and engineers, eagerly accepted the new Soviet challenge and the consequent redefinition of competition. An alternative could have been to point out that, even if the Russians had a small lead in rocket booster technology,

America remained far ahead of the Soviets in all other aspects of technology and economy. The American hysteria over Sputnik, according to the historian Walter McDougall, was caused by Americans who wished to see the government play a stronger role in education, R&D, and even social issues such as segregation and poverty.[11]

For McDougall, the legacy of Sputnik was the growth of government power in the 1960s. From the perspective of competitiveness, the Sputnik episode redefined national competitiveness in terms of high technology instead of in other terms such as equity of income distribution or economic growth. The massive government investment in new high-technology weapons, with which the military had then become infatuated, was justified in part by this point of view. It is difficult to argue against the assertion that the American preoccupation with magical weapons has diverted resources and talent away from more economically significant technologies. From this point of view, it is not surprising that the Germans and Japanese, who have been barred from this realm of competition, have done so well in other areas of technology. The Cold War, then, had two important impacts on the American economic values: a rededication to individualism and competition as the key to success, and a redefinition of economic strength in terms of high technology.

The current debate over American competitiveness has focused on the threat of Japanese products and culture to American economic prosperity. Japan offers a wonderful mirror to the American and western European experience. Yet the picture we see is distorted by our own values and ideologies, particularly those that emphasize the importance of competition. On one level, we see ourselves competing with the Japanese, not only to make better cars, but in all aspects of life. This represents a vestige of the Cold War and leads to paradoxical conclusions. The life of the average Japanese salaryman would be intolerable to Americans, as well as would be the lives of their wives and children.[12] The Japanese system of education which emphasizes long hours of memorizing information at the expense of play, sleep, and all other activities— playing baseball excepted—simply would not work in America. Yet, proposals to make American children go to school year round, so that they can keep up with the Japanese, are increasingly popular.[13]

Generally, Americans select only certain aspects of Japanese culture for emulation in order to advance their own long-established agendas. Critics of American management attitudes toward workers as being appendages to machines and as being motivated only by wages, paint a picture of Japanese workers and managers solving problems together harmoniously. At the same time, American managers point to the subservience of Japanese workers to management prerogatives that are often bitterly contested by American labor unions. Which scenario is right? In the Japanese context, both are; in the American, neither.

A clever twist to the cultural debate was added by James Fallows, who lived in Japan for almost three years.[14] Observing the dynamics of Japanese society, Fallows concluded that theirs is such an alien culture that we should not try to emulate the Japanese, but should closely scrutinize our own culture and try to strengthen those aspects that make it work. In response to Japanese collective effort and social hierarchies, Fallows recommends making America truly individualistic and socially fluid by removing impediments to those principles. Fallows attacks credentialism of every variety. For example, SAT scores have been shown to correlate with family income, so these exams do not measure scholarly potential, but socio-economic status instead. So, Fallows says that SAT tests should be abolished. Another example from education is teaching. Becoming an elementary or secondary school teacher requires taking education courses. Teachers' unions and university education departments support requiring these courses, the former as a way to limit entry into the profession and the latter as a justification for their existence. Without these requirements, Fallows argues, some people who majored in academic disciplines in college would be attracted to teaching. In general, Fallows' arguments assume that an American society that is as open as possible will lead to the best possible situation socially and economically. This conclusion results from his interpretation of the history of America and his own family. It is an updated version of Federick Jackson Turner's famous frontier thesis, that on the frontier there exists the most egalitarian form of culture because the frontier has the fewest barriers to success for those who work hard and are intelligent.

At the other extreme from Fallows are those who want America to adopt the Japanese approach to many issues, especially in the area of business-government relations.[15] Because of the major role that American government has played in regulating business and the way government regulates business, an adversarial relationship has been built into the structure of government-business relations. The American regulatory apparatus contrasts sharply with Japanese institutions with similar missions, especially the Ministry of International Trade and Industry (MITI), which have had a major impact on the development of business and technology in Japan.[16]

Of course, the United States, which maintains an ideological commitment to laissez-faire economics, allows such interference with private enterprise only in the area of defense. The Defense Advanced Research Projects Agency has been a miniature MITI, giving out research funds for technologies that the military might use in the future, among them artificial intelligence and high-definition television.[17] American advocates of an industrial policy would like to see government play a stronger role in the direction of American industry, but how this would happen is less clear. The sometimes heavy-handed approach of MITI would never be acceptable to Americans. Probably the farthest the United States government could go would be to subsidize research in particular fields of interest or to impose tariffs to protect industries judged important to the national interest.

Rather than focus on individual behavior or broad cultural values, the competitiveness issue is probably best addressed at the level of the corporation, the actual producer of wealth in America and Japan. Investigating the dynamic operation of these institutions provides an opportunity to focus the competitiveness issue on the terrain in which the battles are actually being waged. Of course, corporations are also cultural entities that have to balance individual initiative with cooperative endeavor.

To understand why modern large-scale business enterprise evolved has been the quest of the business historian Alfred D. Chandler, Jr. Chandler began his work from an organizational rather than an economic point of view.[18] His novel approach led him to ask new questions and to gain new insights into the origins and evolution of big business. He argued that in the second half of the nineteenth century, entrepreneurs discovered that by investing in new, high throughput, technologies manufacturing costs could be lowered dramatically. They empirically discovered what has become known as economies of scale, which could be quite dramatic, sometimes lowering the cost of production by an order of magnitude. To insure that the expensive new technology was fully employed, the entrepreneurs then had to invest in marketing organizations in order to maintain high levels of sales. In some industries these sales organizations gave the companies what is called economies of scope. That is, once the expense of setting up a distribution network has been incurred, then other similar products could be marketed through the same network.

For Chandler, the key to long-term success in industries offering potential economies of scale or scope has been the development of organizational capabilities.[19] To reap the rewards of scale and scope requires hierarchically organized institutions. Once these institutions are put into place, they can provide the basis for ongoing product diversification and geographical expansion that provide long-term stability and growth for the firm. In industries that evolve along these lines, there is competition, but not the price competition that neoclassical economics demands. In reality, large firms compete for market share, to be the lowest-cost producer in established lines of business, and to be the leader in new-product innovation. In sum, Chandler's model provides an alternative to market-oriented economic models for explaining the evolution of modern industrial economies.

Just as American history has been skewed by focusing primarily on the individual, American economic theory has been built on the concept of the competitive market. Yet these economic theories have not been very successful in explaining the persistence of large businesses around the world. In fact, economic arguments based on the assumption that resources are most efficiently allocated through perfectly competitive markets can only explain the success of big business in terms of "market failure" and "monopoly rents," meaning that big business has essentially destroyed the market and earns higher profits than it would under competitive conditions. According to this theory, a company earning such high profits will draw new capital into the industry, leading to a more competitive situation. If this does not happen the economist can argue that the industry has erected high barriers to entry in order to discourage newcomers. Although this explanation is the logical outcome of the assumptions about markets allocating resources efficiently, it really says nothing about the dynamics of the firm itself. The Yale economist Oliver Williamson has attempted to develop an economic model to explain why large firms persist and are apparently efficient.[20] Williamson has developed the concept of transactions costs that are incurred because buyers and seller must inform themselves about what the market really looks like in terms of prices and qualities. The point here is that buyers and sellers have to define for themselves what the market is. In a similar vein, the economic historian Richard Sutch has argued that

The power of neoclassical theory derives from the strong assumptions it makes about the presence of competition, the absence of transactions cost and uncertainty, and the stability of underlying economic institutions. Many of the most interesting problems in economics, however, revolve around the absence or imperfections of competition, the consequences of substantial transactions cost and uncertainty, and changes in the economic institutions of society.[21]

When examined analytically, the market emerges as an idealized concept which in reality is never fully realized. What Williamson argues is that firms that are vertically integrated have internal "markets" where the information to make decisions can be obtained more cheaply, thus leading to efficiences in large organizations. Overall, transactions costs do not correspond exactly to economies of scale and scope, which remain primarily empirical phenomena gleaned from the historical record.

Chandler's analytical framework can be applied to understand the balance between competitive and cooperative forces in modern industrial economies. Below, I will use this framework to discuss the British and American competitiveness crises of the late-nineteenth and late-twentieth centuries, respectively.

The current Japan versus America debate is in some ways a repeat of an earlier competitiveness crisis, that of Great Britain in the second half of the nineteenth century. At mid-century, Britain stood unchallenged as the premier industrial power. It had led the way in the industrial revolution characterized by the steam engine–coal–iron complex, cotton textile production machinery, and the development of sophisticated metal-working skills. The steam engine was initially developed by Thomas Newcomen about 1712 to pump water from increasingly deep coal mines. At about the same time, Abraham Darby was learning how to smelt iron with coal instead of increasingly expensive charcoal. Cheaper coal and iron gave Britain two important tools for industrialization. British mechanicians such as Henry Maudslay, inventor of the modern lathe and many other machine tools, developed skills in using these materials that made Britain the world's center of metal-working and machine building.[22] One example was the modern paper-making machine that was perfected in England by Brian Donkin.[23] The most famous and economically important machines were those were developed to spin, and later to weave, cotton. By the 1790s, the cotton-spinning factory, first installed by the inventor-entrepreneur Richard Arkwright, had revolutionized textile production by increasing the labor productivity of cotton spinning by thousands of percent over traditional spinning wheels. This innovation led Britain to develop extensive overseas markets for cotton thread and fabric, in the process providing jobs for one and a half million people and generating enormous wealth in the first half of the nine-teenth century.[24]

In 1851 Britain held an international world's fair, the first of what would become a continuing tradition, to advertise the goods that the "workshop of the world" was making. The fair building was a monument to British ingenuity. Designed by an estate manager, Joseph Paxton, it was a large-scale version of greenhouses which he had earlier designed and built. The Crystal Palace, as it was dubbed, was built with cast-iron columns, cast- and wrought-iron girders, and 250,000 panes of glass. It covered twenty-two acres, but its modular design allowed it to be constructed in only thirty-nine weeks.[25] Although the Crystal Palace was a success, the excellence of American-manufactured goods exhibited inside it, such products as Colt's revolvers and McCormick reapers, shocked British manufacturers. Samuel Colt's disingenuous boast that his guns were made with interchangeable parts astounded fairgoers. Actually, the United States government arsenal at Springfield, Massachusetts, was making small arms with interchangeable parts, the result of decades of effort to achieve a military objective of guns that could be repaired in the field. The high cost of achieving inter-changeability, compared to other methods of production, prevented it from being used by private arms makers or other manufacturers of complex machinery. In response to the American challenge, the British organized a committee and sent a commission to the United States to investigate the new production technology in place there. The commissioners were impressed with the American's machine-building in general and went home with the depressing news that Britain had fallen behind in a critical technology that had been central to the initial phase of the industrial revolution.[26]

Although competition had arisen in its older technological base, Britain might have pinned its hopes for the future in new technologies invented in the 1850s. Henry Bessemer discovered how to liquefy pure iron, something that was impossible using blast furnace technology. The product of a blast furnace, namely, pig or cast iron, contained 4% carbon and could easily be liquefied. As the percentage of carbon in iron is reduced, as is necessary to make wrought iron or steel, the melting point rises significantly. Because of this, pure or wrought iron and steel had to be produced and worked as a solid. To attain the high temperatures needed to melt pure iron, Bessemer surmised that the carbon in pig iron could be used as a fuel if air were blown through the molten product. The resulting process not only produced magnificent pyrotechnics, but also made possible the production of cheap steel.[27]

At about the same time Bessemer was experimenting with iron, a young British chemistry student, William Perkin, was naively trying to synthesize quinine, which had been shown to be effective against malaria. For raw materials Perkin used coal tar chemicals, the residue that remained after coal was heated to high temperatures to create gases that were piped throughout London for lighting. One of his experiments produced a purple-colored liquid that led Perkin to pursue its development as a dye. As luck would have it, purple was at that time the high-fashion color and could be made only from exotic and expensive materials. Perkin's discovery led other chemists to try similar experiments, and soon other synthetic dyes were discovered. The first important one was alizarine, which replaced the natural red dye, madder, in the 1860s. Development of these dyes led to the creation of the organic chemical industry.[28] In addition to these new technologies and the industries that grew up around them, the late-nineteenth century also witnessed the rise of electrical technology. The dynamo, first conceived by Micheal Faraday in Great Britain in the 1830s but developed in Germany in the 1860s, made electricity available in sufficient quantities and at low enough cost that it became a viable power source. By the 1890s electricity had become a rapidly expanding industry. Not only did it provide the basis for new lighting systems and motors, which had a major impact on factories, it also provided a method for manufacturing metals and chemicals, such as aluminum, refractory metals, oxygen, and chlorine.[29] These new technologies were exhibited at the Paris Exhibition of 1867, at which the naval engineer Scott Russell commented that, "We then learnt, not that we were equalled, but that we were beaten—not on some points, but by some nation or other on nearly all those points on which we had prided ourselves."[30]

These new technologies of the second half of the nineteenth century have been called the Second Industrial Revolution and provided the basis for the United States and Germany to surpass Great Britain as an industrial power by the First World War.[31] The loss of competitiveness by Great Britain has been widely discussed, then and now. Contemporary observers linked technological and economic progress to the work of inventors and engineers, so the system of technical education in Great Britain came under intense and ongoing scrutiny. In its universities, Britain had some of the greatest scientists and engineers in the world. *It is important to remember that in the quality of its technological and scientific ingenuity Britain was in no way inferior to any other nation.* The list of late-Victorian British scientists and engineers included

James Clerk Maxwell, Charles Wheatstone, Charles Parsons, Osborne Reynolds, J. J. Thompson, Lord Kelvin, William Rankine, and Ambrose Fleming.[32] In the twentieth century Britain continued to be an important source of new science and technology, but too frequently did not capitalize on the industrial and economic opportunities that they presented.[33] To explain these failings, contemporary observers and historians have focused on the insufficient quantity, rather than the quality, of British scientists and engineers.

The most persistent explanation of the relative decline of British industrial performance has thus been to attribute it to the lack of adequate support for technical education in Great Britain.[34] This argument was first made by the chemist Lyon Playfair, who was in charge of commissioning the construction of the Crystal Palace, in 1852. In a lecture at the new School of Mines, Playfair compared unfavorably the state of science in Britain to its state in France and Germany, where government supported education. Playfair called for the establishment of an industrial university that would "grant degrees involving high social recognition to those who attained them, and would draw off the excess of talented men, to whom the Church, the Bar, and Medicine, offered only a slender chance of attaining eminence."[35] In the following decades, one commission after another would echo Playfair's argument with increasing urgency as Britain fell further and further behind, both industrially and educationally. In an 1869 book, Russell claimed that Britain spent more than five times as much on pauperism and crime as it did on education, while Switzerland spent seven times as much on education as on pauperism and crime.[36] Linking education to competitiveness, educator Thomas H. Huxley, an eminent Darwinist and educator, in 1887 portrayed the future in Darwinian terms: "We are entering, indeed we have already entered, upon the most serious struggle for existence to which this country was ever committed. The latter years of the century promise to see us in an industrial war of far more serious import than the military war of its opening years."[37]

For a number of reasons, including a commitment to laissez-faire principles, the British government did not act until it passed the first Technical Education Act in 1889. But Great Britain would never catch up with the European countries or the United States, which saw the number of engineers increase dramatically after the 1862 Morrill Act gave federal land grants to state universities that would teach agricultural and mechanical arts subjects. In 1913, all of the universities of England and Wales together graduated 1129 engineers, which was about one-tenth the number graduating from

German universities, and represented the output of the three or four largest American engineering schools.[38]

The connection between the number of university-trained engineers and industrial performance, however, remains controversial.[39] One view is that the more people who are working in science and technology the more progress there will be in those areas. The cases of Germany and the United States suggest that, in both countries, significant numbers of university-trained engineers and scientists became available just at the time when large industrial enterprises had openings for them. Some historians, notably David A. Noble, see this occurrence, not as a happy coincidence but as a takeover of educational institutions by industry to provide it with suitably trained personnel.[40] Of course, the obvious counterexample is Great Britain, where the educational establishment retained its commitment to classical education and to the creation of proper gentlemen. In America and Germany, engineers became probably the single most important professional group in industrial enterprises. These engineers filled the ranks of middle management in industrial firms, helping them establish the organizational capabilities Chandler sees as essential for the ongoing evolution of technology and successful industrial enterprise. From the historical point of view, therefore, the decline of the competitiveness of Great Britain was only indirectly connected to the shortage of engineers and scientists. Without an appropriate institutional setting—particularly the modern corporation—even large numbers of technical personnel could not have kept Britain competitive. The key factor was that technical activity had to be organized and directed toward long-term goals.

What separated Britain from the United States and Germany with regard to the technologies of the second industrial revolution was the relatively smaller size of British firms. Preferring what Chandler calls personal capitalism, British businessmen continued to manage their firms directly, and consequently did not build organizational hierarchies. As the effective integration of mass-production technology and mass marketing required such hierarchical organizations, the British were overwhelmed by American and German competition in many important industries. British economic historians argue about whether their country suffered from "entrepreneurial failure," beginning in the second half of the nineteenth century. This approach misses the point. Entrepreneurial activity is the necessary *first* stage of the development of a new industry, but it is not sufficient to insure long-term survival and growth.[41]

If the British competitive crisis dates from the Crystal Palace Exhibition of 1851, the American one originated in 1957 with the launching of the Soviet satellite, Sputnik. More generally, as discussed above, the concept of national competitiveness may have its origins in the Cold War. In the 1950s the United Sates and the Soviet Union held up their respective political and economic systems as the model for other countries around the world, especially the former colonies in Africa and Asia which at the time were becoming independent. In this competition it was imperative to argue superiority in all areas: economic, political, social, and cultural.[42] Of course, the United States had been in competition with western European countries in all these areas before World War II, but no one expected the United States to be superior to them across the board.

To understand the development of science and technology in that era, it is probably best to view the United States and Europe as a single Atlantic community; each country specialized in particular fields or subfields and borrowed heavily from others if more advanced knowledge or technique existed elsewhere. The major advantage of America in the pre-World War II era appears to have been its ability to commercialize technologies that would have a broad market appeal. This strategy capitalized on America's enormous market and its vast middle class which had considerable purchasing power. Even during the Depression, the American market remained the largest and broadest in the world. The forced savings of World War II, when combined with the new infrastructure built during the war, catapulted the American domestic economy forward in the postwar era. The health of the American economy in the 1950s was a major advantage for the United States in the Cold War.[43]

A dramatic and economically important example of Cold War competitiveness was the Silicon Valley phenomenon in the electronics industry. Until recently, the small- to medium-sized companies in the semiconductor industry were hailed as a new American approach to business, which thrived on entrepreneurial activity and avoided large market dominating firms of the IBM-type. Silicon Valley proudly represented the Cold War values of individualism and competition. This assessment, however, ignored the institutional framework within which Silicon Valley originated, grew, and prospered. The semiconductor entrepreneurs depended on Bell Labs for basic science, technology, and personnel, and on the military for product development money and initial markets.

To justify its monopoly status, AT&T had a long-term policy of arguing that it was a corporation that valued the public interest highly in its decision making. In short, it was a good monopoly, not a bad one. Ever since its founding in 1925, the Bell Research Labs had been a cornerstone of this strategy. Research, in general, was viewed as being in the public interest, and AT&T was quite generous in licensing new technology for non-telecommunications applications. In fact, AT&T did research of a very general nature that might have ramifications for all kinds of other technologies.[44] Before the breakup of AT&T, Bell Labs was probably the closest thing to a national laboratory that the United States has ever had. American semiconductor research began there and, of course, the transistor was invented there in 1947. Since then, the company has played a leading role in the development of semiconductor science and technology. A family tree of the Silicon Valley companies shows that most lines go back to AT&T: transistor co-inventor William Shockley left to form his own firm, and some of the employees who left to form Fairchild Semiconductor eventually formed Intel. Even though Bell Labs did not make all the breakthroughs, it developed the field generally and trained people who would staff other companies' laboratories. Bell Labs acted as a resource center for the entire industry.[45]

The other key to the success of Silicon Valley was the fact that the military took much of the risk out of innovation, a risk that for many firms threatens survival. In any innovation, the development phase is the critical one because large sums of money are needed to develop prototypes, manufacturing processes, and markets. Generally, the amount of money spent during this phase is much greater than in the earlier research phase. Using modern accounting techniques, such as discounted cash flow analysis, money invested in development is treated as a loan that accumulates interest charges as long as it is not paid back. Therefore, if the initial investment is large and sales are slow to develop, large "interest" payments, when combined with the initial capital input, may keep the product permanently in the red. For a small company the problem is even greater, because it might actually have had to borrow money to develop a new product. Failure in this instance can lead to bankruptcy. The military helped the Silicon Valley companies over the development hump by providing capital and by buying the initial small batches of product at relatively high prices.[46]

Another important aspect of the military investment in semiconductor technology is that it funded the development of expertise that could be applied to other applications. Empirical studies have shown that the cost of manufacturing a given product trends downward over time, and economists have labeled this phenomenon "the learning curve." Historians of technology explain learning in terms of accumulated experience with a particular technology leading to ongoing improvements. By pushing semiconductor development, the military simultaneously pushed companies down the initially expensive and risky parts of the learning curve more rapidly.

Through the 1960s, the original institutional sources of the American semi-conductor industry—Bell Labs and the Pentagon— were sufficient to maintain the health of the industry, but the 1980s witnessed the rise of the Japanese semiconductor industry. In that decade the United States share of the world market in semiconductor devices fell from 60% to 35%. Silicon Valley has not been able to compete with the large Japanese firms such as Sony, Matsushita, NEC, and Canon. From the point of view of neoclassical economic theory, it is difficult to explain this shift except by claiming that the Japanese collude to avoid free-market competition and, therefore, get unfair advantages. In the longer run, however, such interference with the free operation of competitive markets will lead to inefficiencies compared to American producers. One problem with this argument is that, except for IBM, there may not be any American semiconductor producers left to exploit this competitive advantage. The demise of Silicon Valley and the rise of the Japanese can be explained by Chandler's theory of organizational capabilities. One semiconductor industry analyst recently argued that the Japanese dominance of the industry is based on the organizational capabilities that exist in the large vertically-integrated Japanese firms but that are absent in the large U.S. firms, except IBM and at AT&T.[47]

The key factors in the industry today are diversification, vertical integration, innovation capability, and access to capital. The driving forces behind these factors are the digitization of a wide variety of technologies and the development of mass-produced, standardized digital components. These two phenomena are related, because it is the cheapness of the components that allows the digitization of cameras, stereos, photocopiers, televisions, typewriters, and other electronic goods. In the future, these devices will all have a common technological basis that will provide a lucrative opportunity for diversification for vertically-integrated firms that are manufacturing one or more of these products. For example, Canon can move from its base in cameras and photocopiers into a wide range of products built with the same standardized components. This process is called technological convergence and has occurred at least twice previously: in machine-building in the nineteenth century, and in the chemical industry since World War II. In these earlier cases, the firms that were diversified and vertically integrated profited from technological convergence.[48]

Vertical integration is important because manufacturers can combine basic component manufacture with specific end products to take advantage of technological convergence. The combination of state-of-the-art process technology, knowledge of end-product design, and marketing are an unbeatable combination. It is likely that mass production, as it did for automobile manufacturing in the 1910s, is raising the amount of investment needed to be competitive. One industry expert has estimated that since the mid-1970s each generation of new semiconductor devices has required twice as much R&D and capital investment as the previous one. Since a generation lasts about five years, the cost of staying competitive is rising rapidly. In research, work on a new generation of technology must begin just as the current generation is moving into production. Needless to say, companies will need to be well organized and have large amounts of reasonably priced capital to stay in this business. Once again, this condition favors large firms.[49]

Whereas current production of both components and final products is essential to be competitive, in the future the component part of the business might become the dominant part. If the process of convergence follows the previous two occurrences, the electronics industry will eventually be controlled by those who make the standardized components. If the manufacture of end products evolves toward assembly of these components, this part of the business might become very competitive, especially if the capital and technological requirements needed to enter it become low enough. At this juncture the future course of events is not clear. The Japanese manufacturers have built their dominating position in electronic products on the base of process technology, which represents innumerable man-years of learning by doing. Although it is always quicker and cheaper to copy the leader rather than to pioneer, it is unclear whether American firms will be able to catch up with the Japanese. But, if the entire technological structure of electronic product manufacture changes dramatically, say, to one in which standardized electronic components are assembled into a wide variety of products, then the cost of entering and competing in this industry might become quite low. This is exactly what happened to the chemical industry in the postwar era.

The convergence of chemical technology around petrochemicals and polymers after World War II dramatically altered the relationship between chemical companies and their downstream consumers, and the competitive structure of the industry itself. Petrochemical-based polymer technology allowed chemical companies to become the raw material suppliers to many large industries, such as rubber and textiles. Because the chemical companies invested heavily in R&D and production technology, the downstream processors became dependent on the chemical companies for raw materials and basic processing know-how. Not surprisingly, the chemical industry reaped rather high profits, whereas their customers found themselves in very competitive industries. By the late 1950s, high profits in the chemical industry attracted many newcomers who could enter the business with modest investments, because a number of process engineering firms had developed standardized plant designs and could sell turn-key plants to customers. Companies as diverse as the shipping company W. R. Grace, the food processor Borden, and the drug chain Rexall became major chemical producers in the 1950s and 1960s. This invasion of the industry by newcomers sent prices tumbling by the early 1960s and created a generally chaotic situation that has taken several decades to stabilize. At this point it is unclear whether a similar situation will occur in electronics products manufacture. It does not appear to be happening yet in semiconductor technology, perhaps because the scale of production is still increasing significantly, thereby raising the cost of entrance into the business.[50]

The phenomenon of technological convergence introduces another complicating factor into the issue of economic performance and competitiveness. Ultimately, industries consist of collections of firms who interact with each other as well as with customers. The overall technological configuration of an industry transcends the firm. In other words, at any given time an industry has a structure, but that structure can and has changed dramatically. At the firm level, sometimes changes can be anticipated and appropriate actions initiated. Frequently, however, industries for one reason or another get caught sleeping, as did the American steel industry. With regard to industry structure, the Japanese have an enormous advantage over Americans in that MITI studies industry structure and tries to keep Japanese industry abreast of change. In America, the concept of industry structure, which is based primarily on technology, has received little interest because our analysts are primarily economists who think in terms of markets, not larger socioeconomic systems.

Rather than focus on culture or economic systems at one extreme, or factors that motivate individuals at the other extreme, the most appropriate place to compare America and Japan might be at the firm level. Both countries rely on corporations to produce economic wealth. What seems most relevant here is that the concepts developed by Alfred D. Chandler, Jr. to explain the large-scale enterprise in the United States, Great Britain, and Germany, also appear to hold in the Japanese case. Americans need to recognize the importance of collective activity—organizational capabilities—in order to understand how the world economy is changing. We need to separate cultural values from economic realities. This does not entail either emulating the Japanese or rededicating ourselves to competition and individualism. What we should strive to achieve is methods of maintaining the health of American economic institutions, so that we can afford to have a culture that supports values, such as individual dignity and initiative.

If there has been an American Dream, it has probably been the idea that each succeeding generation of family will move at least one step up the socio-economic ladder. For a long time, American economic and social spheres were nearly congruent. In many ways, what was good for General Motors *was* good for America. GM assembly-line workers were paid high wages for unskilled work, which allowed them to achieve middle-class status and send their children to college, if they so desired. As recent corporate restructuring has shown, American corporations have had bloated bureaucracies. But, again, corporations offered well-paying jobs to the large numbers of Americans who sought college educations in the postwar era. All of this made GM cars somewhat more expensive than they would be in an idealized economic world, but the spending of GM employees on all kinds of goods helped to keep wealth circulating in America. The extra GM profits also went to American shareholders. From the standpoint of neoclassical economics, this system may not have been the optimum for the consumer, but economics consists of two functions, production and consumption. In an essentially self-contained system, there was no need to optimize it around any particular item, such as lowest cost production. Of course, what has changed is that GM is now an international company and the American market has been invaded by foreign producers.

In the old system, private enterprise accomplished important social objectives by providing large numbers of good jobs for unskilled and college-trained workers. If that system has broken down, the question remains as to how American social objectives will be accomplished in the future. We are now competing in an international economy, and American wages and working conditions might trend downward toward some kind of world average if we assume that lowest-cost production is the sine qua non of economic activity. As the organization of business increasingly transcends national boundaries, the problems of wealth generation and distribution are becoming much more complex. To comprehend the operation of this international economy, we need to use concepts such as organizational capabilities, industry structure, and national industrial priorities, which are not part of neoclassical economic theory and which contradict long held American beliefs about the efficacy of individual effort and competition.[51]

NOTES

1. *Time,* 15 September 1990.
2. On the historical debate about economic growth and individual freedom see John F. Kasson, *Civilizing the Machine: Technology and Republican Values in America, 1776–1900* (New York: Penguin, 1977.)
3. On the work ethic in America see Daniel T. Rodgers, *The Work Ethic in Industrial America, 1850–1920* (Chicago: University of Chicago Press, 1974).
4. Robert Whiting, *You Gotta Have Wa* (New York: Vintage, 1989).
5. For a good discussion of American and Japanese values see Clyde Prestowitz, *Trading Places* (New York: Basic Books, 1988).
6. A good introduction to big business and American attitudes toward it is Glenn Porter, *The Rise of Big Business, 1860–1910* (Arlington Heights, Ill.: AHM Publishing Company, 1973.)
7. Andre Millard, *Edison and the Business of Innovation* (Baltimore: Johns Hopkins University Press, 1990).
8. Ibid. 82.
9. On American cold war values see chapter 1 of Prestowitz, *Trading Places: How We Gave Our Future to Japan and How to Reclaim It* (New York: Basic Books, 1988), and Tom Wolfe, *The Right Stuff* (New York: Bantam, 1980).
10. On American anti-trust policy see Ellis W. Hawley, "Anti-Trust," in Glenn Porter, ed., *Encyclopedia of American Economic History* (New York: Scribners, 1980), vol. 2, 780.
11. Walter A. McDougall, . . . *The Heavens and the Earth: A Political History of the Space Age* (New York: Basic, 1985).
12. On life in Japan see James Fallows, "The Hard Life," *Atlantic Monthly* (March 1989): 16–25.
13. On year-round education see Michael J. Barrett, "The Case for More School Days," *Atlantic Monthly* 226, No. 5 (November 1990): 78–106.
14. James Fallows, *More Like Us: Making America Great Again* (Boston: Houghton Mifflin, 1989).
15. For example see Thomas K. McCraw, *America vs. Japan* (Cambridge, Mass.: Harvard Business School Press, 1986).
16. On the role of MITI in Japanese industry see Chalmers Johnson, *MITI and the Japanese Miracle: The Growth of Industrial Policy, 1925–1975* (Stanford, Calif.: Stanford University Press, 1982).
17. On DARPA see, "America's Answer to Japan's MITI," *New York Times,* 5 March Sec. 3, 1, 1989.

18. Chandler's concepts are developed in his books *Strategy and Structure: Chapters in the History of American Industrial Enterprise* (Cambridge, Mass.: MIT Press, 1961); *The Visible Hand: The Managerial Revolution in American Business* (Cambridge, Mass.: Harvard University Press, 1977); and *Scale and Scope: The Dynamics of Industrial Enterprise* (Cambridge, Mass.: Harvard University Press, 1990).

19. For a general discussion of Chandler's concepts see *Scale and Scope,* chapter 1.

20. Oliver Williamson, "Modern Corporation: Origins, Evolution, Attributes," *Journal of Economic Literature* 19: (December 1981) 1539–44.

21. Richard Sutch, "Douglas North and the New Economic History," in R. Ransom, R. Sutch, and G. M. Walton, eds., *Explorations in the New Economic History* (New York: Academic Press, 1982).

22. For an overview of technology and the British industrial revolution see David S. Landes, *The Unbound Prometheus: Technological Change and Industrial Development in Western Europe from 1750 to the Present* (New York: Cambridge University Press, 1969).

23. On Donkin and his paper machine see George Escol Sellers, *Early Engineering Reminiscenses (1825–40),* ed. Eugene Ferguson (Washington, D.C.: Smithsonian Press, 1965), 108–34.

24. Friedrich Klemm, *A History of Western Technology* (Cambridge, Mass.: MIT Press, 1964), 291.

25. Folke T. Kihlstedt, "The Crystal Palace," *Scientific American* (October 1984): 132–43.

26. Brooke Hindle and Stephen Lubar, *Engines of Change: The American Industrial Revolution, 1790–1860* (Washington, D.C.: Smithsonian Institution Press, 1986), chapter 15. On British views of the American system see David A. Hounshell, *From the American System to Mass Production, 1800–1932: The Development of Manufacturing Technology in the United States* (Baltimore: Johns Hopkins University Press, 1984), 61–65.

27. Landes, *Unbound Prometheus,* 255.

28. Anthony S. Travis, "Perkin's Mauve: Ancestor of the Organic Chemical Industry," *Technology and Culture* 31 (January 1990): 51–82.

29. On the importance of electricity in the late nineteenth century see Landes, *Unbound Prometheus,* 281–90.

30. George S. Emmerson, *Engineering Education: A Social History* (New York: Crane, Russak & Company, 1973), 174.

31. Paul Kennedy, *The Rise and Fall of Great Powers* (New York: Vintage: 1989), 198–202.

32. Emmerson, *Engineering Education,* chapters 7 and 9.

33. British scientists and engineers made important contributions to radio, radar, penicillin, jet engines, and nuclear technology.

34. Robert R. Locke, *The End of the Practical Man: Entrepreneurship and Higher Education in Germany, France, and Great Britain, 1880–1940* (Greenwich, Conn.: JAI Press, 1984).

35. Emmerson, *Engineering Education,* 170.

36. Ibid., 177.

37. Ibid., 187.

38. Chandler, *Scale and Scope,* 293.

39. On this issue see Part I of Robert R. Locke, *The End of the Practical Man:*

Entrepreneurship and Higher Education in Germany, France, and Great Britain, 1880–1940 (Greenwich, Conn.: JAI Press, 1984).

40. David F. Noble, *America by Design: Science, Technology, and the Rise of Corporate Capitalism* (New York: Oxford University Press, 1977).

41. Chandler, *Scale and Scope,* Part III.

42. McDougall, *Heavens,* chapter 6.

43. On the world economy in the postwar era see Kennedy, *Rise and Fall,* 413–37.

44. On Bell Laboratories see Lillian Hoddeson, "The Roots of Solid State Research at Bell Labs," *Physics Today* (March 1977): 22–30.

45. On the development of the semiconductor industry see Ernest Braun and Stuart Macdonald, *Revolution in Miniature: The History and Impact of Semiconductor Electronics,* 2nd ed., (New York: Cambridge University Press, 1982).

46. Thomas J. Misa, "Military Needs, Commercial Realities, and the Development of the Transistor," in Merritt Roe Smith, ed., *Military Enterprise and Technological Change* (Cambridge, Mass.: MIT Press, 1986).

47. Charles H. Ferguson, "Computers and the Coming of the U.S. Keirtsu," *Harvard Business Review* (July–August 1990): 55–70.

48. Ibid.

49. Ibid.

50. Peter H. Spitz, *Petrochemicals: The Rise of an Industry* (New York: John Wiley and Sons, 1988), chapters 8 and 13.

51. Robert Reich has recently argued that in the context of international business the most important factor will be the skill of the workforce and the national infrastructures that link people together. For him, organizational capabilities are no longer relevant. He sees the world economy evolving toward close relationships between small specialized problem solvers and customers. The key players in this economy, ironically, become the largest organizations—national governments, which must invest in education and infrastructure to insure economic growth. Robert Reich, "The Real Economy," *Atlantic Monthly* 267, No. 2 (February 1991): 35–53.

Political Economy of Competition
in a Global Economy

LAURA KATZ OLSON

What is good for the country is good for General Motors, and
what's good for General Motors is good for the country.
  —Charles E. Wilson, Chairman of the Board, General Motors,
    testimony before the Senate Armed Forces Committee, 1952

This essay seeks to address the meaning of competition in the
context of an increasingly global economy. It will argue that American concepts of, and goals for, competition are seriously at odds
with the values, objectives, and strategies of other industrialized
nations in the 1990s, disadvantaging the United States in the global
market economy. Further, the United States has suffered from increasing unemployment as jobs flow overseas, decreasing real wage
levels and standards of living, declining productivity, and other
serious economic woes. In order to meet the real needs of the
nation and its people, the United States must redefine both the
nature of a competitive political economy and the goals on which
it is based.

The unprecedented economic growth in the United States, the
superiority of the U.S. economy, and global American economic
and industrial hegemony, from the 1940s until the late 1960s, was
the result of extraordinary worldwide circumstances and the
growth of corporate monopoly power, rather than U.S. business
managerial skill, or U.S. economic, social, or political expertise.
Over the last several decades the United States has steadily lost
its world economic hegemony, and concomitantly its geopolitical
influence. American companies, which must now compete interna-

tionally as well as nationally without such advantages, have become increasingly less successful.

American views on the nature of competition include such value judgements as the primacy of individualism over communitarianism, the inviolability of private property and business rights, and corporate preoccupation with profit maximization, short-term financial gains, and the priority of shareholder entitlements at the expense of other participants in the production process. This essay contends that such values, inextricably linked to American capitalism, have contributed to the country's competitive deterioriation in the world economy today. These pervasive attitudes also have served to divert public attention away from a sense of social responsibility.

In the face of their declining economic position, American corporations have attempted since the 1970s to maintain high short-term profits through strategies that have had increasingly deleterious effects on the national interest, as well as on workers, consumers, and local communities. Efforts to cut labor costs by relocating firms nationally and internationally in order to retain or secure special economic protections and concessions, and by investing in mergers and acquisitions rather than in new plants and equipment, have not served community and social needs.

It is the view within this essay that a truly productive society seeks to meet social needs, to utilize human resources fully, and to improve its people's quality of life overall.

In addition, the rise of the multinational corporation and new technological innovations allowing for rapid, inexpensive worldwide communication and transportation, have altered significantly the meaning of competition in the international economy. The emergence of global firms operating outside national boundaries and interests, and the growing integration among transnational corporations, have rendered traditional nation-centered concepts of competition less relevant to current realities.

The greater integration and interdependence of the world's economic and financial systems suggest that national self-interest lies in international synergism. For example, a nation attempting to improve its own short-term competitive position through protectionist trade policies will generate negative ramifications worldwide, resulting in long-term problems for the country originating the policy.

Competition should thus be a means to achieve larger ends rather than an end in itself. Such ends comprise higher living standards, more equitable distribution of wealth and income, expanded and upgraded employment opportunities, and an enhanced living and working environment.

THE U.S. ECONOMIC POSITION AFTER WORLD WAR II

From the beginning of World War II until the early 1970s, the U.S. was predominant in the international economic order, accounting for 50% of total world GNP and controlling nearly three-fourths of world monetary assets, mostly in the form of gold.[1] In addition, American firms produced almost 50% of the world's manufactured goods.[2]

The unprecedented economic growth experienced by the American economy, as well as American economic and political hegemony during this period, could not be sustained given both the unusual circumstances of the era and U.S. corporate responses to them. The strength of American firms was not based on superior managerial skills or other capabilities. Rather, it was due primarily to the commanding economic position held by the U.S. as a result of a war that incapacitated its competitors. The economies of Europe and Japan had been devastated, leaving the United States with over 50% of the usable productive capacity worldwide.[3] According to George Lodge, "the nation's economic strength was so vast and unchallenged that it could do essentially everything that it wanted, without counting the costs." There was little necessity to establish priorities and to work efficiently to achieve them.[4] Since the scientific establishment elsewhere was in disarray, American firms faced only limited technical competition. However, American dominance diminished significantly as the war-torn nations rebuilt their economies.

During this period, from 1945 to 1973, an increasing share of the productive capacity of the U.S. economy came under the control of fewer and larger corporations. The most significant part of the economy, particularly in manufacturing, was dominated by large firms competing with only a few other companies. The percentage of total manufacturing assets held by the 200 largest corporations grew from 45% in 1947 to 69.4% in 1968, reaching approximately 80% by 1989.[5] Even in areas where there were many companies, the markets tended to be geographically fragmented, thus creating monopoly-like conditions.

The growth of monopolies and oligopolies allowed, among other things, substantial corporate influence over prices. As there was only limited competition from overseas until the mid-1970s, such companies were able to enjoy unusually high profits without having to improve significantly the efficiency or effectiveness of their production processes.

In addition, after the war, U.S. consumers had both pent up demands for goods and the savings to pay for them. At the same time, there was a desperate need that could not be satisfied locally for goods and services by war-ravaged nations rebuilding their industrial bases.

Finally, the Bretton Woods Conference in 1944 produced an international economic order dominated by American interests. In fact, it was generally assumed by the United States that whatever benefitted American manufacturing and financial interests was good for the country, for other nations, and for the international economy overall.[6] The dollar emerged as both a domestic currency and the international standard, contributing to the predominance of American corporations domestically and worldwide. At the same time, U.S. financial institutions became both banker and creditor for the capitalist world economy. By the 1970s, however, the United States could no longer shape global market rules to conform to its national needs.

AMERICA'S DECLINING ECONOMIC POSITION

Since the early 1970s, other industrialized countries, and newly-industrializing countries such as Taiwan, South Korea, Mexico and Brazil, began competing successfully with the United States. By producing goods more efficiently and effectively, nations such as Japan and Germany have steadily reduced the American productivity edge. During the 1980s, U.S. productivity growth lagged behind nearly all of the industrialized nations.[7]

The United States steadily lost its worldwide market shares to other countries in nearly every industry, from traditional manufacturing to high-technology electronics. In 1943, U.S. firms produced 52% of the world's steel; by 1982, the United States was importing 22%, and four years later 37% of its total domestic usage. In 1960, U.S. firms manufactured nearly half of all the world's motor vehicles, with imports totalling only 1%; by 1987, imports primarily from Japan accounted for nearly one-third of U.S. car sales.[8] Although American companies controlled virtually the entire international consumer electronics market during the early 1950s, by the

1980s they produced only 5% of the total.[9] Some products, such as VCRs and compact disc players, were not produced domestically at all. U.S. semiconductor production, which had dominated the world market for nearly thirty years, fell to 40% of the total by 1987.[10]

The U.S. machine tool industry, which accounted for over 25% of world production in the 1960s, fell to less than 10% by 1986. The commercial aircraft industry lost ground as well. European Airbus Industrie represented only about 7% of total new orders for commercial aircraft worldwide late in 1980. By 1987 its share had grown to approximately 23%, including over 50% of the world's wide-bodied aircraft sales.[11] The U.S. share of world trade overall declined 16% between 1960 and 1970; during the 1970s it was reduced by another 23%.[12] The country also began experiencing a steady growth in its trade imbalances. In 1985, the previously largest creditor nation in the world emerged with a net debtor status. The U.S. trade deficit grew to an astounding $110 billion by 1989, of which over one-third was with Japan.[13]

Moreover, as Bluestone and Harrison have sardonically observed, by the late 1970s the largest Japanese exports to the United States were such items as automobiles, iron and steel plates, radios, motorbikes, and audio and video tape recorders. U.S. exports to Japan were primarily soybeans, corn, hemlock logs, coal, wheat, and cotton.[14]

WORLD COMPETITION SINCE THE 1970S: ALTERNATIVE NATIONAL VALUES AND CORPORATE PRACTICES

Although it is generally acknowledged that the United States has lost its international economic and industrial superiority, alternative views on the causes of and, consequently, the solutions for reversing the situation have been offered. Primarily blaming macroeconomic factors, public officials, business leaders, economists, and others have responded by suggesting ways to make U.S. industry more competitive: altering domestic monetary and fiscal policies, and halting "predatory" practices of other nations.

Blame has also been placed on exchange rate misalignments, consumption and savings patterns, unfair national protective practices (especially by Japan), the Middle Eastern oil cartel, the comparatively high cost of American capital, overly restrictive U.S. tax laws and business regulations, the domestic budget deficit, international trade imbalances, and especially the high cost and lack of motivation of American labor. These factors, however, are not the fundamental causes of the declining competitive position of the United States in the world economy. Consequently, micro- and macroeconomic adjustments cannot solve the U.S. economic crisis.

U.S. institutional arrangements under capitalism are simply ill-suited to the needs of modern industrial society. American concepts of, and values related to, competition, as well as U.S. corporate practices, have failed to serve U.S. domestic and international interests. The sanctity of private property and individualism in the American culture, together with corporate values that prioritize short-term goals and maximize profits and shareholder rights, have diverted attention from critical social and community needs such as improved wages, employment opportunities, environmental protection, adequate health care, and the like. Moreover, as Richard Ellsworth concludes, the unquestioned dominance of shareholder interests and profit maximization in the United States over other goals has seriously undermined American competitiveness in the world economy.[15]

Since Americans venerate individualism and private property rights, corporate leaders are allowed to control nearly all aspects of production. Instead of setting national economic goals and addressing these goals through public policy initiatives, U.S. political leaders presume that community interests will be best served through unconstrained competition among corporations.

Governmental supports for the business sector, whether at the national, state or local levels, generally are not tied to, nor do they imply business obligations to the community or nation. Overall, under American capitalism, businesses are not expected to attribute a high priority to public needs or to concern themselves with the social costs imposed by their actions.

The steel industry was given substantial government benefits and special protection for decades. However, instead of modernizing their operations, corporate executives invested in nonsteel ventures, closed steel plants, and cut their work force dramatically.[16] Although profits were protected, workers, communities, and the national interest have suffered.

Importantly, the performance of American companies as well as that of its managers, is measured almost exclusively by the firm's current stock price and by its ability to reach high targeted rates of return on investment, usually on a quarterly basis.[17] This is an extremely short time frame, especially since major product innovations in most firms take from seven to fifteen years before they

become profitable.[18] More recently, if quarterly profits are not sufficiently high, the company may become susceptible to hostile
takeover.

Pressure for a short managerial time frame is further buttressed
by the American tendency to reward senior executives for immediate results. These executives, who tend to stay with a firm only
five or six years, are too often motivated by their profit-related
bonus and stock option plans. Moreover, middle-managers usually
are promoted and rewarded based on the quarterly earnings of their
particular profit centers.[19] Consequently, corporate managers tend
to pursue projects with short-term profits and to avoid long-term
commitments, including new technology and new products. As
Thurow sums it up, "short time horizons are produced by an economic environment where everyone responds rationally to individual incentives, but the sum total of those individually rational
choices is social stupidity."[20]

In Asian and European countries, communitarian ideologies are
favored to varying extents. The Japanese in particular presume, as
reported by George Lodge, that "the community as a whole has
special and urgent needs that go beyond the needs of its individual
members. The values of survival, justice, self-respect, and so forth,
depend on the recognition of those needs. . . . It is . . . difficult to
translate the word 'individualism' into Japanese with any other
meaning than selfishness and egocentricity."[21] Individuals tend to
identify more with the larger entity, fostering greater productivity
growth and competitive success.

In contrast to the U.S., public and corporate leaders in other
industrialized countries assume that economic competition is
among nations rather than among firms. Not only are political guid-
ance and support integral to business decisionmaking, but firms
also are expected to serve social needs as well as the national
interest. Consequently, domestic rules for each industry often are
based on how a particular product serves or is expected to contribute to the social, political, or economic requirements of the nation.

The Japanese government supports industry by such diverse
means as ensuring the availability of capital, providing research
and development funds, and educating and training workers. Government subsidization of steel production in Japan, as well as in
western Europe, Brazil, and Mexico over the last two decades, has
been based on the presumption, shared among political leaders,
corporate executives, and workers, that it is in their national interest to have a strong, viable steel industry. At the same time, domestic market rules in Japan and most European countries guarantee
that workers and consumers will be protected.[22]

In fact, the goals of business itself are intricately linked with those of the national community in most other industrialized nations. European firms, for example, are less preoccupied with earnings, dividends, and share prices than their American counterparts. The MIT Commission on Industrial Policy reports that managers of European firms tend to have commitments "to the larger community of employees, customers, neighbors, and suppliers, and to the continuity and growth of the firm itself."[23] Business executives seek adequate rates of return rather than profit maximization.

The Japanese, in particular, view the corporation as a partnership among executives, employees, political leaders, and lenders/stockholders. The prevailing precept is that all of these groups contribute to the firm's productive process, have mutual obligations, and consequently have a right to share in the firm's successes, including its profits. On the other hand, the goal of profit maximization is balanced against other goals, such as improving the general welfare of society and furthering national interests.[24]

When a Japanese company is forced to restructure itself in order to meet technological and other changes, employees are assigned to new jobs within the firm, receiving training to upgrade their skills if necessary. In fact, there tends to be a high level of worker mobility and employer-financed training *within* the company in general. Employees are rarely laid off; if absolutely necessary, the company assists them in finding new jobs. Moreover, as raises and bonuses are based on such factors as loyalty, service to the company, and hard work, employees are willing to sacrifice for the firm.[25] Because full-time Japanese workers tend to be assured employment, and their economic rewards are tied to the success of the firm, they embrace modernization and technological innovations such as robots. Interestingly, studies show that American workers, when given a workplace environment similar to those of the Japanese, tend to produce as much and as well.[26].

Japanese companies take a long-range point of view, as well. They are expected to retrench from declining industrial sectors without negatively affecting specific communities or overall employment levels.[27] They are also willing to endure periods of heavy investment and meager returns in order to secure a foothold in a growing market or to increase their market share worldwide. In some cases, Japanese firms have incurred economic losses for up to five years, only to break even for a few years after that.[28]

In its research on the consumer-electronics industry, the MIT Commission found that "the longer time horizons of the Japanese electronics companies helped them to dominate the market for

videocassette recorders (VCRs). The Japanese are now virtually
unchallenged as makers of what has become the most important
single product in the consumer-electronics market."[29] In fact, U.S.
firms had pursued higher market returns elsewhere, dropping out of
that industry entirely. The Commission concluded that American
companies, which have been unwilling to forego short-term returns
for long-term gains, have been encountering similar problems in
industry after industry since the early 1970s.[30]

Japanese corporations also have been willing to reinvest profits
within the firm. In contrast, the collapse of the American steel
industry stems in part from the failure of managements to make the
necessary capital investments to modernize their plants. Similarly,
instead of reinvesting the high profits earned prior to the 1970s,
American machine-tool makers used the gains for other ventures
and corporate overhead. According to the MIT Commission, the
industry "concentrated on building high-volume products on steadily deteriorating equipment, eventually making the machine-tool
producers vulnerable to commodity competition." As the Commission argues, "excellent machine tools are a key to the nation's
manufacturing strength."[31]

The inherent character of competition in other industrialized
countries such as Japan and those in Western Europe precludes an
exclusive focus on profit maximization. Although Japanese firms
experience intense domestic inter-corporate rivalry in key industries, price is not the only stimulus; managers also compete for
domestic and worldwide market shares on the basis of such factors
as the performance, reliability and overall quality of commodities,
proficiency at product upgrading and innovation, repair service,
availability of parts, and the number and type of new product lines.
Japanese businesses also vie with each other for productivity leadership positions.[32] Their success in consumer electronics, for example, can be attributed to a certain extent on innovative products.[33]

Western European companies, especially in Germany, also have
been able to build market share and reputation by improving product quality, modernizing plants through technical innovations, and
maintaining capacity to assure timely distribution of products.[34]
Such investments are possible because, unlike the U.S. situation,
these executive have the option of focusing on long-run gains at the
expense of short-run profitability. Consequently, in comparisons
of product quality, service to consumers, and speed of product
development, an increasing number of non-American companies
consistently outperform U.S. companies.[35]

Additionally, in other industrialized nations, managers generally are not rewarded on profit-based incentives. Richard Ellsworth found that German and Japanese corporate executives rarely receive stock options, and own only limited amounts of the firm's stock, if any. Moreover, their salaries are not tied to company profit levels.[36]

AMERICAN CORPORATE STRATEGIES SINCE THE EARLY 1970S

Faced with international competition beginning in the early 1970s, and declining profits, the major strategies of American firms have been to concentrate on cutting costs, particularly those of labor, and on mergers and acquisitions. The former tactics have included reducing union influence and rules, wage give-backs, the search for low-cost labor through relocation inside and outside the U.S., offshore sourcing of components and finished products, and divestment. As the MIT Commission found, "[t]he history of the American textile industry is essentially a search for low wages. The industry moved first from New England to the Southeast and then went offshore, but the quest for cheap labor has not brought success in the marketplace. . . . The route to success in the modern garment trade is not low wages."[37] The Commission stresses that Germany, which was the third largest exporter of textiles in the world, had higher wage levels than the United States. Their textile industry achieved success primarily by investing in new technologies, machinery, and plants.

U.S. firms have tended to treat labor as a cost to be controlled rather than as an asset to be developed. This attitude has fostered an unskilled, inflexible workforce unprepared for the rapid technological changes that have taken place over the last several decades. As Thurow points out, "with the introduction of more flexible computer-aided design and manufacturing processes, it is clear that the penalty for an inflexible labor force is going to increase."[38]

In their pursuit of high profits, along with new capabilities for capital mobility and public policies allowing business to move whenever and wherever it wants, U.S. companies relocate or reinvest without considering the impact on workers or on the communities in which they live. In fact, a significant number of plants are closed in the United States simply because profitable firms have not been profitable enough. In order to gain even higher earnings, a productive firm may move to another domestic or international location, generating massive unemployment in, and devastating the overall economic vitality of, the original city.

U.S. corporations also have attempted to attain or maintain high short-term profits through mergers and acquisitions, a strategy that has accelerated since the 1970s. Resources devoted to the promotion and/or prevention of mergers and takeovers have been at the expense of investments fundamental to the long-range health of the company, including technological improvements, and other innovations. Thurow argues that "instead of engaging in the lengthy process of creating and fine-tuning new products or processes at home, top managers come to feel they can get rich quick and expand their company with a well timed takeover. . . ."[39] As Barry Bluestone and Bennett Harrison summarize the situation, "the essential problem with the U.S. economy can be traced to the way capital—in the form of financial resources and of real plant and equipment—has been diverted from productive investment in our basic national industries into unproductive speculation, mergers, and acquisitions, and foreign investment."[40]

In New York, New Jersey, and Pennsylvania, over 75% of the Fortune 500's new manufacturing plants during the 1970s emanated from acquisitions and mergers rather than from investments in new plants and equipment.[41]

Takeovers tend to be in diverse products and services bearing little or no relation to the original industry. Thus, there tends to be minimum interest in or knowledge about the products themselves. For example, Bluestone and Harrison report that during the late 1970s the steel industry systematically began procuring companies unrelated to steel, including cement, natural gas, chemicals, nuclear power parts, and other products. General Electric and Mobil Oil diversified into a wide variety of new businesses such as toaster ovens, and a department store chain, respectively. Moreover, many companies acquire a profitable firm, and "milk it" of its resources, concentrating on its more profitable product lines. Depleted of its productive capital, the acquired plant eventually is shut down.[42]

In addition, the goals of management in the United States must conform increasingly to the guidelines of lawyers and financiers who buy a portfolio of companies; they tend to have limited knowledge of, or interest in, the long-term health of the company, its employees, the community in which the company is situated, or even the actual product produced. Ellsworth remarks that "shareholder's interests have become more and more removed from concern for institutional integrity and economic vitality. . . . In this environment, the market overvalues short-term profits and under-values the cost of long-term competitive decline."[43]

Significantly, the turnover rates of stocks have been increasing; the turnover rate on the New York Stock Exchange rose from 12% in 1960 to 51% by 1983. In contrast, German and Japanese bankers who govern investments in manufacturing firms view themselves as managing institutions rather than portfolios, so they rarely sell their equity holdings.[44]

MULTINATIONAL CORPORATIONS AND THE GLOBAL ECONOMY

As suggested earlier, in addition to their involvement with merg-ers and acquisitions, American companies have reconstructed pro-duction by relocating operations abroad. This multinationalization of American business has been supported and encouraged by U.S. public policies, particularly through substantial tax benefits se-cured by firms for overseas investments. These tax advantages, which significantly increased the company's after-tax profits, did not stipulate corporate obligations to the nation or to its commu-nities.

Direct foreign investment by U.S. firms rose from $12 billion in 1950 to $192 Billion in 1980.[45] By 1988, nearly 50% of all new manufacturing ventures involved the acquisition of facilities overseas.[46]

American multinational firms have fared considerably better in producing for world markets than their domestic counterparts. In fact, Harry Magdoff and Paul Sweezy contend that "U.S. manufac-turers are not competing for export business against foreign firms but against their own branches and affiliates located abroad. . . . U.S. manufacturing firms located abroad are selling almost three times as much as is being exported by the United States."[47] Concur-rently, American multinationals generated a growing percentage of all profits earned by the leading 100 U.S. domestic firms, reaching approximately one-third of the total by the late 1970s.[48] According to Wolfe, these firms became increasingly less likely to repatriate profits back to the U.S.[49]

Many domestic manufacturing firms, as Ezra Vogel explains, "became in large measure marketing firms for goods produced overseas."[50] For example, in 1983 Kodak announced the invention

290 LAURA KATZ OLSON

of its small lightweight video camera; the product eventually was manufactured abroad.[51]

Japan, on the other hand, has relied primarily on the export of manufactured products from its own country rather than seeking low-cost labor abroad. Japanese companies have built subsidiaries, such as Honda plants, in the U.S. However, such efforts are partly in response to threats of American protectionism. Additionally, unlike the aim of some U.S. companies, the purpose of overseas Japanese investments generally is to manufacture products at the intended market rather than for export back to Japan.[52]

New technologies allowing for rapid and inexpensive worldwide communication and transportation have contributed enormously to the rise of the global firm. It is now feasible to scatter corporate headquarters, managers, workers, shareholders, and markets throughout the world. In fact, national borders are becoming increasingly irrelevant. As Robert Reich notes, "American industries no longer compete against Japanese or European industries. Rather, a company with headquarters in the U.S., production facilities in Taiwan, and a marketing force spread across many nations competes with another similarly ecumenical company."[53]

Airbus Industrie, which is owned by a consortium of European governments, uses engines made by U.S. firms; it competes primarily against Boeing, which uses Rolls Royce engines. Data entry facilities for American airlines currently are located in Barbados and in the Dominican Republic.[54] Ford Motor Company and General Motors both manufacture diverse parts for their automobilies throughout Europe, Brazil, Mexico, the U.S., and other countries.

American multinational firms also have embarked on joint commercial and technical ventures with, and/or have invested directly in, foreign firms over the last several decades. American corporations have often used these tactics as a means for gaining access to overseas markets. They have also boosted short-term profits by selling or swapping advanced technology.[55] In the longer term, however, these companies contributed to their own future competition. As suggested by Bluestone and Harrison, "in the 1970s this competition came back to haunt them in virtually every major industry: steel, automobiles, shipbuilding, and electronics, to name a few."[56]

Such alliances include General Motors and Toyota, Ford and Toyo Kogyo-Mazda, IBM and Kaematsu Gosho, Hewlett-Packard and Samsung, AT&T and Olivetti, Eastman Kodak and Matsushita, and General Electric and Rolls-Royce. Additionally, Ford Motor Company owns 25% of Mazda and 10% of Korean Kia Motors;

GM owns a substantial share of Isuzu, Suzuki, and Daewoo Motors; and Chrysler, which bought out Italian car manufacturer Maserati in the late 1980s, owns 30% of Mitsubishi Motors.[57]

Importantly, the interests of the American economy and those of American multinational corporations are not necessarily the same. The inappreciable national loyalty of American multinationals further compounds U.S. economic problems. As a Colgate-Palmolive Company executive explicitly stated, "The United States does not have an automatic call on our resources. . . . There is no mindset that puts this country first."[58]

In actuality, greater productivity and profits abroad have generated greater domestic unemployment. While GM expended over $7 billion for its European ventures during the 1980s, and despite its even greater investments in U.S. facilities, tens of thousands of GM workers lost their jobs. Similarly, Chrysler cut its work force significantly while at the same time it was investing in such nations as Italy, Mexico, and Brazil.[59] Arnold Hax estimates that the U.S. deficit in its balance of payments in 1987 represents a contribution of over four million jobs overseas.[60]

Multinational companies have gained such economic power that they are, at times, capable of defying both the home and host governments and their interests. The ability to operate their own global communications systems enables them to bypass both a nation's services and regulations as well as to evade trade restrictions.

The growing integration and interconnectedness of key industrial sectors around the world have produced entirely new modes of competition. Consequently, in lieu of concentrating on the competitiveness of American industry per se, U.S. leaders should be addressing issues related to the global corporation.

The interdependence of the world economic and financial systems in the 1990s compels the United States to alter its concept of competition in additional ways. Leonard Silk aptly remarks, "the line between domestic and international economic policy has been rubbed out. . . . [T]he unit for policy thinking must become the world economy rather than the national economy, although this flies in the face of traditional national politics and economic pressures."[61] Because of the need for a global perspective—along with the realities that the United States is no longer self-sufficient, nor can it any longer mold the world monetary system to its own design—national self-interest lies increasingly in international synergism.

It has become more difficult for individual nations to control their own economies, or to solve their domestic problems unilaterally; nations must act within the context of the wider, international system. Furthermore, policy interventions designed to have an impact on specific, circumscibed national problems often activate interdependencies, with unanticipated and significant outcomes for other countries. These consequences can also reverberate, affecting the nation originating the measures.

Accordingly, policies providing for short-term gains at the expense of other countries can threaten international stability overall as well as produce serious long-term domestic crises. Given recent trends, including public policies aimed at protectionism, a new definition of competition incorporating international synergism will not be achieved easily.

U.S. HEGEMONY AND DEFENSE SPENDING

In order to protect growing overseas investments, and to ensure American economic hegemony, the U.S. has steadily expanded its military power over the last several decades. Defense spending has served both as an economic stimulus and as the primary means for insuring U.S. influence worldwide. By fiscal 1990, the nation was spending some $300 billion, or about 7% of its GNP, on defense.

As Wolfe argues, "Relying on overseas expansion as an alternative to needed domestic reconstruction, America, slowly at first, rapidly later, sacrificed more and more of its domestic strength in order to keep alive its overseas influence."[62] Although defense spending did stimulate the economy in the short-run, it eventually contributed significantly to the country's growing budget deficit, rampant inflation, negative balance of payments, and other economic problems.

The U.S. also concentrated its engineering talent, along with its research and development efforts, on defense industries and products, siphoning human and capital resources from the civilian commercial sector. Almost half of U.S. research and development is sponsored by the national government, with two-thirds of these funds spent on defense. Moreover, since the 1960s, commercial spin-off from military research has decreased enormously.[63]

Despite America's declining economic position world-wide, and the depletion of the country's resources by defense spending, the United States has continued to rely on military power as its major tool of foreign policy; the defense budget has continued to escalate unabated.

WINNERS AND LOSERS IN THE CORPORATE GAME

This essay argues that competition should be a means toward larger ends and not the goal in itself. Accordingly, it contends that the U.S. should strive for greater competitiveness in order to attain a rise in living standards, an expansion and upgrading of employment opportunities, improved environmental conditions, enhanced quality of life, and a more equitable distribution of national wealth and income. Ends such as these should be used for gauging U.S. competitiveness worldwide, instead of international trade balances, stock prices, or profit levels. As Bluestone has shown, the stock market and unemployment could rise simultaneously.[64]

American corporate strategies to sustain or improve profit levels over the last several decades, along with public policy measures, have had an adverse affect on employment levels, wages, income distribution and overall standards of living in the United States. According to Cornell University economists Robert Frank and Richard Freeman, ". . . every $1 billion of direct U.S. foreign investment seems to eliminate (on balance) about 26,500 domestic jobs."[65] Bluestone and Harrison estimate that total private disinvestment in American business cost the country from thirty-two to thirty-eight million jobs during the 1970s.[66]

The evidence suggests that workers affected by plant closings or layoffs tend to find new work at lower wages and lower status. A Bureau of Labor Statistics study of workers displaced from manufacturing between 1979 and 1984 discloses that just under half of the successfully reemployed workers suffered income loss and two-thirds had decrements amounting to over 20% of their former wages. Many of the unemployed deplete their savings before finding new work, causing such problems as mortgage foreclosures, loss of medical insurance, and reduced physical and mental health.[67] A recent analysis by Gary Hansen concluded that this trend will most likely continue. About 50% of the blue collar workers displaced from manufacturing jobs in the future will not find new employment in their former industries; most will be re-employed in lower paying service jobs.[68]

Communities can also be devastated by plant closings. Local tax revenues are reduced, causing a decline in services. Moreover, as more unemployed workers turn to welfare, public expenses increase. While older industrial cities have been desolated by plant closings, Sunbelt boomtowns have grown haphazardly, with little or no regulations, serious highway congestion, water shortages, overcrowded schools, housing crises, and increases in crime.

Plant closings and other forms of divestment by the business community, as Bluestone and Harrison note, "may be robbing the nation of $200 billion annually in foregone output, and forcing Americans to spend over $12 billion more yearly in income assistance." Research by the U.S. Bureau of Economic Analysis discloses that for every percentage point increase in the unemployment rate in 1980, the nation's GNP and federal tax receipts were reduced by $68 billion, and $20 billion, respectively.[69]

The rights of corporate executives and stockholders over those of other partners in the productive process in the U.S. are exemplified by the difficulty of legislating plant closing protection for workers.[70] A study by the General Accounting Office in the early 1980s showed that one-third of all firms with over one-hundred workers gave less than two-weeks notice and another one-third gave no notice at all to its employees.[71]

American corporate and political efforts also have had an adverse affect on income distribution, poverty and the standard of living in the U.S. From 1973 to 1987, the average American worker's standard of living eroded by nearly 15%.[72] According to the 1990 annual report of the Census Bureau, income inequality has grown steadily over the last two decades. Reich found that between 1978 and 1987 alone, the poorest 20% of America's families became poorer, while the richest 20% became 13% richer. Although the wages of unskilled workers declined, and the number of impoverished workers rose, the income of professionals in the securities industry grew by 21% during that period.[73] Compared to the U.S., Japan has both a higher national income and a more equitable distribution of its national assets.[74]

SUPPLANTING THE MANUFACTURING SECTOR

As the manufacturing sector has declined, the service sector has risen both in absolute and relative terms. By the late 1980s, approximately 75% of all nonagricultural employment in the United States was in services. At the same time, many corporate leaders, economists, and public officials have argued that high-technology industries will replace the manufacturing sector. This transformation of the American economy has been lauded as signifying a change toward a higher level of economic development, or a post-industrial society.

Such a view does not take into account the fact that services, high technology and manufacturing are inextricably linked. Stephen Cohen and John Zysman point out, for example, that "a substantial core of service employment is tightly tied to manufacturing. It is a complement and not, as the dominant view would have it, a substitute or successor for manufacturing. Lose manufacturing and you will lose—not develop—those high-wage services."[75] Or, in Jerry Weaver's words, ". . . without a healthy and prosperous manufacturing industry there will be little to service."[76]

Nor will we be able to export services easily in the future. As Thurow notes, international competition in services is, and most likely will continue to be, intense. Since the structural weaknesses in services tend to be similar to those in manufacturing, it is not likely that under current conditions the United States will be dominant worldwide in this sector.

Furthermore, high technology is interwoven with production, as well. Cohen and Zysman, for example, explain that high-technology products are most often used in other products (micro-chips), or in the production process itself (robots). Moreover, new ideas and innovations cannot be developed effectively or efficiently in isolation from the ability to construct the product. Manufacturing is the linchpin of high technology and American firms cannot expect to compete with other nations unless they can integrate high technology into a strong manufacturing base. The growing manufacturing weakness in the United States, especially in such products as steel and consumer electronics, has thus been eroding the country's technical edge.[77]

In addition, the transformation of the American economy has affected workers unevenly, contributing considerably to the growing income inequalities in American society. In his analysis of non-government U.S. employment, Robert Reich argues that workers can be placed in three functional categories: 20% of the jobs comprise symbolic-analytic service workers such as lawyers, investment bankers, research scientists, management consultants, real estate developers, and design engineers. This group, which is in high demand worldwide, has been experiencing a growing standard of living. The routine production and service employees, which include another 25% of jobs such as those in manufacturing and data processing, have been experiencing unemployment and decreases in their standard of living as their firms move overseas.

The third category, routine personal service workers, account for another 30% of employment in the U.S. Although this sector has expanded rapidly since the 1970s, the work tends to pay poorly, with limited benefits.[78]

CONCLUSION

This essay has argued that under American capitalism, concepts of a competitive society are based on values, strategies, and goals that are not well suited to the world economy today. They are not conducive to meeting domestic social and community needs either. Such cultural and corporate values include individualism, the sanctity of private property rights over community needs, short-term instead of long-range goals, the maximization of profits, and shareholder rights over other partners in the productive process.

American industry, which benefitted from an advantaged U.S. economic and political position following World War II, has steadily lost its commanding worldwide economic position since the early 1970s. Newly industrializing nations and other industrialized countries, especially Germany and Japan, have procured growing market shares in nearly every industry worldwide.

In order to maintain high short-term profits over the past several decades, U.S. industrial strategies have included relocating firms to low-wage domestic and international areas, and investing in mergers and acquisitions rather than in new plants and equipment. These tactics have contributed to rising unemployment and underemployment, declining living standards, and deteriorating communities and working environments.

It also has been argued that both the emergence of the global firm and new forms of transnational affiliations among corporations have produced entirely new modes of international competition. The divergence of interests among American workers and their communities, the domestic economy, and American multinational firms have been fostered even further.

Finally, this essay has maintained that the United States must redefine both the nature of its competitive political economy and the goals on which it is based. Given the prevailing cultural and corporate values, and the economic, social, and political structures supporting these, it is problematic as to whether the United States is capable of confronting these formidable challenges.

NOTES

1. David B. Yoffie, "Protecting World Markets," in Thomas K. McCraw, ed., *America Versus Japan* (Boston: Harvard Business School Press, 1986), 37–38.

2. Alan Wolfe, *America's Impasse: The Rise and Fall of the Politics of Growth* (New York: Pantheon Books, 1981), 154.

3. Jeffrey P. Richetto, "U.S. Industry: Decline and Fall?," *Long Range Planning* 21, No. 1 (1988): 35–37.

4. George C. Lodge, "The United States: The Costs of Ambivalence," in George C. Lodge and Ezra F. Vogel, eds., *Ideology and National Competitiveness: An Analysis of Nine Countries* (Boston: Harvard Business School Press, 1987), 115.

5. Wolfe, *America's Impasse,* 32–33; "The Forbes Assets 500," *Forbes* (30 April 1990), 248–54.

6. Ibid., 154.

7. Michael L. Dertouzos, et al, *Made in America: Regaining the Productive Edge* (Cambridge, Massachusetts: MIT Press, 1989), 26–30.

8. Ibid., 18, 278; Thomas K. McCraw and Patricia A. O'Brien, "Productivity and Distribution: Competition Policy and Industry Structure," in *America Versus Japan,* 91; and Thomas K. McCraw, "From Partners to Competitors: An Overview of the Period Since World War II," in *America Versus Japan,* 6.

9. Arnoldo C. Hax, "Building the Firm of the Future," *Sloan Management Review* (Spring 1989): 78.

10. Dertouzos, *Made in America,* pp. 249–53.

11. Ibid., 209; and Lester Thurow, "Revitalizing American Industry: Managing in a Competitive World Economy," *California Management Review* 27 (Fall 1984): 1:12.

12. Barry Bluestone and Bennett Harrison, *The Deindustrialization of America: Plant Closings, Community Abandonment, and the Dismantling of Basic Industry* (New York: Basic Books, 1982), 140.

13. If investment income is excluded, the deficit would be significantly higher. George C. Lodge, "Introduction—Ideology and Country Analysis," in Lodge, *Ideology,* 1.

14. Bluestone and Harrison, in *Deindustrialization,* 5.

15. Richard R. Ellsworth, "Capital Markets and Competitive Decline," *Harvard Business Review* (September–October 1985): 171–83.

16. By 1979, nearly half of all U.S. Steel's capital investments went into non-steel projects, see Bluestone and Harrison, *Deindustrialization,* 41.

17. The standard pre-tax American target rate of return on investment, according to Thurow, is 20 percent. Thurow, "Revitalizing," 15.

18. Ibid., 9–41.

19. Ibid.; and Dertouzos, *Made in America,* 62.

20. Thurow, "Revitalizing," 25–26.

21. Lodge, "Introduction," in Lodge and Vogel, *Ideology,* 15.

22. Stephen S. Cohen and John Zysman, *Manufacturing Matters: The Myth of the Post-Industrial Economy* (New York: Basic Books, 1987), 247.

23. Dertouzos et al, *Made in America;* see also, Ellsworth, "Capital Markets," 174.

24. Ibid.

25. Ezra F. Vogel, "Japan: Adaptive Communitarianism," in Lodge and Vogel, *Ideology,* 158.

26. Dertouzos et al, *Made in America,* 81.

27. Ezra F. Vogel, "Conclusion," in Lodge and Vogel, *Ideology,* 312.

28. Ellsworth, "Capital Markets," 178.

29. Dertouzos et al, *Made in America,* 53.

30. Ibid., 54, 217.

31. Ibid., 238, 237.

32. Peter Enderwick, "Multinational Corporate Restructuring and International Competitiveness," *California Management Review* (Fall 1989): 44–58; see also Michael E. Porter. *The Competitive Advantage of Nations* (New York: The Free Press, 1990), 408–14.

33. Dertouzos et al, *Made in America,* 228.

34. Ellsworth, "Capital Markets," 174.

35. See, for example, Thurow, "Revitalizing," 17; and Dertouzos et al, *Made in America,* 26.

36. Ellsworth, "Capital Markets," 174.

37. Dertouzos, *Made in America,* 16–17.

38. Thurow, "Revitalizing," 36.

39. Ibid., 23.

40. Bluestone and Harrison, 6.

41. Ibid., 41.

42. Ibid., 40–41, 156.

43. Ellsworth, "Capital Markets," 173–174.

44. Ibid., 173, 180.

45. Bluestone and Harrison, 42.

46. John Maxwell Hamilton, *Entangling Alliances: How the Third World Shapes Our Lives* (Washington, D.C.: Seven Locks Press, 1990), 10.

47. Harry Magdoff and Paul M. Sweezy, *The Deepening Crisis of U.S. Capitalism* (New York: Monthly Review Press, 1981), 94–106.

48. Richetto, "U.S. Industry," 35–37.

49. Wolfe, *America's Impasse,* 41, 166.

50. Ezra Vogel, *Comeback: Building the Resurgence of American Business* (New York: Simon and Schuster, 1985), 21.

51. Thurow, "Revitalizing," 11.

52. McCraw, "From Partners," in McCraw, *America Versus Japan,* 32–33; and Enderwick, "Multinational Corporate Restructuring," 44–58.

53. Robert B. Reich, "As the World Turns: U.S. Income Inequality Keeps on Rising," *The New Republic* (1 May 1989), 26.

54. See Hamilton, *Entangling Alliances.*

55. Dertouzos et al, *Made in America,* 251.

56. Bluestone and Harrison, 15.

57. Enderwick, "Multinational Corporate Restructuring," 6, 36; and Norman Roth, "Why We Need International Trade Union Unity," *Labor Today* 27 (Spring 1988): 12–15.

58. Quoted in Hamilton, *Entangling Alliances,* 14.

59. Roth, "Why We Need," 12–15.

60. Hax, "Building the Firm," 75–81.

61. Leonard Silk, "The United States and the World Economy," *Foreign Affairs* (1987), 463, 473.

62. Wolfe, *America's Impasse,* 109.

63. Dertouzos et al, *Made in America,* 201–16.

64. Barry Bluestone, "Deindustrialization and Unemployment in America," *The Review of Black Political Economy* 17 (Fall, 1988): 29–44.

65. Quoted in Bluestone and Harrison, *Deindustrialization of America,* 44.

66. Ibid., 9; Peter Enderwick calculates that the U.S. lost nearly four million jobs because of plant closings between 1978 and 1982. See Enderwick, "Multinational Corporate Restructuring," 44–58.

67. Patrick J. Ashton and Peter Iadicola, "Financial Impact of a Plant Closing on Displaced Blue-Collar and White-Collar Workers," *Labor Studies Journal* (Spring 1988): 37; for more on the negative affects of plant closings see Bluestone and Harrison, *Deindustrialization,* p. 117.

68. Gary B. Hansen, "Layoffs, Plant Closings, and Worker Displacement in America: Serious Problems that Need a National Solution," *Journal of Social Issues* 44, No. 4 (1988): 157.

69. Bluestone and Harrison, *Deindustrialization,* 77.

70. President Reagan vetoed the 1988 Omnibus Trade Bill, which included a provision requiring larger companies to give workers 60 days advance notice of plant closings or mass layoffs. Moreover, only a few states have passed any type of plant closing legislation. Maine, Connecticut, Wisconsin, Maryland, Massachusetts and New York have attempted to require or encourage some advance notification, but the acts have been largely ineffectual.

71. Masahiko Aoki, "Toward an Economic Model of the Japanese Firm," *Journal of Economic Literature* 28 (March 1990): 1–27.

72. Lewie Anderson, "America Belongs to the People—Not to the Profiteers," *Labor Today* 26 (Fall 1987): 1–2.

73. Despite U.S. economic problems, CEO's from the hundred largest publicly held industrial firms received wages averaging nearly 12 percent in 1988. See Reich, "As the World Turns," 23.

74. McCraw, "From Partners," in McCraw, *America Versus Japan,* 28.

75. Cohen and Zysman, *Manufacturing Matters,* 3.

76. Jerry Weaver, "A New Definition for U.S. Competition," *Metalworking News* (8 June 1987), 6.

77. Cohen and Zysman, *Manufacturing Matters;* see also Masaka Ogi, "Strategies for Competing in a Global Economy," *Chief Executive* (July/August 1988), 54–57.

78. Reich, "As the World Turns," 23–28.